THE UNITED STATES AND TERRORISM

THE UNITED STATES AND TERRORISM

An Ironic Perspective

Ron Hirschbein

ROWMAN & LITTLEFIELD
Lanham • Boulder • New York • London

Published by Rowman & Littlefield
A wholly owned subsidiary of The Rowman & Littlefield Publishing Group, Inc.
4501 Forbes Boulevard, Suite 200, Lanham, Maryland 20706
www.rowman.com

Unit A, Whitacre Mews, 26-34 Stannary Street, London SE11 4AB

British Library Cataloguing in Publication Information Available

Library of Congress Cataloging-in-Publication Data

Hirschbein, Ron.
The United States and terrorism : An ironic perspective / by Ron Hirschbein.
pages cm
Includes bibliographical references and index.
ISBN 978-1-4422-3777-3 (cloth : alk. paper) -- ISBN 978-1-4422-3779-7 (electronic)
1. Terrorism--United States. 2. Terrorism--United States--History. I. Title.
HV6432.H576 2015
363.3250973--dc23
2014048375

Printed in the United States of America

In Aeschylus's "Prometheus Bound," the
chained Titan is pitilessly interrogated by the chorus.
They ask him whether he gave human beings
anything else.
Yes, he says, "I stopped mortals from foreseeing doom."
How did you do that, they ask?
His response is revealing:
"I sowed in them blind hopes."
—Critchley, 2014

Only in a world where irony was dead could
an intellectual class enter war at the head of such
illiberal cohorts in the avowed cause of
world-liberalism and world-democracy.
—Randolph Bourne (Bacevich, 2013)

To Concerned Philosophers for Peace:
Decades of camaraderie, insight, and inspiration.

CONTENTS

INTRODUCTION

The Quest for the Unholy Grail

My barber asked what I was up to. I mentioned writing a book. "Murder or science fiction?" Pondering the strategic fictions improvised in the bloody episodes that inform this study, I answered, "Both."

This is not the first book on terrorism, but it's unique: It recounts recent American encounters with terrorism in an unsettling ironic light. To paraphrase Nietzsche, concepts with a history cannot be defined; they must be narrated. Terrorism is such a concept. A narrative account of terrorism from World War II to the present reveals troubling ironies. Among the most daunting: incongruities in language that would be humorous if they weren't tragic; and incongruous situations in which war planners provoke what they intend to prevent. The ancient Greeks called it hubris.

Six decades have passed since theologian Reinhold Niebuhr chronicled the most troubling ironies of American history: He warned of the consequences of delusions of American exceptionalism.[1] Events vindicate his warning. To cite an example pursued in this study: Nuclear terror weapons ushered in dreams of an American Century, an epoch of unparalleled security, prosperity, and dominion for the elect among nations. The Soviet bomb was a rude awakening; the ensuing arms race left the United States vulnerable as never before. Niebuhr recognized the folly of fantasizing about managing history.

More recently, philosopher Richard Rorty urged us to acknowledge our all-too-human predicament by becoming ironists—recognizing the humbling irony of our socialization. He explains: Beset by radical and persistent doubts, "the ironist . . . [worries] about the possibility that she has been initiated into the wrong tribe [or] taught to play the wrong language game."[2]

I wrote this book because I'm beset by radical and persistent doubts about prevailing accounts of terrorism. The doubts begin where most contemporary accounts of terrorism begin—definitions. Those who control the definition control the argument. *Currently*, all agree: Terrorism is despicable—whatever it is. (Several analysts note 250 competing definitions.[3]) Mainstream analysts invoke definitions that exonerate American officials from charges of terrorism—critics don't. Quests to find the unholy grail, *the* definition of terrorism, share a deficit hidden in plain sight—historical amnesia. What historian Paul Fussell calls "irony-assisted recall"[4] facilitates the return of the repressed.

To begin with the obvious: Terrorism didn't always get bad press. As we'll see, military men such as General Curtis LeMay boasted of the terror, the firestorms, visited upon German and Japanese cities. Prominent politicians and strategists praised nuclear terror in elite journals such as *Foreign Affairs*. And officials such as Secretary of Defense Robert McNamara reckoned what they called the balance of nuclear terror—a delicate balance that purportedly ushered in peace on earth *without* goodwill toward men. In short, terrorism was praised as an indispensable strategy for winning wars (World War II), and for keeping the peace (the Cold War), and for enhancing American dominion (extended deterrence). Who would have thought that a tactic and strategy lauded for such marvels would become the most loathsome of evils?

Once defining terrorism was decidedly unproblematic. During World War II terrorism meant one thing—bombing Axis cities. Likewise, during the bipolar disorder known as the Cold War, terrorism meant one thing: the unprecedented threat posed by nuclear weapons—a threat that putatively preserved peace between the superpowers. Today we war *against* terrorism although we're not entirely sure what it is.

Circa 1972, terrorism became an inchoate, nebulous evil.[5] What happened? A sorely neglected story needs to be told about how terrorism morphed from a clearly defined, praiseworthy strategy into the ultimate opprobrium. As Noam Chomsky quips: "Look at the actual history [of terrorism], not the one that's written . . . I could even maybe suggest it as a research topic to some enterprising graduate student who aspires to a career as a taxi driver."[6]

Even though terrorism is today's *idée fixe*, there is negligible interest in this story, a saga rife with irony. Analysts remain preoccupied with the quest for *the* definition of terrorism, a definition free of historical context and of troubling ironies. Such definitions are sought by attending to current usage in venues such as journalism and political rhetoric both here and abroad. Others turn to officials and their critics. Finally, perhaps philosophers—ever attentive to language—can help.

That terrorism is *the* omnipresent evil is not wasted upon journalists. Consider the irony, the incongruity, in representations of the threat. The chances of being killed by a terrorist are about the same as being struck by lightning. The chances of being killed by everyday hazards such as nicotine and alcohol addiction, automobile accidents, and hospital malpractice are considerably higher. Nevertheless, terrorism is the ultimate, the most formidable evil—a fate worse than death. A family is murdered: It could have been worse—thank God it wasn't a terrorist act. A plane crashes, but survivors take comfort; it wasn't terrorism. A deranged woman injures police at the Capitol—not as unnerving as it seems. Talking heads reassure us—it's not terrorism.

The terrorist epithet is not restricted to jihadists in faraway places with strange-sounding names. The emotive force of the epithet is invoked in tiresome, partisan acrimony. Republicans liken Democrats to terrorists, and Democrats return the favor in rejoinders like "Democratic Leader Likens Republicans to Terrorists."[7] "Vice President Joe Biden, during a private meeting with Democratic House members, reportedly said that Republicans had acted like terrorists." And former Treasury Secretary Paul O'Neill insists he is *not* speaking metaphorically: He "called those who opposed the debt limit increase our version of al-Qaeda terrorists. '*Really*,' he added for good measure."[8]

The terrorist epithet is among the few remaining US exports. Palestinians and Israelis denounce one another as terrorists, as do Syrian officials and rebels. The Egyptian military declares a war on terror against those opposing the overthrow of President Morsi, and so it goes. You'd be hard-pressed to find regimes that *don't* vilify opponents as terrorists. In ordinary usage, terrorism is a shameless, promiscuous epithet. Whatever cognitive meaning terrorism once had is cheapened and denatured—the evil of banality.

Times change. Praised for titrating the "delicate balance of nuclear terror" during the Cold War, today's officials take offense when charged with terrorist practices. Defining terrorism becomes a political act. Officialdom goes to considerable lengths to exonerate itself from charges of terrorism. Their definitions of terrorism are irony-free—no worries about the probity of American decision-makers. According to the State Department, terrorism is the "premeditated, politically motivated violence perpetrated against noncombatants."[9] However, like other official definitions, ad hoc qualifications automatically exclude the possibility that the United States practices terrorism. Terrorism is limited to subnational groups and to unlawful activity. Accordingly, the War on Terror targets subnational groups engaged in activity deemed unlawful.

Critics such as Chomsky argue that if official definitions are applied consistently without qualification, the evidence is clear: America engages in terrorism—noncombatants perish.[10] Officials and their supporters respond that it's obscene to suggest moral equivalence between jihadists killing noncombatants and American forces inadvertently causing collateral damage. They insist that US policymakers and the jihadists inhabit radically different moral universes. American actions are driven by worthy ideals such as deposing tyrants, and exigencies—self-defense. Unlike jihadists, Americans refrain from using all the weapons at their disposal, and they don't intentionally harm noncombatants—that's not their aim. Unlike terrorists, Americans lament civilian deaths. Indeed, sensitive to humanitarian and to public relations concerns, American forces take measures to avoid civilian casualties. (Whether they follow Walzer's injunction and redouble their efforts to avoid such casualties is arguable.)[11] Finally, Americans prescribe rules of war and, on occasion, prosecute violators.

Critics counter by arguing that, despite these restraints and precautions, whether by accident or design, American actions harm noncombatants. And what was "shock and awe" about? Didn't it send the signature message of terrorism: Be afraid, be terribly afraid? Surely noncombatant casualties were foreseen. Officials offer rejoinders. They explain that noncombatant casualties (euphemistically called collateral damage) are justified by the doctrine of double effect: It's permissible, if not ethically obligatory, to commit a lesser evil to promote a greater good.

In the case of Iraq, for example, casualties were justified in the interest of liberating Iraqis from a tyrant. Does this justification exonerate American officials from charges of terrorism? Just what is terrorism? And so it goes—arguments and counterarguments. That officials and critics will agree upon terms is as likely as NRA members voluntarily giving up their guns.

In the aftermath of 9/11, philosophers entered the fray in search of the unholy grail: *the* irony-free definition of terrorism that dissolves any doubt about the notion. The contesting language games are a quest for what Rorty calls a final vocabulary—the last word on a concept. The pursuit of the unholy grail is a quest for a metaphysical first principle, the final answer that reveals the essence of terrorism and determines whether American officials should be condemned or exonerated from charges of terrorism.

Philosopher Stephen Nathanson recounts the debate in *Terrorism and the Ethics of War.*[12] The debate pivots around issues such as legitimacy: Is it permissible for nation-states to harm noncombatants in self-defense or in pursuit of other legitimate goals? Must terrorism be informed by a political or some other ideological agenda? Arguments regarding the doctrine of double effect enter the debate: Should certain actions be condemned regardless of the consequences, or are these actions permissible if they achieve a greater good? And of critical importance: What of intentionality? Certain tactics don't intentionally harm noncombatants. Even so, harm is foreseen; are these terrorist acts?

This quest for the unholy grail leads to neither conceptual nor ethical clarity. (Upon attending one of our philosophy conferences, my son observed: "You know, Dad, groups have collective names such as a parliament of owls; how about a confusion of philosophers?") Understandably, academics want to get it right, even though terrorism is a concept, not a thing like a triangle. A triangle can be defined correctly: its objective status does not vary from time and place. True, certain concepts such as lies have fairly stable meanings. However, context determines the meaning of concepts with a history. Unlike World War II when terrorism had an uncontested, unequivocal meaning, today, as Nathanson illustrates, the meaning is contested. It's tempting to conclude that competing academic definitions are self-confessional—indications of the sort of violence authors find despicable.

Academic struggles to get it right by accurately defining terrorism immerse readers in a never-ending language game.[13] There are no referees, and certainly no authoritative tribunal to settle interpretative disputes to everyone's satisfaction. Not always noted for modesty, academics seldom entertain the possibility that they're playing the wrong language game, and that their definitions reflect their tribe.

Quests for the unholy grail remind me of Montaigne's long-ago insight about academics, an insight that suggests that academics are preoccupied with interpreting one another's interpretations rather than examining salient issues—in this case, harm to noncombatants:

> The hundredth commentator passes it on to the next, still more knotty and perplexed than he found it. When were we ever agreed among ourselves: "this book has enough; there is no more to be said about it"? Do we find any end to the need of interpreting? . . . Is it not the common and final end of all studies? Our opinions are grafted upon another; the first serves as a stock to the second to the third, and so forth.[14]

No wonder Nathanson opts out of the language game as it's usually played. He concludes that definitions of terrorism are neither true nor false; they are persuasive definitions—proposals for adopting a particular perspective. Indeed, why continue the search? Do labels really matter? Does invoking "terrorism" enhance understanding of events, or merely indicate our repugnance? Were it up to me, I'd abandon the search for the unholy grail and discuss painfully concrete particulars— such as harming noncombatants or threatening to do so—call it what you will. *But it's not up to me; I'm not the arbiter of language.* Terrorism discourses, the lingua franca of the political spectacle both here and abroad, can't be ignored.

Nathanson shares this realization, and proposes a pragmatic approach to clarify thinking while promoting understanding: a search for a useful, albeit elusive, definition. He explains that deliberate attacks on noncombatants "are the clearest, least controversial instances of terrorism. . . . [This] keeps the definition closer to ordinary usage and avoids needless controversy."[15] However, focusing solely on what is clearest and least controversial won't satisfy critics who charge US officials with terrorist practices. Their marginalized voices need to be heard. Accordingly, I traffic in operational definitions: What operations, what policies and actions, do officials and critics designate as terrorism, and why do they do so?

I analyze clear and distinct episodes in which American decision-makers called their actions terrorism and acted accordingly—World War II and the Cold War. Rather than dwelling upon the history of these conflicts, my overarching concern involves a neglected but revealing issue: These episodes reveal how elites evaded, then celebrated the harrowing ironies that attend the theory and practice of terrorism—deliberately targeting noncombatants in thought and deed.

What can be said of the critics' charge that the past is prologue? In response, I'm tempted to challenge ordinary usage and to invite controversy. Heeding Oscar Wilde's advice, I deal with temptation by giving in. The terrorist practices—strategic bombing—of World War II continued in wars in Korea, Vietnam, and Iraq. Circa 1972 officials no longer called their strategy nuclear terrorism—the venerable "balance of power" became politically correct. I'm curious about the semantic legerdemain that changed the name of the game.

I revisit conflicts in Korea, Vietnam, and Iraq that critics indict as terrorism. These critics deserve a hearing. These conflicts bear a family resemblance to what is usually deemed terrorism—harming noncombatants or threatening to do so. In so doing, I explore an overlooked irony: Noncombatants in enemy lands were not demonized; on the contrary, they were portrayed as "honorary good guys" longing for regime change. Even so, they perished in staggering numbers.

No discussion of terrorism—especially one attentive to irony—would be complete without a discussion of the War on Terror. How much credence should be given to the critics' claim—the war is an answer to a jihadist's prayer? Finally, nothing surpasses the irony of a culture that simultaneously dreads terrorism while relishing terrorism as captivating entertainment. Given the popularity of *Homeland*—President Obama's favorite show—it seems Americans just can't get enough terrorism.

NOTES

1. Reinhold Niebuhr, *The Irony of American History* (Chicago: University of Chicago Press, 1952).

2. Richard Rorty, "Ironists and Metaphysicians," in *The Truth about the Truth*, Walter Truett Anderson, ed. (New York: Putnam, 1995), 101–102.

3. See, for example, sociologist Lisa Stampnitzky's account in *Disciplining Terror* (Cambridge: Cambridge University Press, 2013), Kindle edition, Location 171–173.

4. Paul Fussell, *The Great War* (New York: Oxford University Press, 1975), 8.

5. Lisa Stamplitzky, 252–254.

6. Noam Chomsky, "Distorted Morality: America's War on Terror?," accessed February 10, 2014, http://www.chomsky.info/talks/200202--02.htm.

7. "Democratic Leader Likens Republicans to Terrorists," accessed February 15, 2014, http://www.mlive.com/news/grandrapids/index.ssf/2013/09/republicans_are_terrorists_dem.html.

8. Ibid.

9. US Department of State, Office of the Coordinator for Counterterrorism, Country Reports on Terrorism, April 30, 2007.

10. Chomsky has made this case for a number of years in various volumes. See, for example, *The Culture of Terrorism* (Boston: South End Press, 1988). Recent studies are found in *On Western Terrorism: From Hiroshima to Drones* (Palgrave, 2013).

11. See Michael Walzer's influential discussion in *Just and Unjust Wars* (New York: BasicBooks, 1977), 132–137.

12. Stephen Nathanson, *Terrorism and the Ethics of War* (Cambridge: Cambridge University Press, 2011).

13. What philosopher Ludwig Wittgenstein dubbed language games aren't trivial; they can be deadly serious. Every language has a specialized subset of unique rules and moves. Imagine contractors communicating in their special shorthand as they build a house; you don't understand but they do. Wittgenstein was exercised by the games philosophers play; unlike our hypothetical contractors, games about the existence of God and free will don't produce tangible, verifiable results. Private language games about the meaning and morality of terrorism have their special rules and move on their own momentum. What are the expected results? See Ludwig Wittgenstein, *Philosophic Investigations*, 3rd ed. Trans. G.E.M. Anscombe (Malden, MA: Wiley Blackwell, 2001), 113.

14. "Michel Montaigne's Letters," cited and explicated in Gayle L. Ormiston and Alan D. Schrift, eds., *Context: Nietzsche to Nancy* (Albany: State University of New York Press, 1990), 1.

15. Nathanson, Chapter 2, 24–28.

Chapter I

WORLD WAR II

Theory and Practice of Terrorism

*There is an argument that says that deliberately mounting military
attacks on civilian populations in order to cause terror and indiscriminate death among them is a moral crime.*

—A. C. Grayling[1]

Terrorism didn't always get bad press. Mainstream historians deem
terror bombing, culminating in Hiroshima and Nagasaki, indispensable
for winning World War II.[2] The familiar history of the war won't be
recounted. I'm concerned with the American theory and practice of
terrorism—namely, terror bombing.[3] Prior to American entry into the
war, Roosevelt condemned Japanese and German terror bombing with
the vehemence reserved for today's jihadist atrocities. Even so, Roosevelt's generals made plans for setting wooden Japanese cities aflame.
During the war British and American terror bombing far surpassed that
of the Axis Powers.

That officials such as the redoubtable General Curtis LeMay resorted to what *they* called terrorism is not a startling discovery. It's
simply an embarrassing fact best ignored by mutual pretense—like that
out-of-control uncle who had to be institutionalized. I intend to do
more than merely reveal family secrets—as if the signature terror
bombing of World War II is a secret. Relying upon what historian Paul
Fussell calls "irony-assisted recall."[4] I recall three questions that speak

to the incongruous discourse and unexpected turn of events that mark the pursuit of victory over the Axis Powers:

1. Why, after twenty years of cold-blooded isolationism, did America engage in hot-blooded warfare? Did the isolationists provoke what they desperately wanted to prevent?
2. Why did US officials condemn then enthusiastically practice fire-bombing civilians? Niebuhr's claim that hypocrisy is the defining moral characteristic of a nation-state can't be discounted. However, the Allies endorsed what I call the Just Terrorism Theory in order to sanctify what I'll charitably call their inconsistency.
3. After revisiting history's bloodiest war, it's worth recounting a salutary irony: Why did enmity suddenly turn to amity? Mortal enemies, namely, the Japanese and Germans, became honorary good guys, virtually overnight, as the occupations began.

FROM COLD-BLOODED ISOLATIONISM TO HOT-BLOODED WARFARE

World War II seemed really so extensively predetermined; it developed and rolled its course with the relentless logic of the last act of a classical tragedy.
—George Kennan[5]

Accounts of World War II almost invariably begin with discussions of World War I (the Great War) and its aftermath—isolationism. World War II was the last act of the Great War, a war that surely did not end all wars, but made the world safe for demagoguery. It was, of course, logically possible for the great powers to intervene to prevent the ascendance of Japanese fanatics and Nazi psychopaths. But what is *historically* possible? One word comes to mind in understanding the isolationist sentiments that emerged from the betrayed utopian promises of World War I—disillusionment. If a phrase is needed, there's none better than poet Philip Larkin's gloss on the Great War, "Never such innocence again."

Fussell finds the folly that was World War I poignantly ironic because the conflict began in innocence: "Irony is the attendant of hope, and the fuel of hope is innocence. One reason the Great War was more ironic than any other is that its beginning was more innocent." Irony is the best medium for grasping the enormity of such a war where "eight million people were destroyed because two persons, the Archduke Francis Ferdinand and his Consort, had been shot."[6]

Fussell, of course, recognizes that the assassinations were the tipping point of a series of ironies beginning in an arms race guided by the clichéd Latin proverb: If you would have peace, prepare for war. The Great War demonstrated the obverse: If you would have war, prepare for war—precisely what the great powers did with entangling alliances and the new weapons of industrial warfare. Everyone knew that dynamite and automatic weapons made war unthinkable. Who would send soldiers to certain death charging machine guns? The war began during the summer of 1914, the last season of innocence. Those who knew best assured a public with a will to believe that the conflict would end triumphantly by Christmas.

Like FDR a generation later, in 1916 Wilson ran on the slogan "He kept us out of war." A year later, Americans joined other combatants trapped in trenches emerging only to be slaughtered by machine guns. To this day, preeminent historians remain mystified by the meaningless slaughter that marks the Great War. To paraphrase Nietzsche, historian John Keegan stares into the abyss of the Great War and the abyss stares back:

> Its origins are mysterious. So is its course. Why did a prosperous continent, at the height of its success as a source and agent of global wealth and power and at one of the peaks of its intellectual and cultural achievements, choose to risk all it had won for itself and all it had offered to the world in the lottery of a vicious and local internecine conflict? Why, when the hope of bringing the conflict to a quick and decisive conclusion . . . did the combatants decide nevertheless to persist in their military effort, to mobilize for total war and eventually to commit the totality of their young manhood to mutual and essentially pointless slaughter?[7]

Isolationism seemed like a prudent response to such deadly folly. It vindicated George Washington's parting counsel: avoid the sordid machinations of European politics. The folly of intervening in European affairs left an indelible impression. Witnessing the war and its aftermath, Freud lamented naiveté about the celebrated, cosmopolitan

European sensibility, redemptive power of science and technology, and Enlightenment faith in inevitable progress: "No event has ever destroyed so much that is precious in the common possessions of humanity, confused so many of the clearest intelligence, or so thoroughly debased what is the highest."[8] Freud incorporated Thanatos—the death wish—into his instinct theory, and concluded that lust for killing is in our blood.

About the same time, Freud's nephew, Edward Bernays, aided the Creel Committee (Wilson's propaganda bureau) in promoting the war. (As we'll see, his techniques were expanded and perfected during World War II.) As the war concluded, he astutely recognized that a war-weary public was sick to death of the sordid affairs of Europe: Promoting compulsive consumption proved more profitable than demonizing the Hun: "Manipulators of patriotic opinion made use of the mental clichés and emotional habits of the public to produce mass reactions against the alleged atrocities, the terror and tyranny of the enemy. *It was only natural after the war ended, that intelligent persons should ask themselves whether it was not possible to apply similar techniques to the problems of peace.*"[9]

In other words, rather than employing propaganda techniques to dehumanize enemies, why not use the same techniques to dehumanize the American public? (Persuading women to smoke proved more profitable than inventing enemy atrocities.) Bernays is often considered one of the most important figures no one knows despite his ancestry and formidable contributions to public relations and advertising as we know it today. To be sure, he's certainly not solely responsible for the dehumanization that occurred during World War II and its aftermath— profound indifference to the death of others (the subject of subsequent chapters). However, Bernays's prescient 1928 edition of *Propaganda* provides a primer for what was to come.

Under the auspices of the ill-fated League of Nations, Bernays's uncle and Einstein corresponded about the causes of war and the prospects for peace. Their correspondence began in 1931 and was published as a booklet titled *Why War?* Only 2,000 copies sold despite the authors' illustrious reputations. There are many questions and few answers; their despair is palpable. Einstein asked:

> How is it possible for this small clique to bend the will of the major-
> ity, who stand to lose and suffer by a state of war, to the service of
> their ambitions? An obvious answer to this question would seem to
> be that the minority, the ruling class at present, has the schools and
> press, usually the Church as well, under its thumb. This enables it to
> organize and sway the emotions of the masses, and makes its tool of
> them. [10]

(Curiously, neither Einstein nor Freud mention Bernays's applica-
tion of his uncle's insights for manipulating the emotions of the masses
and putting them under the thumb of elites. Bernays advised every
president from Wilson to Nixon; Goebbels reportedly also relied upon
his insights and techniques.)

Modern industrial warfare baffled Freud, a thinker rarely reticent
about the reasons for human perfidy: "Wars, as now conducted, afford
no scope for acts of heroism according to the old ideals and, given the
high perfection of modern arms, war today would mean the sheer extermination of one of the combatants, if not of both. This is so true, so
obvious, that we can but wonder why the conduct of war is not banned
by general consent." [11]

Any search for irony needs look no further than the Kellogg-Briand
Pact. Three years prior to Freud's observation, Germany, Italy, and the
United States were among the signatories to the pact banning war by
general consent. They agreed not to use war to resolve "disputes or
conflicts of whatever nature or of whatever origin they may be, which
may arise among them." Unlike the League of Nations treaty that it
rejected, the Senate approved the pact 85–1. (The pact didn't impede
ongoing American military intervention in Central America.) Perhaps
Freud ignored the pact because he believed that primitive instincts, not
sanctimonious phrases, governed elites.

Einstein and Freud advocated world federalism—a central authority
to settle international disputes. They knew they succumbed to wishful
thinking, and even if their wishes were granted, they feared vast con-
centrations of power. In any case, they had no illusions about nation-
states ceding sovereignty to an international authority, and certainly no
illusions about the League enforcing its mandates. Disillusionment
turned to despair. Shortly after their correspondence, Einstein and
Freud fled the Nazis and migrated to the United States and Great
Britain, respectively.

Disillusionment went well beyond intellectual circles. Popular novels such as *All Quiet on the Western Front* exposed the tragedy and futility of the Great War, if not of all wars: "How senseless is everything that can ever be written, done, or thought, when such things are possible. It must be all lies and of no account when the culture of a thousand years could not prevent this stream of blood being poured out, these torture-chambers in their hundreds of thousands. A hospital alone shows what war is."[12]

Dalton Trumbo's hospital scenes in *Johnny Got His Gun* show what war is. Totally disabled by the war, locked in the remnants of a war-torn body, unable to communicate, all that remains of Joe Bonham are his thoughts, questions—much to his regret—he should have asked before going to war:

> "[What] was this freedom the little guys were always getting killed for? Was it freedom from another country? Freedom from work or disease or death? Freedom from your mother-in-law? Please mister give us a bill of sale on this freedom before we go out and get killed."[13]

(Trumbo, however, supported World War II; the book's initial plates were destroyed. Reissued during the Vietnam War, the book went into several printings.)

Works such as *Merchants of Death* influenced those in the halls of power, Republicans and Democrats alike. Senator Gerald Nye investigated the role of military contractors in promoting the war. He warned: "When the Senate investigation is over, we shall see that war and preparation for war is not a matter of national honor and national defense, but a matter of profit for the few."[14] The investigation echoed and reinforced isolationist sentiments, as did General Smedley Butler's condemnation of US foreign policy.

> Upon his retirement, Butler, former Commandant of the Marine Corps, admonished: "War is a Racket. . . . In the World War a mere handful garnered the profits of the conflict. At least 21,000 new millionaires and billionaires were made in the United States during the World War. That many admitted their huge blood gains in their income tax returns. How many other war millionaires falsified their tax returns no one knows."[15]

(Butler's admonition likely reinforced early isolationist sentiments, but his impact on current interventionism is negligible. Pacifist and leftist friends have heard of him; friends and students in the Marines have not.)

Interventionists reminded the isolationists that, unfortunately, emerging belligerents in Europe and Asia didn't share their pacifist sentiments. A war-weary public responded with cool indifference. As the 1930s unfolded, Europe once again became embroiled in conflict. The Versailles Treaty, designed to humiliate the Germans while seeking reparations and territorial concession, provided a pretext for Hitler's perversity. Reviving Teutonic mythology, the Nazis armed and conquered in violation of the treaty. Perhaps the earlier fabrications of propagandists such as the Creel Committee made it difficult to convince politicians and allies of Japanese and German atrocities. Recalling these fabrications, reports of Nazi atrocities were dismissed as interventionist propaganda. Credible reports regarding atrocities against Jews and other "non-Aryans" were met with disbelief, if not indifference. Indeed, even members of the well-assimilated German Jewish community were in denial.

Nazi airpower mercilessly slaughtered civilians in Spain followed by a blitzkrieg in Poland, and once again, German subs sank American ships. The threat to American allies and interests was obvious for anyone who cared to look. FDR devised programs to circumvent the neutrality acts—programs such as Lend-Lease and other programs for channeling military supplies to Great Britain.

Rather than isolationist ideology, perhaps events closer to home contributed to indifference to international affairs—namely the Great Depression. And lest interventionists yield to temptation, beginning in 1935 Congress passed a series of neutrality acts designed to keep the United States out of another war: neither friend nor foe could receive aid. FDR and the interventionists were exercised about events in Europe and Asia—as Japan wreaked havoc in China and Manchuria. The president warned: "I tell the American people solemnly that the United States will never survive as a happy and fertile oasis of liberty surrounded by a cruel desert of dictatorship."[16] Accordingly, the president tried to isolate Japan. He explained: "As you know, I am fighting against a public psychology of long standing—a psychology which comes very close to saying 'Peace at any price' . . . The most practical and most peaceful thing to do in the long run is to quarantine them [the Japanese]."[17] FDR had his justification: The Japanese committed atrocities in what they called—apparently without irony—their "Co-Prosperity Sphere." Even now they are reluctant to acknowledge their sheer barbarism.

Irony of Deterrence

Seemingly reasonable actions designed to deter aggression often produced disastrous results. The Roosevelt administrations responded with an oil embargo and other measures after the Japanese allied themselves with Germany. In addition to inflaming jingoism, the embargo put Japan in a seemingly untenable position: conquer, negotiate, or starve.

Japanese thinking was also rife with irony. A limited war to secure Asian assets and gain American concessions seemed to be the answer. Optimism regarding such a venture didn't seem unreasonable: Given their victory in the Russo-Japanese war, unopposed conquests in Asia, and American isolationism, the Japanese were confident of a favorable outcome.[18] Any war with America would be limited and brief. The Japanese stereotypes of Americans, along with wishful thinking, had ironic consequences. Japanese leadership assumed Americans were merchants who would never find it profitable to pursue a protracted war with impassioned Japanese willing to fight to the death. And surely arrogant Americans would never recover from a humiliating attack on Pearl Harbor and the Philippines—they would cut their losses and sue for peace. The irony proved tragic for both sides.

The Japanese had no monopoly on self-deception. Dispatched to Pearl Harbor, surely the Pacific Fleet would deter Japanese ambitions. In September 1941, a columnist in a Honolulu paper reassured nervous readers:

> A Japanese attack on Hawaii is regarded as the most unlikely thing in the world, with one chance in a million of being successful. Even if an attack occurred, American naval men would like nothing better than to see the Japanese fleet outside of Pearl Harbor where they could take it on.[19]

The gods punish those who believe their own propaganda: The ancient Greeks appreciated tragic irony—they called it hubris. Elites entertained narcissistic notions of American exceptionalism and racial superiority; American stature itself was the ultimate deterrent. The consequences proved worthy of Greek drama. Decision-makers ignored the obvious and indulged in wishful thinking. Unchastened by Japanese victory in the Russo-Japanese War and Asian conquests, most American planners couldn't believe that the "little yellow bastards" were capable of successfully attacking American assets in the Pacific. Surely, the American colossus would defeat "primitive yellow midgets" in a matter of weeks—and (supposedly) the Japs knew it.[20] The Japanese seemed like a joke, not a foe.

There were, however, concerns about local saboteurs. In a seemingly minor tactical move that had momentous strategic consequences, base commanders Kimmel and MacArthur parked American ships and planes in close proximity both at Pearl Harbor and in the Philippines—creating a target-rich environment. Kimmel was charged with dereliction of duty. MacArthur was not although he had adequate warning—the Japanese attacked MacArthur's installation nine hours *after* the attack on Pearl Harbor. MacArthur couldn't believe the "inferior" Japanese sunk his ships and destroyed his aircraft—must have been German pilots.

Prior to Pearl Harbor, the interventionists were more concerned with events in Europe, especially in 1939 as the Nazi juggernaut began to roll over the continent. With the Great War still fresh in memory, the isolationists advocated a fortress America immune from yet another European conflagration. Conflicts between isolationists and interventionists were seldom thoughtful, deliberative debates. In 1940 two social psychologists saw the dispute degenerate into a contest between propagandists. In the authors' words, such propaganda confuses, rather than clarifies, and translates power politics into mythology while portraying the world as a kind of Manichean cartoon. In short, "The modern world has become the propagandists' paradise."[21] Propagandists, the authors observed, don't lie in vain. Bernays couldn't have agreed more. In what he called a democracy, Bernays argued that consent needs to be manufactured for the horde. World War II mass-produced ordnance and consent.

Writing at the cusp between war and peace, a time when "history marches at a double speed," the authors, Lavine and Wechsler, didn't predict the outcome of the contest between the isolationists and interventionists, but two predictions proved prescient. If war came, war with Japan would be a pretext for engaging in world war. "There was another door to war of which most Americans were only vaguely conscious, but which the propagandists could not overlook. It was labeled Japan." A variety of military men and pundits asserted that war against Japan was inevitable: US entry into the war will be through "the back door of the Pacific." In effect, a war against the Yellow Peril and the Hun would be "extremely saleable merchandise."[22] They also predicted that, if war came, a propaganda campaign unprecedented in scope and power would emerge—America would speak with one voice. Pearl Harbor ended the debate.

BAD JAPS, GOOD GERMANS, AND RUSSIAN COMRADES

[Pearl Harbor] inspired a thirst for revenge among Americans that the Japanese, with their own racial blinders, had failed to anticipate.
                                                                          —Dower[23]

Japan declared war on the United States just after the attack on Pearl Harbor. The next day, December 8, 1941, the United States declared war on Japan. Allied with Japan, Germany followed suit; the United States declared war on Germany on December 11. Influential isolationist groups, such as America First, disbanded within days.

The surprise attack and consequent shift from isolationism to interventionism are obvious ironies. That "yellow midgets" could destroy much of the Pacific fleet in a matter of hours seemed incongruous indeed! World War II, however, also raises puzzling, largely overlooked ironies, ironies that even now raise unsettling questions.

- Why, for example, did American and British leaders denounce terror bombing prior to the war, only to orchestrate massive terror bombing during the conflict?
- According to official US Department of State accounts: "The Allied leaders came to Yalta [from February 4 to 11, 1945] knowing that an Allied victory in Europe was practically inevitable."[24]

Nevertheless, the most massive, destructive terror bombing of Germany and Japan occurred in 1945. What accounts for these gratuitous air raids?

- Japan didn't pose an existential threat to the United States; the Nazis were more formidable. Why then did the United States Army Air Force (USAAF) engage in attacks on Japan that far surpassed the European campaign? Specifically, why did the USAAF expressly target Japanese noncombatants while making some effort—at least during the early phases of the war—to avoid harming German noncombatants?

- No account of the irony of World War II could omit the newfound friendship with the formerly despised Soviet Union: no mystery here—my enemy's enemy is my friend.

- The occupations of Japan and Germany present a salutary, albeit puzzling, irony—giving aid and comfort to former enemies. Generals MacArthur and Marshall played key roles in destroying *and* rebuilding Germany and Japan. The occupations reinvented these former, mortal enemies as honorary good guys—destined to become trusted allies—virtually overnight.

Never Such Propaganda Again

We are governed, our minds are molded, our tastes formed, our ideas suggested, largely by men we have never heard of. This is a logical result of the way in which our democratic society is organized. Vast numbers of human beings must cooperate in this manner if they are to live together as a smoothly functioning society.

—Edward Bernays[25]

World War II propaganda successfully dissolved these ironies—at least in the minds of most Americans. Even now, many scholars along with the general public see nothing ironic in the "Good War." The cause was just: The surprise attack on Pearl Harbor and the Nazi juggernaut prompted declarations of war. But a just war isn't necessarily fought justly in a manner consonant with a nation's peacetime core values—namely, sparing the lives of noncombatants. Propagandists had their work cut out.

The ironies just mentioned were not mere linguistic incongruities. Absent effective propaganda, authorities and their constituents would have experienced the incongruity in American actions as unnerving *cognitive dissonance.*[26] *Overcoming cognitive dissonance is the key to understanding wartime propaganda.* Social psychologist Leon Festinger coined the term to describe the dissonance aroused by the clash of core beliefs. He presupposed an innate drive to sustain cognitive consistency; unfortunately, the drive can condone maladaptive behavior—in this case, terror bombing.

Cultures that embrace a will to truth cannot abide contradictions in core values. To be sure, wartime propaganda promoted falsehoods essential for overcoming dissonance. But lies mean nothing unless one cares about the truth. Evidently, propagandists believed—rightly or wrongly—that truth mattered so much that stressing the truth about enemy civilians targeted for destruction—namely, their humanity—would demoralize the Greatest Generation and undermine the war effort. In effect, propagandists told the public *you can't handle the truth!*

The irony of condemning terror bombing civilians while setting Axis Power cities aflame is undeniable. Prior to American entry into the war, President Roosevelt echoed virtually universal revulsion regarding German and Japanese terror bombing. In the president's words: "The ruthless bombing . . . of civilians in unfortified centers of population . . . has resulted in the deaths of thousands of defenseless men, women, and children. [It] has sickened the hearts of every civilized man and woman, and has profoundly shocked the conscience of humanity."[27] Responding specifically to the Nazi destruction of Guernica, Roosevelt appealed "to every Government which may be engaged in hostilities publicly to affirm its determination that its armed forces shall in no event, and under no circumstances, undertake the bombardment from the air of civilian populations."[28] Likewise, Roosevelt condemned the "Japanese bombing of civilians in China as 'barbarous' violations of the 'elementary principles' of modern morality."[29] Churchill echoed this revulsion when he condemned the Nazi blitzkrieg visited upon Poland as an act of terror and destruction.

All the ideological resources were marshaled to promote the war effort. Terror bombing Japanese cities was not merely condoned, it was celebrated. The entire culture spoke with one voice. Propaganda was ubiquitous—inescapable. The War Department and Office of War Information mobilized virtually every institution in the campaign against the Axis Powers. Mickey Mouse got into the act as well as the staid *New York Times*. I admit to perverse nostalgia. The Big Lie about the bestial nature of the Japanese people ignited all-too-human hot-blooded hatred. Does latter-day, cold-blooded indifference to the death of others demonstrate our moral superiority?

Just Terrorism Theory

> *Recently a number of liberal political theorists, including Rawls and Walzer, have argued for a "supreme emergency exemption" from the traditional just war principle of discrimination which absolutely prohibits direct attacks against innocent civilians, claiming that a political community threatened with destruction may deliberately target innocents in order to save itself.*
>
> —Christopher Toner[30]

As if to confirm Niebuhr's observation that hypocrisy is the signature of international relations, American and British strategists fashioned extensive plans for bombing enemy cities if war came as Roosevelt and Churchill condemned Japanese and German terror bombing. Prior to the Pacific War, for example, General George Marshall instructed aides to devise plans to burn Japanese cities.[31] American forces operationalized these plans in 1942 by attacking Japanese and German cities, air raids culminating in firestorms in Hamburg and Dresden, and in Tokyo, Hiroshima, and Nagasaki.

It is unfair, however, to reduce British and American actions to sheer hypocrisy. Sometimes, exigent circumstances demand choosing the lesser evil. The Allies devised a conceptual strategy that rationalized the incongruity between denouncing and practicing terror bombing—Michael Walzer calls it the doctrine of "Supreme Emergency." I call it Just Terrorism Theory. Leaders *do* have principles; they change to suit the occasion. Churchill and Roosevelt didn't ignore the terror bombing they orchestrated. Sometimes they lied, but on other occasions they proffered good reasons for their actions; whether they were entirely sincere, I cannot say.

British terror bombing—at least prior to about 1944—is understandable given exigent circumstances. Whether, in retrospect, it was justified is difficult to assess—although some speculate that it galvanized Nazi resolve. In any case, in his seminal work in ethics and warfare, Michael Walzer forgives but doesn't forget. Churchill, for good reason, insisted his island confronted a "Supreme Emergency," an existential threat to British civilization. Walzer characterizes a Supreme Emergency as:

1. Omnipresent danger: Nazi victories on the continent along with the bombing of their isle revealed the mortal danger. The threat wasn't hypothetical; it was ongoing and worsening. The British rightly feared further terror bombing, an invasion, and the destruction of their civilization.
2. Unprecedented threat: such as the Nazi peril, a uniquely horrifying saga of conquest and destruction. For once, propaganda and reality aligned: Simply put, Nazism was as bad as it gets. Amid the rubble in Coventry and London, the British knew that the terrible already happened.

Walzer argues that the British were justified in struggling to save their civilization, if not their lives, by any means necessary, including terror bombing.[32] The pure morality of sparing noncombatants cannot be sustained amid such exigent circumstances. British planners hoped that terror bombing would shorten the war by undermining popular support for the Hitler regime. It would force the enemy to divert resources from the battlefront to devastated cities, and demolish key industries along with their workers. Terror bombing might also shatter Hitler's promise of German invincibility by fomenting dissention among German elites, possibly bringing down the regime. The vast majority of the British supported the campaign—the Germans had it coming. Finally, the Royal Air Force Commander Arthur (Bomber) Harris seemed to argue that two wrongs might not make a right, but three do: All wars kill civilians, blockades kill civilians; therefore, it is permissible for terror bombing to kill civilians.[33]

American Policy

Every war is ironic because every war is worse than expected. Every war constitutes an irony of situations because its means are so melodramatically disproportionate to its presumed ends.

—Fussell[34]

My concern, however, is with American policy: Did American planners believe *they* faced a Supreme Emergency? Did propaganda and reality align? A citizen couldn't make it through the day without total immersion in the sights and sounds of a Supreme Emergency. The draft called up hundreds of thousands as sacrifice and rationing began. Unlike today, Americans knew a war was on. Menacing Huns and Japs were everywhere: in posters, newscasts, fireside chats, movies, and papers.

What did American planners believe? Apparently, they didn't construe the War in the Pacific as a Supreme Emergency. Planners saw Japan as the weaker, junior partner in the Axis alliance, a power incapable of destroying American civilization. The Japanese didn't pose an existential threat to the United States. To be sure, turning the Pacific into a Japanese lake was inimical to American interests as was the Co-Prosperity sphere. Japs, however, marched down Pennsylvania Avenue only in propaganda, not in the elite imagination.

In the case of the British, national survival trumped noncombatant immunity. In the case of the Americans, national interests, and hot-blooded passion for avenging Pearl Harbor, trumped noncombatant immunity. America waged war against Japan as if the Empire of the Sun presented a Supreme Emergency, an exigency demanding the extermination of all that was Japanese. The uninhibited air war leveled scores of cities, killing hundreds of thousands of noncombatants. Just Terrorism Theory seemed superfluous. It could be argued that payback drove the excesses in the war against Japan; strategic concerns were secondary.

American planners recognized the obvious: The Nazis were more formidable. At times, FDR worried about the prospect of a Nazi conquest—a *possible* Supreme Emergency. It was clear that, unopposed, the Nazis could conquer Europe, North Africa, and the Soviet Union, a calamity of catastrophic proportions. In a fireside chat, FDR warned: Nazis planned for ultimate domination, "not of any one section of the

world but of the whole earth and the oceans on it. When Hitler organized his Berlin-Rome-Tokyo alliance, all these plans of conquest became a single plan."[35]

Given the magnitude of the threat, why was FDR, in the words of
one historian, a "cautious crusader" reluctant to engage in full-scale
terror bombing of Germany, while encouraging virtually uninhibited
bombing of Japan? (During the latter phases of the war, however, the
USAAF became less inhibited and joined the RAF in igniting the firestorms that incinerated Hamburg and Dresden.) Compared to the punishment visited upon Japan, the American bombing of Germany was
relatively restrained—terrorism-lite. Why was this the case?

Terrorizing the Japanese

*In Europe, we felt that our enemies, horrible and deadly as they
were, were still people. But out here [in the Pacific theatre] I soon
gathered that the Japanese were looked upon as something subhuman or repulsive: the way some people feel about cockroaches or
mice.*

—Journalist Ernie Pyle[36]

Due to the shock of the horrific events in Hawaii and the Philippines, no propaganda was necessary to rally support for declarations of
war against the Axis Powers. I'm not certain a massive propaganda
campaign was necessary to condone, if not celebrate, bombing enemy
cities. Nevertheless, World War II marks the apotheosis of death and of
propaganda. As Dower explains: Noncombatants became legitimate targets; firestorms incinerated hundreds of thousands of Germans and
Japanese.[37] It's one thing to battle despised enemy soldiers; it's quite
another to violate the venerable rules of just war by raining incendiaries
upon noncombatants after stridently condemning such actions.

Dower's magisterial *War Without Mercy* disabuses the reader of the
congenial notion that strategic decisions are informed and tempered by
a strict, cost/benefit/risk analysis of military exigencies. Massing evidence from a variety of sources, Dower gives considerable weight to
racism, bloodlust, and narcissistic injuries to American pride in ac-
counting for the hot-blooded hatred of the Jap.[38] No precise estimate of
Japanese deaths is possible. There is consensus, however, that terror

bombing destroyed cities resulting in hundreds of thousands of civilian deaths.[39] The estimates of those who orchestrated the raids reveal the magnitude of what the official *United States Strategic Bombing Survey* called history's greatest slaughter.[40] In 1944 and 1945, the defeat of Japan appeared imminent—not only did cities and industries lie in ruin, but the enemy's military was also decimated. Recalling the March 1945 firestorm Robert McNamara and General LeMay orchestrated upon Tokyo, McNamara estimates that about 100,000 civilians burned to death. Interviewed in the documentary film *Fog of War*, he equivocates regarding what he and his government visited upon Japan:

> Killing 50 percent to 90 percent of the people of sixty-seven Japanese cities and then bombing them with two nuclear bombs is not proportional . . . [Nevertheless] I don't fault Truman for dropping the nuclear bomb. The US–Japanese War was one of the most brutal wars in all of human history. . . . You shouldn't bomb, shouldn't kill, shouldn't burn to death 100,000 civilians in one night. LeMay said, "If we'd lost the war, we'd all have been prosecuted as war criminals." And I think he's right. He, and I'd say, we're behaving as war criminals. LeMay recognized that what he was doing would be thought immoral if his side had lost. But what makes it immoral if you lose and not immoral if you win?[41]

Overcoming Cognitive Dissonance

Dehumanizing the Jap resolved the cognitive dissonance that would attend incarcerating American citizens of Japanese descent in concentration camps and incinerating Japanese cities. As social psychologists Anthony Pratkanis and Elliot Aronson explain: "The cognition '*I and my country are decent, fair, and reasonable*' is dissonant with . . . '*I and my country have hurt innocent people.*' . . . Dehumanization succeeds in resolving any dissonance that may be aroused by our cruelty toward our enemies."[42]

Propagandists, and intellectuals who should have known better, promoted a cognitive illusion, a falsehood intuitively accepted as true—the Big Lie about the subhuman, treacherous nature of *all* Japanese. In so doing, they humanized Americans, depicting us as the very exemplars of humanity: a resolute people fearlessly and selflessly engaged in combating evil.[43] (As Churchill quipped: "In wartime truth is so precious that it should always be attended by a bodyguard of lies.")

Cognitive illusions are immune from criticism, and yet they are not indelible—as the occupations of Japan and Germany illustrate. Amid the war, the illusion prevailed due to confirmation bias—people see what they want to see. The Japanese provided ample examples of atrocities by torturing and beheading soldiers and civilians. Both sides committed atrocities. *Life* magazine, for example, featured a full-page photo of a young American woman caressing a Japanese skull—a souvenir sent by her fiancé fighting the Japanese.[44] Neither side considered the distinct possibility that young soldiers were thrown into a terrifying, atrocity-producing situation. The Japanese depicted American atrocities as the work of white devils. In the world according to American propaganda, Japanese atrocities were proof positive of the intractable, vile nature of the Japanese race.

Both sides ignored or denigrated counterevidence. Most Americans experienced what social psychologists call "availability bias": No one remembered long-ago gifts of Japanese cherry trees festooning the Washington Mall; Jap Zeroes screaming over Hawaiian waters were fresh in memory. Japanese prisoners seldom had the decency to conform to the stereotype of rabid fanatics; their docile behavior made no difference. Ernie Pyle observed Japanese prisoners "wrestling and laughing and talking just like normal human beings." He couldn't believe his eyes: "They gave me the creeps, and I wanted to take a mental bath after looking at them."[45]

Given racist stereotyping, and the shock and humiliation of Pearl Harbor, Americans had an unquenchable thirst for revenge. The Japanese became wholly other, another species—the Yellow Peril. Everyone knew that *all* Japanese, regardless of citizenship or locale, got what they deserved! It was obvious to most Americans: The Jap wasn't a human deserving moral consideration; he was a plague reviled as a louse or rat. (I'm reminded of science fiction films in which cheerful, idealistic Americans battle pernicious insects on alien planets.)

Social psychologist Melvin Lerner analyzed the comforting notion that people get what they deserve—it's a just world after all. Those who embrace what he called the "Just World Hypothesis" are strong in the faith that the world is a harmonious, just place, a moral universe in which people get what's coming to them.[46] Ironically, "belief in a just world may take the place of a genuine commitment to justice. . . . It is simply easier to assume that forces beyond . . . [our] control mete our justice. . . . The result may be abdication of personal responsibility, acquiescence in the face of suffering and misfortune, and indifference toward injustice."[47]

The dehumanized image of the Jap pervaded American culture. Propagandists referred to the enemy with singularity: The Jap denoted a homogenous, undifferentiated herd. Indeed, it would be difficult to find popular *or* scholarly media that didn't dehumanize the Jap. Even progressive periodicals such as the *Nation* featured cartoons portraying the Jap as a crazed monkey hidden in dark jungles. And those who should have known better—anthropologists such as Margaret Mead— asserted that Japs were "childish and pathological."[48]

Popular music featured titles such as:

> "Taps for the Japs," "We've Got To Do a Job on the Japs, Baby," "Oh, You Little Son of an Oriental," "When Those Little Yellow Bellies Meet the Cohens and the Kellys,". . . and "We're Going to Find a Fellow Who Is Yellow and Beat Him Red, White, and Blue." In an act of selective racism, one recording, "The Japs Haven't Got a Chinaman's Chance," producers renamed "The Japs Haven't Got a Ghost of a Chance," out of sensitivity over America's Chinese allies. In an era of overt racism, there were now good and bad Orientals. [49]

It would be redundant to go into detail about the spate of popular films dehumanizing the Japanese. Suffice it to mention that, in the formulaic narratives, subhuman, savage Japs stab trusting Americans in the back. The savages delight in torturing those unfortunate enough to survive. As communication theorists Koppes and Black conclude in their study of wartime films: "It was a rare film that did not employ terms such as . . . *beasts, yellow monkeys, nips, or slant-eyed rats.*"[50] Three films, however, merit special mention.

Purple Heart ends with a portentous vow: "[We'll] blacken your skies and burn your cities to the ground. . . . This is your war—you wanted it—you asked for it. And now you're going to get it—and it won't be finished until your dirty little empire is wiped off the face of the earth!"[51]

Behind the Rising Sun brought editorials such as those in the *Los Angeles Times* to life on the big screen: "A viper is nonetheless a viper wherever the egg is hatched—so a Japanese American, born of Japanese parents, grows up to be a Japanese, not an American."[52] The film is rare, perhaps unique, in portraying a young Japanese man as an individual, not a clone. Affable young Taro Saki studies engineering at Cornell and returns to his native land seeking employment with an American firm. He almost seems like a typical, ambitious young American—until his blood cries out for savagery. Betraying the Americans who selflessly helped him, Taro joins the Nippon military and relishes skewering Chinese babies on bayonets—vintage Creel Committee imagery.

Many consider *Know Your Enemy—Japan* as the culmination of the wartime propagandist's art: the American equivalent of Leni Riefenstahl's bravura celebration of Nazism, *Triumph of the Will*. Three years in the making, the script was continually revised to satisfy War Department objections, objections such as portraying ordinary Japanese as victims of fanatical militarists. In a perversely brilliant distillate of racist stereotyping, we witness the sordid history of the Jap, a being bereft of individuality, let alone of the tolerance and compassion treasured by Americans. The Jap was a print from the same negative—an image of a defective, fanatical race.

Our search for irony leads to the film's premiere on August 9, 1945, the day the second atomic bomb obliterated Nagasaki. General MacArthur had the film withdrawn two weeks later as the occupation was about to begin. As Dower concludes: The film is an iconic revelation of the hot-blooded hatred that drove the war in the Pacific.[53]

Taken as a whole, the popular music and films insisted that incarcerating Japanese Americans and destroying Japanese cities was not merely permissible—it was mandatory. Roosevelt's Executive Order 9066 authorized concentration camps (called "relocation centers"). The terror visited upon the Japanese homeland was unrestrained. Terror bombing was widely accepted as just retribution for Pearl Harbor and much else. It is difficult to determine what was worse in the American mind-set: the tragic loss of life and destruction at Pearl Harbor, or the inconsolable humiliation at the hands of a supposedly inferior race. As Dower illustrates, those who questioned, let alone criticized, the terror bombing were usually denounced as fools or traitors.[54]

The bombing began with the Doolittle raid in April 1942, a small-scale operation, but a harbinger of the massive terror bombing that followed. The daring attack on Tokyo was of negligible strategic value, although it symbolized Japanese vulnerability. The raid—like the massive bombing that would follow—was a much-needed response to the despair of Pearl Harbor. The *Doolittle Website* makes this point, a point applicable to the gratuitous bombing of Dresden and Hamburg, and of Hiroshima and Nagasaki: "By spring 1942, America needed a severe morale boost. The raid on Tokyo [an attack on Japanese civilians] on April 18, 1942, certainly provided that—cheering the American military and public."[55]

Gratuitous Terror Bombing

> *Blow up or burn 53 percent of Hamburg's buildings . . . and kill fifty thousand people into the bargain. Mutilate and lay to waste the Polish and the Dutch cities. . . . And explode Japanese industry with a flash of magnesium, and make the canals boil around bloated bodies of the people. Do Tokyo again.*
>
> —Curtis LeMay[56]

According to official documents and the reckoning of a variety of historians, the Axis Powers were doomed by 1944. Why did the most destructive bombing—such as the firebombing of Tokyo mentioned above—begin at this juncture? One obvious answer: By 1944 enemy air defenses were decimated; attacks occurred with impunity. This realization does not impugn the bravery and idealism of the RAF and USAAF crews who, amid the flak and gunfire, attacked the enemy during the early phases of the war. They deemed their cause righteous. Some who planned the gratuitous raids expressed regret after the war: Churchill had second thoughts about Dresden, and Oppenheimer expressed deep regret about Hiroshima and Nagasaki. Others had no remorse, at least in public. Bomber Harris seemed to believe that terror bombing means you never have to say you're sorry. And Truman claimed he never lost a night's sleep after authorizing Hiroshima and Nagasaki.

Still smarting from Pearl Harbor, Americans longed for a fitting climax for the war against Japan. Some claimed that only utter devastation would assure unconditional surrender and assure the world that the Japs would never rise again. Dreams of revenge became a Japanese nightmare. General Henry (Hap) Arnold dreamed of hot-blooded vengeance, not icy-cold strategic calculation. He envisaged a grand finale— hitting Tokyo with a thousand planes—a fitting coda to the war. As darkness fell on August 14, 828 B-29s accompanied by 186 fighters bombed the remnants of Tokyo. President Truman announced the sur-render before many of the fighters returned.[57]

Was Hiroshima Gratuitous?

Humanist and pacifist refugees from the Nazi threat first envisaged the ultimate terror weapon. Ongoing research verified Einstein's cele-brated equation $E = mc^2$. (Newtonian particle logic described matter in motion; Einstein calculated *annihilation*—annihilating matter. Annihi-lating a miniscule bit of uranium isotope could destroy an entire city.) Fearful of research leading to nuclear weapons in Nazi hands, refugee physicists—Leo Szilard and Edward Teller—prevailed upon Einstein to write an appeal to Roosevelt stressing that the Nazis might develop nuclear weapons that would determine the outcome of the war; accord-ingly, the United States must move decisively and secretly to get the weapon first. Einstein came to regret his decision. Initially, the eccen-tric longhairs weren't taken seriously; the government only allocated $6,000 for nuclear research. However, the Manhattan Project began after British intelligence corroborated and reinforced the physicists' apprehension.[58] The rest is history, or what some feared might be the end of history.

A truism: Generals are always fighting the last war. However, as historians such as Gar Alperovitz suggest, on occasion the generals are fighting future wars. He argues that, in no small measure, nuclear weapons were designed to intimidate the Soviets in future confronta-tions. Hiroshima and Nagasaki demonstrated awesome American pow-er and unflinching resolve.[59]

Physicist Joseph Rotblat—the only scientist to leave the Manhattan Project—lends credence to the argument. Evidently, General Leslie Groves, the Project director, fought a future war. Rotblat experienced "disagreeable shock" after Groves told him: "The real purpose in making the bomb was to subdue the Soviets." In explaining his dismay, Rotblat stresses that the Soviets were allies battling Nazis—their losses were horrific. He thought his efforts were solely intended to prevent a Nazi victory.

By 1944 Rotblat realized that the European War would end before the bomb was ready; moreover, fears that initially motivated the Man-hattan Project proved groundless—no German bomb existed. Never-theless, efforts to build the bomb accelerated. He quit and returned to

England, not without enduring considerable harassment. He devoted the remainder of his life to alerting the public to the danger of nuclear war. He won the Nobel Peace Prize in 1995.[60]

General Groves was equally candid about the bureaucratic and technological imperatives that prompted dropping the atomic bomb after Japan lay in ruins. As we'll see shortly, the official *United States Strategic Bombing Survey* concluded that nuclear weapons didn't prompt the Japanese surrender; the defeat of Japan was a foregone conclusion in summer 1945. Planners chose Hiroshima and Nagasaki because they were among the few cities that remained intact. The destruction of Hiroshima displayed the incredible power of the uranium mechanism; Nagasaki proved the plutonium mechanism equally effective.

Groves also had more mundane concerns. He realized that Congress would follow the money: After investing $2 billion on the Manhattan Project, they expected payback. If Congress didn't get something in return, Groves feared he would spend the rest of his life testifying on Capitol Hill. Indeed, politicians and military men who sponsored the project would also pay a high price if it seemed the money was wasted.[61]

Commentators seldom discuss the morality of burning hundreds of thousands of civilians to death with conventional weapons; historians, however, remain preoccupied with the morality of destroying Hiroshima and Nagasaki. Mainstream historians such as John Gaddis contend: "Having acquired this awesome weapon, the United States used it against Japan for a simple and straightforward reason: achieve victory as quickly, as decisively, and as economically as possible."[62] In short, atomic weapons proved indispensible for ending the Pacific War.

These historians claim that, despite their losses, the Japanese had no intention of surrendering in 1945; they made preparations to defend their homeland. It is estimated that Operation Olympiad, the planned invasion, would prolong the war and cost tens of thousands of American lives and many more Japanese lives. Revisionist historians such as Gar Alperovitz counter that "by July 1945, a combination of assurances from the Emperor and the shock of a Russian declaration of war appeared quite likely to bring about surrender long before an invasion could begin."[63]

At the risk of being preemptory, the debate should have ended in July 1946 with the publication of the *War Department Strategic Bomb-*

ing Survey. This official account, drafted by noted "hawks" such as Paul Nitze, recognizes that Japan lay in ruin due to conventional bombing. The document concludes that the Japanese would have surrendered under virtually any circumstances:

> Based on a detailed investigation of all the facts, and supported by the testimony of the surviving Japanese leaders involved, it is the Survey's opinion that certainly prior to 31 December 1945, and in all probability prior to 1 November 1945, Japan would have surrendered even if the atomic bombs had not been dropped, even if Russia had not entered the war, and even if no invasion had been planned or contemplated.[64]

The *Survey*'s implication is clear: Hiroshima and Nagasaki were gratuitous acts of terrorism: "As might be expected, the primary reaction of the populace to the bomb was fear, uncontrolled terror, strengthened by the sheer horror of the destruction and suffering witnessed and experienced by the survivors."[65]

Not surprisingly, LeMay participated in planning the destruction of Hiroshima and Nagasaki. His regret *is* surprising. Taking the Nuremburg defense, LeMay explained that using atomic bombs was unnecessary—just following orders. "We went ahead and dropped the bombs because President Truman told me to do it. He told me in a personal letter."[66]

Good Germans

Will you destroy the good with the wicked? If there be fifty just men in the city, will you then destroy the place and not spare it for the sake of the fifty just men within? Far be it from you to do such a thing as kill the just with the wicked, treating just and unjust alike! Far be it from you! Shall not the judge of all the Earth act justly?
—Abraham beseeching God not to destroy Sodom and Gomorrah

Commencing on the night of July 24, 1943, the bombing continued until August 3. Operation Gomorrah destroyed a significant percentage of the city of Hamburg, leaving over one million residents home-

less and killing 40,000–50,000 civilians. In the immediate wake of the raids, over two-thirds of Hamburg's population fled the city. The raids severely shook the Nazi leadership, leading Hitler to be concerned that similar raids on other cities could force Germany out of the war.

—Military historian Kennedy Hickman[67]

God didn't have a Christian attitude—no forgiveness. He called off the deal struck with Abraham to spare the innocent after His undercover angels discovered gross iniquity. God destroyed the place; Genesis notes collateral damage—the innocent perished. Anglican Bishop George Bell displayed a more Christian attitude. As early as 1939, he condemned retaliating against enemy atrocities with terror bombing. Even after the Luftwaffe attacked England, the bishop urged his countrymen to resist terrorizing German noncombatants. He and other members of the small community opposing night raids were denounced as naïve pacifists, perhaps traitors.[68]

It is noteworthy, however, that Liddell Hart, an influential British strategist, initially believed terror bombing would shorten the war, thereby saving Allied and Axis Power lives. The horrific toll exacted on German noncombatants gave him second thoughts:

It will be ironical if the defenders of civilization depend for their victory upon the most barbaric . . . way of winning a war that the modern world has seen . . . We are now counting for victory on success in the way of degrading war to a new level—as represented by indiscriminate (night) bombing.[69]

Hart realized it's disingenuous to claim that joint RAF and USAAF actions were intended solely to shorten the war. The most extensive and destructive bombing occurred toward the end of the war, 1944–1945, when German air defenses were decimated, and the Allies enjoyed more planes and advanced technology. Nevertheless, in January 1945, according to a British historical site, the RAF planned to destroy Dresden:

Dresden, the seventh largest city in Germany and not much smaller than Manchester, is also by far the largest unbombed built-up city the enemy has got. In the midst of winter with refugees pouring westwards and troops to be rested, roofs are at a premium. The

intentions of the attack are to hit the enemy where he will feel it
most, behind an already partially collapsed front, to prevent the use
of the city in the way of further advance, and incidentally to show the
Russians when they arrive what Bomber Command can do.[70]

On February 13, 1945, the RAF and USAAF began a two-day assault
on Dresden. No longer overly concerned about noncombatant casual-
ities, the USAAF sent 527 heavy bombers. Tens of thousands perished
in the ensuing firestorm. The American role in European terror bombing raises questions that plague us to this day. As Grayling and others
illustrate, there's no question about the intentions of the British. Led by
"Bomber Harris," the RAF targeted noncombatants. By most accounts,
during the early phases of the war, the USAAF intended to spare noncombatants by practicing precision, daylight bombing of military targets. Initially, they didn't intend to kill noncombatants en masse in the
manner of the RAF. Even so, tens of thousands of noncombatant
deaths were foreseen. And American actions contributed to the firestorms that engulfed Hamburg and Dresden. In pursuit of Allied victory, the USAAF bombed extensively behind enemy lines: noncombatants perished in Belgium, France, and Italy, and of course these deaths
were foreseen. My concern is more immediate: What accounts for the
differences in British and American strategy? To reiterate, compared to
the RAF, the USAAF ordinarily practiced terrorism-lite. The less formidable Japanese enemy endured the greatest slaughter in human history: Why were the Germans and Japanese treated differently?

Two obvious responses: The Nazis didn't attack the American homeland, and it wasn't a race war—the Germans were "just like us." Unlike
the Japanese, the Germans weren't deemed an evil, subhuman race;
nurture, not nature, explained Teutonic, lockstep militarism. Unlike the
Jap, Nazis had individuality; they were represented in the plural. FDR,
of course, was not indifferent toward electoral politics: locales like my
hometown of Milwaukee had substantial German-American populations. Despite fifth columns like the German American Bund and the
real possibilities of sabotage, there were no concentration camps.

The irony is rather obvious: the Nazis posed a more formidable
threat than the Japanese. Even so, the war against the Nazis lacked the
hot-blooded passion of the Pacific War. Pearl Harbor, to understate the
case, made the public painfully aware of Japanese perfidy. However, as
FDR allowed, the public had to be educated about the Nazi threat—a

threat difficult to exaggerate. (The public was self-educated about the Japanese threat, real and imagined.) Even so, as historian Steven Casey illustrates in his aptly titled *Cautious Crusade . . .* a deeply ambivalent FDR equivocated about the Nazi threat, and succumbed to wishful thinking amid Hitler's rise to power.[71] FDR was an optimist, not an ironist. Prior to the war, he predicted the collapse of Hitler's regime—his domestic agenda would fail. Apparently, as late as 1938, the president and many of his associates believed—or hoped—that Hitler had limited objectives such as easing objectionable clauses in the Versailles Treaty. Even after Great Britain and France declared war on Germany following the Polish invasion, FDR hoped for a European stalemate between the great powers: Surely the Maginot line would hold. The Nazis overran France in a matter of days. Nevertheless, American officials sought signs that Nazism would collapse due to internal problems.

Hitler's astonishingly quick victories in Europe and early successes on the Eastern Front convinced FDR that Hitler had to be eliminated. Nazi atrocities made news. However, given the anti-Semitism endemic to American culture, the Holocaust was underplayed. Compared to the vitriol hurled at the Jap, anti-Nazi propaganda seems halfhearted. Nazis were seldom called vermin or subhumans. Dubbing Nazis Jerries, Krauts, or hinnies sounds almost affectionate. In popular films, the Jap was a clone of a defective, subhuman race. Nazis, however, were redeemable with proper education—a point brought home in an unusually somber Disney cartoon.

Education for Death reveals that Nazis are not inherently evil; only relentless indoctrination makes young Germans succumb to the dark side. A villainous Nazi schoolmaster humiliates little Hans for doing what comes naturally—pitying a bunny devoured by a wolf. The master's relentless hectoring, along with peer pressure, forces Hans to ignore his better angels. Curiously, Hans becomes schooled in the political realism dominant in American political thought, a truism Thucydides expressed long ago: "The strong do what they have the power to do, and the weak must accept the consequences."

Typically, however, Disney made the Nazis laughable—Bavarian buffoons. Donald Duck dreams he lives under the Nazi regime, a world driven by a collective Tourette syndrome: Nazis spend their days shouting "Heil Hitler," saluting, and marching—they can't help themselves. The dream becomes a nightmare: Donald finds himself enslaved by the demanding, mindless routines of a production line—much like American workers in Chaplin's iconic vision in *Modern Times.*

Chaplin's first sound movie, *The Great Dictator*, debuted in 1940—an unforgettable parody of Hitler. Chaplin played upon his resemblance to Hitler. Whether Hitler saw *The Great Dictator* is not known. However, Hitler's recently discovered *Juden Sehen Dich An* (*The Jews are Watching You*) inscribed his death list of prominent Jews: "The fact that Chaplin was not Jewish didn't save him from being a target; he was branded pseudo-Jew."[72]

The film reflects a somewhat reassuring isolationist view of Hitler: a raving narcissist bound to fail; a pathetic little man bullied by the likes of Mussolini. Chaplin changed his story as the war began—Hitler was taken seriously; he withdrew the film from circulation. Chaplin plays a humble, Jewish barber *and* Hitler. In a case of mistaken identity, Hitler is imprisoned as a Jew, and the barber becomes the Great Dictator invading Austria. Chaplin's coda extolling the end to national boundaries and universal brotherhood spoke to posterity. The House Un-American Activities Committee listened; it was among the factors leading to Chaplin's exile.

Albert Speer, Hitler's architect, saw the film, and according to one historian, "commented that it was the most accurate representation of Hitler ever put on screen. Speer also claimed that Hitler had also owned a globe in the form of a balloon, though it was much larger than the one Chaplin danced with in the film."[73] The balloon pops—obvious yet memorable symbolism.

Frank Capra's seven-part *Why We Fight* series (commissioned by the War Department and Office of War Information) took the Nazis very seriously. The theme in the first installment, *Prelude to War*, echoes throughout: World War II is a fateful battle between the "slave world" of fascism and the "free world" of American liberty. In the "slave world," the entire populations of Germany, Italy, and Japan are hoodwinked by madmen, opportunists who capitalize on their people's desperation and weakness to rise to power. (Capra makes the point with frequent newsreels of German and Japanese rallies.) Demagogues like Hitler promise to avenge past humiliations. They convince the masses to give up their rights and embrace dictatorship. In the free world, Washington, Jefferson, and Lincoln embody the cherished principles of equality, freedom, and liberty. This freedom is a threat to the fascist dictators of the Axis Powers who claim that democracy is weak and must be eradicated. Ultimately, the Axis Powers strive to enslave the free world. Along with the other media, these films depicted the European war as primarily an ideological struggle, a campaign against a particularly aggressive foe bent on conquest.

The war, of course, was also about Nazi atrocities. General Eisenhower came to recognize the magnitude of the atrocities as his troops liberated the concentration camps. He compelled nearby German citizens to share his recognition by removing corpses and digging graves. Confronting the unthinkable prompted Hollywood to produce a series of gruesome documentaries about the camps and somewhat fictionalized accounts of painfully real events—such as *Schindler's List*. Of course, as entertainment became the métier of popular discourse, a Nazi prisoner of war camp became a laughing matter on television sitcoms such as *Hogan's Heroes*. Once again Nazis became nothing more formidable than Bavarian buffoons.

Russian Comrades

In Russia [Ambassador] Davies meets the leaders . . . He talks cracker-barrel philosophy with them on political issues and finds them genuine. He tours Russia and sees its vast resources, its similarities in many ways to "home," and soon acquires an honest admiration and respect for it all.
        —*New York Times* review of *Mission to Moscow* [74]

The irony of newfound Soviet friendship—amity that portrayed Soviet villages as just another American town—emerged against a backdrop of relentless anticommunism. American elites did not take kindly to the Bolshevik Revolution of 1917. Despite Wilsonian rhetoric about a League of Nations preventing war and protecting national autonomy, the United States secretly aided Bolshevik adversaries in their attempts to overthrow the new regime. Following the armistice, Wilson dispatched thousands of American troops to Siberia in support of communist opponents. As historian Carl Richard argues in *When the United States Invaded Russia*, the invasion bolstered Russian nationalism and proved the Bolsheviks correct about the intentions of the capitalist powers. The irony doesn't go unnoticed: The invasion strengthened the regime it was meant to overthrow.[75]

As the Palmer Raids illustrate, it exaggerates little to suggest that the American response to the Bolshevik Revolution verged on the paranoiac. The suppression of dissent that marked the war years continued after the 1918 Armistice. Labor unrest, alleged anarchist bombings, and even women's suffrage were attributed to Bolshevik influence. Wilson's attorney general, A. Mitchell Palmer, took it personally when his home was partially destroyed by a bomb.

Palmer makes "The Case Against the Reds" in no uncertain terms. The Red menace is "eating its way into the homes of the American workmen . . . licking the altars of the churches, leaping into the belfry of the school bell . . . seeking to replace marriage vows with libertine laws, burning up the foundations of society." Subversives must be watched, disrupted, imprisoned, and deported if possible.[76]

The Red Scare waned as propagandists heeded Bernays's counsel and turned their efforts from constructing enemies to promoting consumer society. Amid isolationism and the Great Depression, the machinations of the Kremlin—real and imagined—were of little interest. However, during the latter half of the 1930s, the Soviets became aggressive and troubling. Stalin signed a Non-Aggression Pact with Hitler, carved up Poland, and invaded Finland: Concern with Soviet capabilities and ambitions was not unfounded.

Popular films portrayed the evils of communism. *Once in a Blue Moon* features an itinerate clown victimized by the Bolsheviks—not a laughing matter. *Confessions of a Nazi Spy*, aside from portraying the brutality of Nazi regime, indicts the Soviet invasion of Finland. It was quickly withdrawn from circulation when the Soviets became honorary good guys. Clark Gable played a reporter covering Stalin's purge trials in *Never Let Me Go*. Since it was not politically correct to indict Stalin when he became an American ally, the film was remade and reissued in 1953.[77]

As the Palmer Raids, popular films, and Soviet aggression illustrate, they were no ordinary enemy; the Soviet Union was *the* archenemy for twenty-five years. Suddenly, they became an ally of convenience—honorary good guys battling Nazis. As if to confirm the plasticity of public opinion, propagandists relied upon government backing, unlimited access to popular media, and collective amnesia to prevent cognitive dissonance. Newfound friendship with Russians was promoted at the highest levels of government and by the popular media. The reasons are clear.

In perhaps his most foolhardy decision, Hitler invaded the Soviet Union in 1941. As the Nazis neared Moscow and laid siege to Stalingrad, Stalin urged FDR and Churchill to distract Hitler by creating a second front—an invasion of Europe. Rather than invade, FDR spent an estimated $11 billion to arm the Soviets through his Lend-Lease program and promoted a pro-Soviet campaign any commissar would envy.[78]

Army films depicted Stalin as the George Washington of the Ukraine. *Life Magazine's* March 1943 issue—an avuncular Joe Stalin as the cover boy—celebrated the Soviet police state. The magazine featured colorful images of a Potemkin nation—too good to be true. Ambassador Davies turned his favorable depictions of Soviet life into a best seller, *Mission to Moscow*. He lauded Soviet progress, marveled at the gaiety of the Soviet people, and concluded that Soviet leadership desires peace in an egalitarian society governed by ethical principles. FDR urged Hollywood to turn the book into a movie. The movie followed the text, proving that, while God can't rewrite history, propagandists can. The viewer learns that, despite the Non-Aggression Pact between Stalin and Hitler, the Soviets viewed the Nazi threat with socialist realism. The Trotskyites tormented and executed in Stalin's purges were actually German and Japanese spies. And finally, the invasion of Finland was designed to protect hapless Finns from the Nazis.

Glad tidings about the Soviet Union were short-lived. Arguments about occupying Germany ensued; disputes raged about spheres of influence; and the House Un-American Activities Committee (HUAC) couldn't countenance pro-Soviet propaganda—expedient but perhaps necessary lies. HUAC blacklisted Howard Koch, the film's screenwriter.[79] Adding yet another ironic twist, suddenly, the Soviets were so wicked that they had to be encircled with nuclear bases. America's mortal enemies, the Japanese and the Germans, became trusted allies.

FROM ENMITY TO AMITY: THE OCCUPATIONS

*After such a merciless war, how can one explain the peaceful nature
of the Allied occupation of Japan, and the genuine goodwill that soon
developed between the Japanese and the Americans. . . . How could
the race hates dissipate so quickly?*

—John Dower[80]

Pundits—who never met a cliché they didn't like—never tire of
warning: Things don't change overnight. Even social psychologists lament the enduring, if not indelible, nature of stereotypes. Not so. In
late summer 1945, Japs were irredeemable subhumans bent on destroying civilized life—extermination was the only answer. The incineration
of Hiroshima and Nagasaki was cause for celebration—"they had it
coming." In early fall, suddenly, the Japanese became a polite, industri-
ous people. GIs, who recently burnt Japs alive with flamethrowers,
shared chocolates with Japanese kids.

Occupied Japan

MacArthur greeted the emperor at the entrance to the reception
room, shaking his hand and saying, 'You are very, very welcome, sir.'
The emperor kept bowing lower and lower until MacArthur found
himself shaking hands with him over the emperor's head.[81]

General Douglas MacArthur ("the American Caesar") took charge of
the occupation and reconstruction. After years of merciless warfare
against the Jap, the general facilitated the construction of a prosperous
new Japan, a regime free of feudalism and militarism. He became, in
Dower's words, the "Caucasian Emperor," as remote and mysterious as
Hirohito, who ruled in name only.

For strategic and humanitarian reasons, decision-makers decided
that the occupation would rebuild Japan without punishing ordinary
citizens. The Allies held several conferences to discuss the fate of postwar Japan. The occupation, however, was the primary responsibility of
the United States. The United States began systematic planning for the
occupation in 1942, planning complemented by courses in Japanese
culture and language and various universities.[82]

Propagandists fell in line and, once again, prevented cognitive dissonance. During the war, the official Marine publication *Leatherneck*
portrayed the Jap as a crazed gorilla. The September 1945 issue depicted a smiling Marine with an affectionate pet chimp on his shoul-
der.[83] As the occupation began, public opinion proved remarkably
malleable. Vicious stereotypes of the Jap vanished, an easy sell for a
war-weary public eager to forget. It was refreshing, not disconcerting,
to watch newsreels portraying a grateful people welcoming American
occupiers.

There were, of course, triumphant overtones: An iconic photo portraying an oversize General MacArthur beside a diminutive Hirohito
put the humiliated emperor in his place. Belligerent propaganda disap-
peared; Disney removed wartime comics mocking the Japanese from
circulation. (They became trophy collectors' items in consumer culture.) Caricatures of buck-toothed, kamikaze pilots vanished. Japan was
about delicately lovely geishas, manicured gardens, tea ceremonies, and
ancient temples.

Dower suggests that enmity turned to amity because the occupation
disabused both sides of demonic, wartime stereotypes. The 250,000
American soldiers deployed to Japan were war-weary combatants,
grateful to be occupiers, not invaders. Not always paragons of virtue,
they certainly weren't the white devils depicted in Japanese propaganda.

A benign racism informed the seven-year occupation. The emperor
remained a symbol of Japanese tradition and unity, but Hirohito, de-
mystified and humanized, was beholden to the American proconsul,
General MacArthur. MacArthur wisely kept the existing bureaucracy in
place to aid him in educating his "children" in Western ways. The "education" unfolded in three stages: punishing and reforming Japan; reviving the economy; and concluding a formal peace treaty while negotiat-
ing various alliances.

Acting in accord with the Potsdam Declaration, American authorities demilitarized Japan, punished war crimes, and encouraged democratic aspirations.[84] In addition to dismantling the means of military
production, Article 9 of the new constitution prohibited resorting to
warfare. As mandated, the Tokyo trials punished war criminals. Some
ironies, of course, are predictable. The trials in Tokyo and Nuremburg
are notable for what was left unsaid: Any mention of Axis Power terror

bombing would prompt discussions of Hamburg and Dresden, of Hiroshima and Nagasaki.

MacArthur instituted reforms, a "New Deal" for Japan: the emancipation and enfranchisement of women, unionization of workers, liberalized education, a reformed justice system, an economic system that encouraged a wider distribution of income and ownership.[85] Certain stereotypes prevailed during the early phases of the economic recovery: Americans associated "Made in Japan" with cheap toys, cocktail napkins, and kitsch tapestry. Hondas, Nikons, and Sony TVs caught Americans by surprise. Once again, Americans felt threatened, but this time the Japanese adversary wore an expensive business suit rather than khaki.[86]

The Japanese lionized MacArthur—for a time. Many mourned his departure after Truman relieved him of his command in April 1951—due to insubordination during the Korean War. MacArthur's stateside attempts to compliment the Japanese backfired. Germany, in the general's view, was a jaded, mature civilization that didn't inspire trust. However, Japan, like a twelve-year-old boy, a properly raised pre-adolescent, could mature into a responsible, trusted ally. The Japanese cancelled plans for a monumental likeness of the American proconsul in Tokyo harbor.

Occupied Germany

I love Germany so much I'm glad there are two of them.
                                                 —François Mauriac[87]

Draconian best describes early American plans for postwar Germany. Such plans are disturbing, yet understandable, in light of the two world wars and revulsion at Nazi atrocities. Among the extremes: University of Chicago Professor and Rhodes Scholar Bernadotte Schmitt advocated reducing Germany from eighty million to thirty million—he didn't say how. Another academic, Theodore Kaufman, did—sterilize all Germans.[88]

Turning to those with more influence and credibility, Treasury Secretary Henry Morgenthau proposed deindustrializing Germany, creating two rural, agricultural states; territory would also be given to Poland and France. Amenable for a time, FDR ultimately rejected the proposal; evidently, he wanted Germany restored to avoid the folly of the Versailles Treaty. Accordingly, he desired to promote humanitarian efforts and to ensure German allegiance in the anticipated confrontation with the Soviet Union. While controversy continued in elite circles, enthusiasm remained for the vindictive Morgenthau plan. Ever pragmatic, and chastened by the lesson of World War I, FDR decided that in addition to preventing the resurgence of fascism and militarism, Germany must become an industrialized, prosperous nation.

Unlike the war in the Pacific, virtually an American campaign, the struggle against the Nazis involved the British, French, and the Soviets—who endured more than their share of casualties. The Allies debated and negotiated the fate of Germany at conferences in Potsdam and Yalta. At Yalta, the Soviets pressed for the dismemberment of Germany and heavy postwar reparations—half to go to the Soviet Union. While FDR acceded to this demand, Truman (perhaps emboldened by the new American nuclear monopoly) urged considerably more modest reparations: Each ally would exact reparations from its occupied territory. (The Soviets didn't hesitate to extract their spoils from occupied East Germany.)

Discussion of spheres of influence faced obdurate realities: The Red Army occupied much of Eastern Europe, and—given the invasions endured during two world wars—the Soviets desired buffer states. Stalin agreed to conduct fair elections in these buffer states, but—as American politicians must have realized—campaign promises are seldom fulfilled. Germany itself was divided into four zones of occupation.

Once again, a military man, General Dwight Eisenhower—the architect of D-Day—took charge. During his brief (seven-month) tenure as military governor, he faced complications unknown to MacArthur. Indeed, disputes emerging from an occupied, divided Berlin plagued the world for two generations. The camaraderie of American GIs embracing Red Army soldiers as they met in Torgau, Germany did not endure. Despite—or because of?—the tension, the Allies negotiated agreements as they came face-to-face with the Red Army. The negotiations deferred the matter of the reunification of Germany. Reunification finally occurred in 1990 after a series of harrowing crises. Prior to that time, not only did Berlin remain in Soviet occupied territory, Berlin itself was divided into four quadrants. As the occupation unfolded, the Americans, British, and French controlled West Berlin; the Soviets controlled East Berlin.

Unlike Japan, where MacArthur remained the uncontested, supreme commander for almost the entire occupation, five military governors and four high, civilian commissioners presided over the occupation. That officials usually served for only a few months suggests difficulties. Dissention within the Truman administration was almost as irksome as dealing with the Soviets. In short, the occupation of Germany was far from seamless, especially during the early phases. I suspected that certain historians exaggerated the difficulties until I read the official *US Army Report* on the occupation: It concludes that the occupation was almost as harrowing as the war itself.[89]

The Army administered the early phases of the occupation amid the rubble and disease of what Grayling aptly calls the dead cities. The *Report* effects a bland, fact-filled, authorial strategy expected in this genre. Nevertheless, portions read like a Cormac McCarthy dystopian novel. In describing the refugee problem, we learn that the displaced person, pitied as an individual, "in the mass he becomes a menace, clogs roads, imposes potentially ruinous burdens on already strained civilian services, and spreads panic."[90] Roving gangs of refugees raped and pillaged as did Nazi soldiers reluctant to surrender.

The *Army Report* indicts the actions of many of the occupying soldiers without explaining the circumstances that may account for their behavior. (Perhaps the Army is reluctant to report on the trauma and post-trauma of war.) American soldiers had something in common with the refugees. Perhaps their behavior can be understood—but not condoned—by recognizing they had been thrown into an atrocity-producing situation—the occupation offered payback: "Looting was so widespread as to be regarded as a soldierly sport."[91] The report laments the occupiers' exploitation of the black market—soldiers exacted a high price for food and cigarettes. Worse yet, "of crimes committed by US troops, the best—though by no means most accurately—documented was rape." Indeed, for a time, the occupiers were seen as terrorists. As the *Report* concludes: "Incidents caused by US troops, if no more numerous than they had been in the last months of 1945, were certainly no fewer; they included, as they had earlier, wanton killing, looting, and threats and assaults on German police and civilians."[92]

The Army had some success in pacifying the situation and meeting the basic needs of the German people. The official conclusion is worth noting in some detail:

> Policy statements [were] harsh to the point of being vindictive, but the practice was humane as a defeated enemy had a right to expect . . . Soldiers looted and played the black market [however] the Army protected and restored the country's art treasures . . . and imported three-quarters of a billion dollars worth of relief supplies. The DPs [displaced persons] were returned to their homes, the concentration camp inmates were cared for, and the numerous services . . . were put back into operation and kept running. . . . The Army had demonstrated its competence to manage a major occupation in the national interest and the interest of a conquered people.[93]

Eisenhower's August 6, 1945, address to the German people—a valedictory perhaps—marks a turning point. He warned of continued shortages in food and coal for heating. After encouraging the Germans to unionize and to engage in local politics, he promised conditions would eventually improve. Eisenhower resisted Potsdam agreements designed to punish Germany. He believed German industry should be restored (under careful supervision) not demolished. He and Marshall corresponded about conditions in Germany and what must be done; Eisenhower may have had something akin to the Marshall Plan in mind.

The Marshall Plan

The most unsordid act in history.

—Churchill[94]

Ironically, another five-star general, George C. Marshall, gets credit for rehabilitating the most formidable Axis Power foe. After orchestrating the destruction of Germany, the general successfully promoted a plan to remedy the devastation in the war's aftermath—the Marshall Plan. He unveiled the plan at Harvard's graduation in 1947. Eleven months later Congress put aside qualms about giving aid and comfort to mortal enemies and passed the plan (the European Recovery Act of 1948).

Naturally, the George C. Marshall Foundation praises the plan for energizing Germany's recovery, and not without reason. It is indeed noteworthy that Marshall was the only general to receive the Nobel Peace Prize. The foundation enumerates the plan's accomplishments and indicts critics who claim the plan was motivated by self-interest as "anti-American."[95] Both the celebrants and the critics are right: The plan's accomplishments were driven by high ideals *and* by calculated self-interest.

The accomplishments are legion. Food and fuel flowed to desperate populations. The aid, reconstruction, and shared technological know-how proved catalytic: Within four years European economic production soared 200 percent above prewar levels. The Brooking Institution reports that a survey of 450 historians and political scientists lauds the plan as the federal government's greatest postwar achievement. The survey's author offers an apt gloss on the Marshall Plan: "The roads, railroads, bridges, and factories . . . were rebuilt. And the hunger, homelessness, and unemployment that marked the end of the war were dispatched as the war-torn continent healed."

Documents obtained from the Truman Library reveal the plan's mixed motives. Writing in the *Department of State Bulletin* as Under Secretary of State, Dean Acheson mentions that, upon his return from Europe, Marshall seemed indifferent to ideology and military concerns. His concern involved necessities: the food and fuel essential to assure the survival of beleaguered Europe. Natural disasters—a brutally harsh winter—worsened the plight of hapless Europeans.

However, Acheson reminded the reader that "These measures of relief and reconstruction have been only in part suggested by humanitarian interests. . . . Your Government is carrying out a policy of relief and reconstruction today chiefly as a matter of national self-interest." Reconstruction involved lucrative contracts for corporate America, and a revitalized Europe was essential to prevent communist subversion. In his 1952 retrospective on the Plan, Marshall himself revealed his concern with "the dreadful situation in Europe." But he allowed that, in promoting the Plan, he sought "the cooperation of special interest groups." As the Department of State's official history concludes: "Fanned by the fear of Communist expansion and the rapid deterioration of European economies in the winter of 1946–1947, Congress approved funding for reconstruction."[96]

The Marshall Plan proved catalytic: A revitalized German economy benefitted ordinary Germans while establishing markets for American goods. Germany once again became a citadel of European culture and the economic powerhouse of Europe. No wonder a student returning from a summer in Germany asked—I want to assume sardonically—"Who won the war?"

Nuremberg

> *Since both sides had played the terrible game of urban destruction—the Allies far more successfully. . . . Aerial bombardment had been used so extensively and ruthlessly on the Allied side as well as the Axis side that neither at Nuremberg nor Tokyo was the issue made a part of the trials.*
>
> —Telford Taylor, Chief Counsel, Nuremburg Trials[97]

The occupation, however, is of course remembered for the Nuremberg Trials begun in 1945. In accord with agreements reached at Yalta, Nazis were tried, convicted, and punished for their shockingly heinous deeds. Twelve trials occurred during the ensuing four years. Attention focused on the opening trial of twenty-one of the most prominent Nazis. The four indictments proffered by prosecutors reflected these deeds. All defendants were indicted on at least two of the counts; several were indicted on all four counts. The indictments included conspiring to wage aggressive war, waging such a war, war crimes (such as mistreatment of prisoners of war), and most notably, crimes against humanity—Nazi attempts at genocide committed against Jews and other minorities—the Holocaust.

Justice Robert Jackson served as Chief Prosecutor. His opening statement discloses that, at first, he was skeptical of reported Nazi atrocities. He was shocked and sickened by the evidence amassed for the trials: He suspected defendants would deny their responsibility for an undeniable fact—Germany had become one vast torture chamber.

Nuremberg was not the last time those accused of atrocities claimed they had no choice—they were merely following orders. There were no indictments for terror bombing for obvious reasons. Even so, Jackson realized that American pilots were following orders on those missions over Hamburg and Dresden, and Tokyo and Hiroshima: "We must never forget that the record on which we judge these defendants is the record on which history will judge us tomorrow. To pass these defendants a poisoned chalice is to put it to our own lips as well."[98]

And somehow Adolph Hitler survived the war, shape-shifted, and acquired astounding linguistic skills. Reincarnated in America's real and imagined enemies, he spoke Russian, Chinese, Korean, Vietnamese, Spanish, Arabic, and Farsi. And the poisoned chalice was imbibed as World War II-style carpet-bombing continued in Korea, Vietnam, and Iraq.

NOTES

1. A. C. Grayling's *Among the Dead Cities: The History and Moral Legacy of Bombing Civilians in Germany and Japan* (New York: Walker & Company, 2006), 4.

2. See, for example, John Lewis Gaddis, *We Now Know* (New York: Oxford University Press, 1987).

3. In addition to Grayling, see John W. Dower, *War Without Mercy* (New York: Pantheon Books, 1986). Dower offers a magisterial account of the war against Japan. John Tirman's *The Deaths of Others* (New York: Oxford University Press, 2011), Chapter 3 recounts firebombing in Europe and Japan. Justin George Lawler offers a Catholic perspective in "Terror Bombing," *America: The National Catholic Review*, August 28, 2006, accessed February 1, 2014, http://americamagazine.org/issue/581/bookings/terror-bombing. General Curtis LeMay was the most enthusiastic, uncritical advocate of terror bombing. See, for example, Robert Higgs, "On Winning the War," in *The Independent Review*, November 1, 2009, accessed February 2, 2014, http://www.independent.org/pdf/tir/tir_11_01_09_higgs.pdf.

4. Paul Fussell, *The Great War and Modern Memory* (New York: Oxford University Press, 1975), 8.

5. George F. Kennan, *American Diplomacy* (Chicago: The University of Chicago Press, 1984), 56.

6. Fussell, 12.

7. Quoted by Fussell, 337.

8. Sigmund Freud, *Standard Edition, Vol. 14: On the History of the Psychoanalytic Movement, Papers on Metapsychology and other Works* (New York: Vintage, 1975), 275.

9. Edward Bernays, "Propaganda History is a Weapon," accessed February 15, 2014, http://www.historyisaweapon.com/defcon1/bernprop.html.

10. *Why War? The Einstein-Freud Correspondence* (1931–1932), accessed February 14, 2014, http://www.public.asu.edu/~jmlynch/273/documents/FreudEinstein.pdf.

11. Ibid.

12. Erich Maria Remarque, *All Quiet on the Western Front*, accessed February 17, 2014, http://www.goodreads.com/work/quotes/2662852-im-westen-nichts-neues.

13. Dalton Trumbo, *Johnny Got His Gun*, accessed February 17, 2014, http://www.goodreads.com/work/quotes/180461-johnny-got-his-gun.

14. Quoted in *United States Senate History*, "Merchants of Death," September 4, 1934, accessed February 18, 2014, https://www.senate.gov/pagelayout/history/one_item_and_teasers/1941.htm.

15. General Smedley Butler, "War is a Racket," accessed February 18, 2014, http://www.informationclearinghouse.info/article4377.htm.

16. Quote accessed February 18, 2014, http://secularist10.hubpages.com/hub/Isolationism-and-Interventionism.

17. Franklin D. Roosevelt, "Quarantine Speech (October 5, 1937)," digitally archived by the Miller Center, University of Virginia, accessed August 15, 2014, http://millercenter.org/president/fdroosevelt/speeches/speech-3310.

18. Dower, 106–11.

19. Charles Beah, *Honolulu Star-Bulletin*, September 6, 1941.

20. Dower, 111.

21. Harold Lavine and James Wechsler, *War Propaganda and the United States* (New Haven: Yale University Press, 1940), 352.

22. Ibid., 335–36.

23. Dower, 36.

24. "The Yalta Conference," US Department of State website, accessed February 20, 2014, http://www.state.gov.

25. Edward Bernays, *Propaganda* (Brooklyn: Ig Publishing, 2005), 1.

26. Social psychologist Leon Festinger devised the concept to explain his 1957 participant observation in a doomsday cult. The leader prophesized that aliens would destroy the earth on December 21 (a favored date for the apocalypse). According to Festinger, the failed prophecy didn't destroy the cult; it strengthened it. The leader prevented cognitive dissonance by explaining that the aliens moved by cultist devotion opted to save the world. Ad hoc rationalizations and changing the meaning of beliefs are among the techniques to avoid cognitive dissonance. See Leon Festinger, *A Theory of Cognitive Dissonance* (Stanford: Stanford University Press, 1957).

27. *The Public Papers and Addresses of Franklin D. Roosevelt, 1939 Volume: War and Neutrality* (New York: Macmillan, 1941), 511–12.

28. Quoted in "Strategic Bombing during World War II," *The Choices Program*, Brown University, accessed August 15, 2014, http://www.choices.edu/resources/supplemental_fogofwar_ww2.php.

29. Tom Englehardt, "Air War, Barbarity, and the Middle East," accessed August 15, 2014, http://www.tomdispatch.com/post/106273/.

30. Christopher Toner, "Just War and the Supreme Emergency Exemption," *The Philosophical Quarterly,* Vol. 55, #221, 54.

31. See Dower's discussion, 39–41.

32. Michael Walzer, *Just and Unjust Wars* (New York: Basic Books), Chapter 16.

33. See Grayling, especially Chapters 1, 2, and 7.

34. Fussell, 5.

35. Gideon Rose, *How Wars End* (New York: Simon & Schuster, 2010), 69.

36. Quoted by Dower, 78.

37. Ibid., 93.

38. Ibid.

39. See, for example, Yuki Tanaka and Marilyn B. Young, *Bombing Civilians: A Twentieth-Century History* (New York: The New Press, 2010).

40. *United States Strategic Bombing Survey: Summary Report (Pacific War)* (Washington D.C. Department of War, July 1, 1946), 26, accessed February 20, 2014, accessed February 20, 2014, file://Volumes/NO%20NAME/R%20&%20L%20AUGUST/United%20States%20Strategic%20.

41. Accessed February 20, 2014, errolmoris.com/film/fow-transcript/html. Actually rules of war granting noncombatants immunity date back to the thirteenth-century writings of St. Thomas Aquinas.

42. Anthony Pratkanis and Elliot Aronson, *Age of Propaganda: The Everyday Use and Abuse of Persuasion* (New York: Henry Holt, 2001), 46–47.

43. I recognize the horror visited by Japanese combatants, and don't disparage the courage and sacrifice of the American military in the Pacific theater. However, I reject the Manichean view of the struggle that depicts the war as combat between the forces of good and evil. To paraphrase theologian Reinhold Niebuhr, World War II was a contest between greater and lesser evils.

44. See Dower's discussion of American and Japanese atrocities, 33–73.

45. Ernie Pyle, *Last Chapter* (New York: Henry Holt & Co., 1945), 5.

46. Claire Andre and Manuel Velasquez summarize Lerner's work in "The Just World Theory," accessed February 21, 2014, http://www.scu.edu/ethics/publications/iie/v3n2/justworld.html.

47. Ibid.

48. Cited by Clayton R. Koppes and Gregory D. Black in *Hollywood Goes to War* (Berkeley: University of California Press, 1990), 252.

49. Accessed February 21, 2014, www.audiohistory/com/1939-1945/4-music/04/PH-Reaction.

50. Ibid., 253.

51. Ibid., 269.

52. Quoted by Dower, 80.

53. Dower, 23.

54. Ibid., 41.

55. James Harold Doolittle (2014). The Biography.com website, accessed February 22, 2014, http://www.biography.com/people/jimmy-doolittle-9277305.

56. Quoted by Gregg Herken in *Counsels of War* (New York: Alfred Knopf, 1987), 82.

57. In addition to Dower's discussion on p. 301, see Wesley Frank Craven and James Lea Cates, eds. *The Army Air Forces in World War II* (Office of Air Force History, 1953), 732–33.

58. See my account of these developments in *Newest Weapons/Oldest Psychology: The Dialectics of American Nuclear Strategy* (New York: Peter Lang, 1989), 48–51.

59. See, for example, Gar Alperovitz, *The Decision to Use the Atomic Bomb* (New York: Vintage Books, 1996).

60. Joseph Rotblat, "Leaving the Bomb Project," *Bulletin of Atomic Scientists*, August 1985, 16–19.

61. See Rose's discussion, 114.

62. Gaddis, 86.

63. Ibid., 643.

64. "The Effects of the Atomic Bomb," *Strategic Survey*, 26.

65. Ibid., 27.

66. Quoted by Alfonso A. Narvaez, "Gen. Curtis LeMay, an Architect of Strategic Air Power, Dies at 83," *New York Times*, October 7, 1990, accessed February 12, 2014, http://www.nytimes.com/1990/10/02/obituaries-curtis-lemay-an-architect-of-strategic-air-power-dies-at-83.html.

67. Kennedy Hickman, "Operation Gomorrah: The Firebombing of Hamburg," retrieved from http://militaryhistory.about.com/od/aerialcampaigns/p/gomorrah.htm.

68. See A. C. Grayling's account, 179–83.

69. Cited by C. A. J. Cody, "Bombing and the Morality of War," in *Bombing Civilians*, Yuki Tanaka and Marilyn B. Young, eds. (New York: The New Press, 2009), 200.

70. Accessed February 23, 2014, www. Historylearning site.co.uk./bombing_of_dresden.html.

71. Steven Casey, *Cautious Crusade: Franklin D. Roosevelt, American Public Opinion, and the War against Nazi Germany* (New York: Oxford University Press, 2001).

72. Accessed February 23, 2014, http://www.dailymail.co.uk/news/article-520648/Nazi-propaganda-book-reveals-Charlie-Chaplin-Hitlers-death-list.html.

73. Accessed February 23, 2014, http://www.tcm.com/tcmdb/title/76858/The-Great-Dictator/articles.html.

74. Bosley Crowther, "Review of *Mission to Moscow*"; *New York Times*, April 3, 1943: accessed February 23, 2014, http://www.tcm.com/tcmdb/title/76858/The-Great-Dictator/articles.html.

75. See, for example, Carl H. Richard, *When the United States Invaded Russia: Woodrow Wilson's Siberian Disaster* (Lanham, MD: Rowman & Littlefield, 2013).

76. A. Mitchell Palmer, "The Case Against the Reds," *Forum* (1920), 63: 173–85.

77. These and other films are described in the following site, accessed February 24, 2014, http://lib.washington.edu/exhibits/AllPowers/film.html.

78. Retrieved from a Library of Congress document: "Revelations from the Russian Archives: World War II: Alliance," accessed February 24, 2014, http://www.loc.gov/exhibits/archives/worw.html.

79. See the *New York Times* review accessed February 25, 2014, http://www.nytimes.com/movies/movie/102572/Mission-to-Moscow/overview.

80. Dower, 301.

81. "When MacArthur Met the Emperor," *Iconic Photos*, accessed August 15, 2014, iconicphotos.wordpress.com/2012/09/28/when-macarthur-met-the-emperor.

82. See Dower's account of this planning in *Cultures of War* (New York: W. W. Norton, 2010), 324–53.

83. Ibid., 302.

84. See John Dower's discussion in *Embracing Defeat: Japan in the Wake of World War II* (New York: W. W. Norton, 1999), Chapter 2. Also see the US Department of State account of Potsdam, accessed February 26, 2014, http://history.state.gov/milestones/1937-1945/potsdam-conf.

85. See Dower's discussion, *Embracing Defeat*, 331–33.

86. Ibid., 552.

87. Accessed February 26, 2014, en.Wikiquote.oe/wk/Francois_Mauriac.

88. See Grayling's discussion, 162–63.

89. Earl F. Ziemke, *Army Historical Series: The US Army in the Occupation of Germany 1944–1946*; accessed February 20, 2014, http://www.history.army.mil/books/wwii/Occ-Gy/.

90. Ibid.

91. Ibid., Paragraph 220.

92. Ibid., Paragraph 437.

93. Ibid., 448.

94. Quoted in *Brookings' Role in the Marshall Plan*, accessed February 26, 2014, http://www.brookings.edu/about/history/marshallplan.

95. Accessed February 26, 2014, http://www.marshallfoundation.org/The-MarshallPlan.htm.

96. Office of the Historian, Bureau of Public Affairs, United States Department of State.

97. Quoted by Mark Selden, "A Forgotten Holocaust: US Bombing Strategy," accessed February 26, 2014, JAPANFOCUS.ordg/=mark=selden/2424.

98. Accessed February 20, 2014, http://en.wikiquote.org/wiki/Robert_H._Jackson.

Chapter 2

CELEBRATING NUCLEAR TERROR

The Irony of the Cold War

By a process of sublime irony [we] have reached a state where safety will be the sturdy child of terror, and survival the twin brother of annihilation.

—Churchill[1]

George Orwell coined the term "Cold War" in October 1945. Anticipating great power confrontations with atomic weapons, he predicted that this "social structure . . . would probably prevail in a state which was at once *unconquerable* and in a permanent state of 'cold war' with its neighbors."[2] The origin and justification of the Cold War—a conflict that embraced nuclear terror—remains contested.

Suffice it to say that mainstream historians hold the Soviets culpable: They extended their hegemony into Eastern Europe and supported regimes inimical to American interests. Such expansion was driven by imperial ambitions and by Marxist-Leninist ideology.[3] The Soviets had the intention and capability of further extending their hegemony throughout Western Europe if not North America. Accordingly they had to be contained—if not rolled back—by credible nuclear threats.

Revisionists hold the United States largely culpable. They argue that the United States provoked Soviet hostility by rebuilding a mortal enemy, West Germany. The Soviets construed the Marshall Plan as a move inimical to their interests. Not surprisingly, surrounding a former ally with nuclear bases proved provocative. True, the Soviets extended their hegemony. However, having endured two German invasions, it was reasonable for the Soviets to create buffer states in Eastern Europe.[4]

I'm concerned with a salient fact beyond dispute, a fact articulated with painful clarity by Bernard Brodie, an early strategist: "Nuclear weapons exist, and they are incredibly destructive."[5] Both sides amassed tens of thousands of these ultimate terror weapons ostensibly to deter the other side. Lewis Carroll said it best as we go through the looking glass to revisit the Cold War:

> Alice stood without speaking, looking out in all directions over the country—and a most curious country it was . . . It's marked out in all directions like a chessboard . . . It's a great huge game of chess being played—all over the world.[6]

This chapter is about the determinative role of the ultimate terror weapon in the Cold War. As Churchill's aphorism indicates, cold warriors' thoughts and actions bespoke of irony and terror. Churchill overlooked another irony: The nuclear arms race precipitated the very situation it promised to prevent—it put Great Britain and America in harm's way as never before. The betrayed promise of the atom became construed as a blessing in disguise—the "sublime irony" of nuclear deterrence. But all was not well. American strategic scenarios envisaged the death of Soviet *and* American citizens "if deterrence failed." Could it be that despite—or because of?—its theoretical and ethical deficits deterrence worked: The dreaded superpower conflagration never occurred.

NUKESPEAK AND DOUBLETHINK

> *I vowed to speak English. . . . No matter how well informed my questions were . . . if I was speaking English rather than expert jargon, the men responded to me as though I were ignorant or simpleminded.*
> —Psychologist Carol Cohn's recollection of a strategic think tank.[7]

Orwell died in 1950. Had he lived, no doubt he would have had much to say about the irony of the Cold War. Cold warriors spoke "Nukespeak."[8] Strategists who prided themselves on their hardheaded realism invoked euphemisms and acronyms that disguised the reality of nuclear peril. Things were not called by their proper names: Nuclear umbrellas protected the vulnerable in an inclement international climate; collateral damage sounded no worse than a bad credit score; and the MX missile was renamed "Peacekeeper." "Fat Man" and "Little Boy" sounded like fast food specials, not weapons that incinerated hundreds of thousands of lives in Hiroshima and Nagasaki. And sardonic acronyms such as MAD (mutually assured destruction) and NUTS (nuclear use theorists) infused Nukespeak with macabre humor.

Nukespeak also bespoke of a cult of secrecy and expertise ineffable to outsiders. Strategists prided themselves as gnostic possessors of ineffable paradoxes that defied logic and the common sense of ordinary mortals. As Churchill's aphorism reveals, deterrence doctrine—the very signature of the Cold War—was "Doublethink." Those who controlled the fate of the earth embraced contradictions and mocked elementary logic. During World War II propagandists struggled to conceal or dissolve cognitive dissonance. Cold warriors celebrated such dissonance— it was nothing less than the hallmark of a brave new logic befitting the irrationality of the nuclear age. Strategists reveled in the irony and congratulated themselves on improvising a cunning strategy to contain the Soviet Union while advancing American interests. I suspect Orwell wouldn't have joined the celebration. He would have recognized that Churchill's renowned eloquence is no substitute for a minimal requirement of rational discourse—logical coherence. Put in Orwell's cherished plain English: Churchill's paradoxical aphorism claims that in order to reduce the risk of nuclear war the risk must be increased.

Despite his uncanny prescience, other Cold War ironies would have confounded Orwell. He presupposed a truism: People must be hated to be targeted for destruction. *1984* famously featured routine hate sessions culminating in Hate Week. There were no hate sessions for Soviet citizens. On the contrary, they were seen as honorary good guys, victims of cruel apparatchiks, longing for regime change. Congress passed resolutions urging Americans to pray for the Soviet people—while strategists plotted their destruction "if deterrence fails."

Finally, and there is a certain finality here, surely there were no hate sessions for the American people. Nevertheless, strategists anticipated the demise of millions of Americans in strategic scenarios, scenarios that held Americans hostage to nuclear terror. Thomas Schelling, a prominent strategist and Pentagon advisor, allows that—given the risks they hazarded—he and his colleagues played "Russian roulette" with the American people.[9] They pulled the trigger during the Cuban missile crisis—somehow we're still here to talk about it.[10]

THE IRONY OF AMERICAN NUCLEAR ENDEAVORS

The atom had us bewitched. It was so gigantic, so terrible, so beyond the power of imagination to embrace that it seemed like the ultimate fact. It would either destroy us all or bring about the millennium. It was the final secret of Nature greater than man himself, and it was, it seemed, invulnerable to ordinary processes of life. . . . Our obsession with the atom led us to assign to it a separate and unique state in the world. So greatly did it seem to transcend the ordinary affairs of men that we shut it out of those affairs all together; or rather tried to create a separate world, a world of the atom.

—David Lilienthal, first chairman of the Atomic
Energy Commission [11]

Claims made regarding the ultimate terror weapon were almost as remarkable as the weapon itself: It won the war in the Pacific, preserved the peace during the Cold War, and assured American hegemony. Lilienthal, however, feared that nuclear weapons might betray their millenarian promise and put the homeland in peril as never before.

During the early heroic days of nuclear endeavors, those "present at creation" were awestruck by the power that binds the firmament. The atomic bomb was a supernatural marvel. Oppenheimer named the test site "Trinity" after reading poet John Donne's "Holy Sonnet"—enigmatic verse about a fearsome "three-personed" God about to batter and burn and yet renew. Upon witnessing the flash—the sky lit for a hundred miles—physicist Ernest Lawrence echoed the *Book of Revelation*: "Time stood still. Space contracted to a pinpoint. It was as though the earth had opened and skies had split. One felt as though he had been privileged to witness the Birth of the World. . . . The big boom came about a hundred seconds after the great flash—the first cry of a newborn world."[12]

Promise Betrayed

Unbridled enthusiasm marked the brief (1945–1949) American nuclear monopoly. Not only did nuclear weapons defeat Japan, they ushered in dreams of an American Century—fantasies of unprecedented power, prosperity, and security for the elect among nations. It seemed magical to Lilienthal, the dawning of a new Earth and a new heaven: "No fairy tale that I had read in utter rapture and enchantment as a child . . . can remotely compare."[13]

As we'll see at the close of the chapter when the efficacy of deterrence is considered, contrary to expectations the American nuclear monopoly didn't temper the ambitions of American adversaries—it probably exacerbated hostilities. The Soviets, for example, blockaded Berlin in 1948. Even so, American officials believed they could encircle the Soviets with nuclear bases with impunity. Despite warnings from military men and scientists, decision-makers refused to believe that the Soviets would soon possess a nuclear arsenal.

Like the Japanese before them, the Soviets were seen as a backward, Asiatic people incapable of formidable, technological accomplishments. As late as 1947, an ever-confident General Leslie Groves (director of the Manhattan Project) quipped that the Russians "can't even make a jeep! . . . The Russians would need fifteen or twenty years to develop an atomic bomb."[14] President Truman was even more emphatic. Robert Oppenheimer told the "president he was unsure about the Soviet's ability to build nuclear weapons. Truman assured Oppenheimer that *he* knew, "Never!"[15]

An atomic explosion above Siberia in 1949 confirmed Lilienthal's worst fears. He joined critics in lamenting wasted opportunities for more cordial relations with the Soviets: "Our obsession with bigger bombs as a cure-all excluded any considerations of such a possibility."[16] The Soviet bomb seemed to preclude the possibility of triumphant warfighting—at least for some. As Brodie explained: "Thus far the chief purpose of our military establishment has been to win wars. From now on its chief purpose must be to avert them. [Nuclear weapons] can have almost no other useful purpose."[17] While strategist Herman Kahn took extreme positions, no one questioned his definition of deterrence: "Deterrence means dissuasion by terror . . . there is a motivation to refrain from an action because of a fearful threat (explicit or implicit) or a warning of fearful consequences."[18]

Nuclear weapons, of course, were created for war fighting, not deterrence; deterrence seems like an afterthought. As Solly Zuckerman, the former chief science advisor to the British government, explains:

> During the twenty years or so that I was myself professionally involved in these matters, weapons came first and rationalization and policies followed. . . . In 1945 no one spoke about "deterrent strategy" or about any other kind of nuclear strategy. . . To those who took the decisions, the atomic, and later the hydrogen bombs were simply immensely powerful weapons . . . nations just had to have.[19]

Could it be that deterrence doctrines were improvised to make the best of a bad situation—unanticipated Soviet nuclear developments? The doctrines, of course, also legitimized elite bureaucracies involved in the development, deployment, and threatened detonation of nuclear weapons. A consensus emerged: Given Soviet intentions and capabilities, nuclear weapons were essential to deter Soviet aggression against America and Western Europe.

In general, there was no enthusiasm for nuclear war-fighting. Nevertheless, strategists hazarded risks. They spoke of deterrence in public and "compellence"—relying upon nuclear threats to compel adversaries to act in accord with US interests—in house. They called it "extended deterrence."[20] Moreover, strategists had nuclear war-fighting strategies in mind "if deterrence fails."

Then as now, it is not politically correct to attribute nuclear endeavors to anything other than deterrence. Even first-use weapons and strategies were called "deterrents." (Other factors driving the arms race such as first-strike scenarios, military contractors, inter-service rivalry, and competition between the national laboratories seldom entered mainstream discourse.) Even presidents gave obeisance to deterrence. In his first Strategic Defense Initiative (SDI) speech, March 1983, President Reagan maligned deterrence for threatening the destruction of Soviet civilians. He claimed that by rendering nuclear weapons "impotent and obsolete," SDI would eliminate the need for deterrence. This pronouncement provoked concern among those accustomed to invoking deterrence to justify their weapons systems and strategic scenarios. Evidently, the president was properly chastened. In his next SDI speech

(March 1988), the president dutifully explained that SDI would "enhance deterrence."[21]

OLDEST PSYCHOLOGY/NEWEST LOGIC

US leaders felt required to take what they saw as a high risk of nuclear war without examining how it would be undertaken or waged to advantage and without confidence that the consequences would be "acceptable."

—Richard Betts[22]

One would hope that weapons created by the greatest advance in science would be managed, if not mastered, by startling advances in psychology and logic. This was not to be. Commenting upon his influential history, *The Evolution of Nuclear Strategy*, Lawrence Freedman regrets invoking "evolution" in the title. He came to understand that "new" insights about deterrence were said yesterday.[23] In his view, Cold War strategizing reiterated the doctrines of the second Eisenhower administration. The deterrence doctrine that informs nuclear strategy goes back further than Freedman suggests. Nuclear endeavors were guided by the oldest psychology, an experiment in Thucydides's applied psychology: credibly threatening terrible punishment in order to give adversaries second thoughts about their ambitions and capabilities.

There is a curious parallel between dramatic changes in ancient Greek accounts of strategy, and equally dramatic changes in the American conceptualization of nuclear weaponry. Decisions about nuclear endeavors are made in halls modeled after Greek architecture, and weapons are named after Greek gods. Less obvious, but more telling: The chronicle of American nuclear endeavors retells an ancient saga about causes of war and prospects for peace.

Initially, Greek bards invoked supernatural imagery—the machinations of Olympian gods—to account for earthly conflicts such as the Trojan War. Thucydides, perhaps the first revisionist historian, relied upon realpolitik to account for the conflict. Prior to his realpolitik, the Greeks invoked mythic/poetic sagas to account for conflicts. Thucydides's account eschews machinations of the gods. In prose that delights any latter-day realist, he insists that Agamemnon's victory was based upon overwhelming military might.

Likewise, during the early heroic days of American nuclear endeavors, those present at creation invoked supernatural metaphors (mostly the Judeo-Christian variety, although as we'll see, Oppenheimer's invocation of Hindu scripture is telling) to account for their noumenal experience—witnessing the uncanny, the "wholly other." This sense of awe soon turned to exuberant millenarianism: American leaders had an exclusive franchise on the power that binds the cosmos—a power that could be put to good use, or so it seemed. After the Soviets unexpectedly got the bomb, and fate no longer smiled on the American nuclear enterprise, strategists took Brodie's advice: "[Strategic thinking] requires appraisal of the atomic bomb as an instrument of war—and hence of international politics—rather than the visitation of a wrathful deity."[24]

The subsequent strategic oeuvre invoked the naturalistic precepts of the ancient historian. Realists claim they understand the world as it is. Resisting the intoxication of wishful thinking, they offer a sober assessment of a deterministic world governed by cruel natural laws operating behind the backs and against the will of decision-makers. The world according to Thucydides and the nuclear strategists is transparent and uncomplicated: It's a jungle out there—no place for high ideals. Amid the international anarchy, states—uninhibited by moral scruples—vie for power. At this point, however, the realists' wishful thinking begins. Despite evidence to the contrary, states are seen as rational actors setting attainable goals and acting accordingly.

While certain strategists were sympathetic to arms control, they all feared they would suffer the same fate of the hapless inhabitants of Melos if they disarmed. Classically grounded or not, strategists were haunted by Thucydides's admonition: "The strong do what they have the power to do, and the weak must endure the consequences." Only the credible threat to use nuclear weapons would give the Soviets second thoughts about their ambitions and capabilities; such a threat could also advance American interests.

Not surprisingly, American realism has a distinctly American accent, an optimistic faith that all problems have solutions—technological solutions. The arms race promised a technological fix, an invincible America no power on earth would dare challenge. The Soviets responded to every advance in weaponry in kind. The sense of the tragic, the cautionary tales, the irony and folly revealed in Thucydides's writings are un-

American. He describes ten attempts at deterrence and compellence. With one exception, these strategies failed and provoked the behavior they were meant to prevent.[25] Might the same be said regarding the irony of post–World War II American military campaigns?

A Brave New Logic

The arms race constantly increased the risk of nuclear war. The proliferation of weapons, the ease of their use, harrowing accidents, and bolder risk-taking heightened anxiety. Making the best of a bad situation, strategists called it MAD (mutually assured destruction). Like the Mad Tea Party in *Alice in Wonderland,* strategists pondered a riddle: Why is it safe to have weapons of a kind and number it is not safe to use?[26] Like Churchill, prominent Pentagon advisors and strategists such as Edward Luttwak answered with paradox.

Luttwak invites participation in a new language game; however, the reasoning and rules are unclear. He invokes the ancient proverb—*Si vis pacem, para bellum.* ("If you would have peace, prepare for war"; of course the dictum "if you want war, prepare for war" better fits the historical record.) Not only must more sophisticated weapons be developed and deployed, the threat must be credible. Decision-makers must convince adversaries *and* themselves that certain provocations will be met with nuclear retaliation.[27] What provocations merited retaliation was subject to considerable debate. However, there was no debate regarding NATO policy mandating the first use of nuclear weapons in response to a conventional Soviet attack in Western Europe.

Admiral Eugene Carroll participated in NATO war games as a commander of US forces. Following long-established policy, NATO authorized the first use of tactical nuclear weapons to repulse a Soviet conventional attack. After the proper codes were released and verified, the game abruptly stopped. The admiral suggested that war-planners were in denial; they could not think of the unthinkable results of detonating 7,000 nuclear weapons. "There were no metaphors for the ensuing paroxysm." Upon his retirement, the admiral became a nuclear abolitionist, lecturing and writing about the urgent need to abolish nuclear weapons.[28] The former NATO commander found nuclear doublethink ironic: The salvation of Europe, if not the entire planet, depended upon

nuclear terror. Salvation from extinction by nuclear weapons was found
in the nuclear weapons themselves.

Luttwak found the irony liberating. He argues that strategizing is
entitled to abandon logic and coherence—but apparently not hope. The
initiated understand that strategy traffics in a unique, contradictory logic all its own. He explains:

> The entire realm of strategy is pervaded by a paradoxical logical of its
> own, standing against the ordinary logic by which we live in all other
> spheres of life. Strategic practice can be liberated from the mislead-
> ing influence of commonsense logic. . . . This offers liberation from
> the false disciplines of consistency and coherence.[29]

Those promoting World War II struggled to avoid cognitive dissonance: condemning while practicing terror bombing. Cold warriors
such as Luttwak celebrate cognitive *insolence*—contempt for sturdy
logic. Lest I be accused of a know-nothing attitude toward the "sublime
irony" of paradox, I hasten to add that with Emerson, I appreciate the
possibility that consistency is the hobgoblin of small minds.

I recognize that theorists of the stature of Hegel, Marx, and Freud
saw contradictions at the center of the human drama. It must be em-
phasized, however, that their theories per se are reasonably coherent—
they don't celebrate internal contradictions *within* their works. Hegelian contradictions, by way of example, are fluid and organic: in his
dialectic, contradictions are incorporated and resolved in a comprehensive synthesis. Luttwak's contradictions are static, ahistorical, and irre-
solvable.

Likewise, the discoveries and theories of twentieth-century physics
are counterintuitive, even paradoxical. Even so, it is difficult to imagine
Einstein and Heisenberg celebrating emancipation from consistency
and coherence. (Imagine Einstein simultaneously claiming that the
speed of light is constant and inconstant.) To paraphrase Einstein, God
doesn't play with dice—but strategists do. Luttwak and the others do
not offer an excursion into the interstices Hegelian dialectic or the
paradoxes of quantum physics. The strategic narrative floats in a mysterious quintessence remote from logic and common sense.

The Strategic Uncertainty Principle

The confidence informing nuclear strategizing is striking and ironic: There's never been a nuclear exchange between belligerents. I'm reminded of a conversation with my friend Mark. When asked what it was like to serve as a medic in Vietnam, he replied, "I had no metaphors, just reality." I suspect strategists suffer the opposite affliction—no reality, just metaphors. To paraphrase Wittgenstein, of that we cannot speak we must remain silent. As the voluminous strategic genre indicates, nuclear terror didn't leave strategists speechless. They used their imaginations. As Derrida observed with uncharacteristic clarity: "A nuclear war has not taken place: one can only talk and write about it."[30]

The talk and writing are indeed prodigious: endless stories ("scenarios" in Nukespeak) about invoking the threat of nuclear terror to give adversaries second thoughts about their ambitions. Some analysts liken deterrence to the icy-cold cost/risk/benefit analysis of rational actors— savvy game players. Glen Snyder, for example, likens deterrence to gaming with a matrix involving precise, numerical calculations that entail rational decisions.[31] This approach lends an aura of scientific credibility to deterrence doctrine. However, it's been said that science begins with metaphor and ends with algebra. Game theory reverses the process. Game theorists begin with mathematics and conclude with metaphors likening decision-makers to players in zero-sum games or Prisoners' Dilemma.

Other analysts propose a more modest view of rational actors. Kenneth Waltz, for example, believes that even intellectually feeble, hot-blooded fanatical leaders of rogue states aren't about to jump in front of fast-moving trucks—or invite nuclear retaliation. Once again, this assertion is based upon faith-based assumptions regarding human nature. Celebrations of the triumph of reason in collective life don't come easily in this post-Freudian age. As we'll see, even President Kennedy—remembered as a pragmatic, rational actor—risked all that he cherished to resolve the Cuban missile crisis. Anthropologist Victor Turner's observation regarding rulers at other times and places applies to those inside the Beltway: "People will die for values that oppose their interest and promote interests that oppose their values."[32]

To reiterate, Herman Kahn didn't mince words when he argued that deterrence works by sending the signature message of terrorism: Be afraid, be terribly afraid. Kahn offers a variety of scenarios for promoting fear and trembling—from limited war-fighting to massive retaliation. His complicated schemata read like tables in the Ptolemaic system.[33]

Fear, of course, has an object. Some strategists consider the possibility that anxiety might be a better deterrent, for anxiety is truly unnerving—it has no object. Convincing adversaries they're dealing with a madman—they know not what to expect—might foment such anxiety. According to Nixon confidant H.R. Haldeman, Nixon toyed with invoking what the president called "madman theory" to deter the ambitions of the Vietnamese:

> I call it the madman theory, Bob. I want the North Vietnamese to believe I've reached the point where I might do anything to stop the war. We'll just slip the word to them that, for god's sake, you know Nixon is obsessed with Communism. We can't restrain him when he's angry—and he has his hand on the nuclear button—and Ho Chi Minh himself will be in Paris in two days begging for peace.[34]

More reflective analysts were troubled by the irony of deterrence doctrine. Karl Deutsche said it best: "The theory of deterrence . . . first proposes that we should frustrate our opponents by frightening them very badly and that we should rely on their cool-headed rationality for our survival."[35]

Despite—or because of?—the incongruities, analysts confidently extol their particular versions of the nuclear canon. As political scientist Philip Green notes: "Almost all works encountered . . . seem invested with a tremendously authoritative air, an air that one associates with scholarly work in the most well-established and systematically researched disciplines."[36] There's no method—short of nuclear war—of testing the strategists' contesting claims. Given this situation, it is not surprising that strategists adopt an authorial strategy rife with irony.

They preface their works with de rigueur professions of academic modesty. Even a dogmatist like Herman Kahn begins by admitting his fallibility and self-doubt. He expresses what I call the strategic uncertainty principle: "Uncertainty is another significant new development of the nuclear age. . . . We have no actual experience from which to make judgments especially on the scale that would be involved in a major war."[37] He underscores this insight by recounting a conversation between a seasoned general and a young defense analyst. Taken aback by the young man's lack of deference, the general scoffed: "How can *you*, a young man who has never fired a gun in anger, have the temerity to argue with me about nuclear war?" Kahn lauds his apprentice's response: "It takes about ten nuclear wars to get a sense of the range of possibilities . . . a very minimal level of experience. Just out of curiosity, how many such wars have you actually fought or studied?"[38]

And yet, despite his professed uncertainty, Kahn can't resist the temptation to pontificate, especially in light of the competition—the American Catholic Bishops' *Pastoral Letter* denouncing many of his nuclear war-fighting doctrines. The bishops' injunction that a nuclear war should never be fought is dismissed ex cathedra: "My views are almost certainly not *wrong* on any of the issues I have raised here . . . though others might not agree that they are entirely right."[39]

Consider the authorial strategy of a highly respected mainstream commentator such as Lawrence Freedman. He reminds us we're in the dark managing nuclear weapons—and there's so much at stake. Rather than humility, strategists display "astonishing confidence in their own nostrums, combined with vindictiveness against those who differ."[40] Even so, he joins other deterrence theorists who—despite Jesuitical differences—confidently eulogize American nuclear endeavors: "My fortunate generation has been allowed to grow up in relative peace. Our peace has been gained at least in part by the sobering prospect of the destruction that would in all probability follow its collapse."[41]

The celebration of nuclear terror is widespread and effusive. Presidential advisor Eugene Rostow lauds deterrence as the Rock of Ages, the foundation of the renaissance of the West since 1945; and journalist William Laurence assures us that the hydrogen bomb makes peace inevitable. Former Secretary of Defense Caspar Weinberger claims that deterrence assured decades of peace in Europe—despite the threat of Soviet nuclear weapons. And prominent academics such as Michael Mandelbaum update Dr. Pangloss when he claims the arms race is the story of the evolution of the best of all possible worlds.[42]

Before evaluating these encomiums to nuclear terror, it's worth considering what might occur if deterrence fails. Accordingly, the next section discusses failures of extended deterrence that actually occurred during the Cold War. Scenarios for the failure of existential deterrence—responding to attacks on the American homeland—are also considered.

FAILURES OF DETERRENCE

I was there; I have had direct experience in trying to handle a nuclear crisis with the fate of the world on the line; and because of my experience, I know—I am not guessing or speculating. I know that we were just plain lucky in October 1962—and that without that luck most of you would never have been born because the world would have been destroyed instantly or made unlivable in October 1962. And something like it could happen today, tonight, next year. It will happen at some point. That is why we must abolish nuclear weapons as soon as possible.

— Robert McNamara's last address on the Cuban missile crisis[43]

Revisiting failures of extended deterrence illustrate that avoiding nuclear war was not always the overarching concern of American leaders—despite their de rigueur public renunciations of nuclear war. Scenarios about imagined failures of existential deterrence—attacks on the American homeland—portend the deaths of hundreds of millions of Soviet *and* American noncombatants.

Failures of Extended Deterrence

While the atom didn't usher in an American Century, strategists expected the American nuclear arsenal would fulfill a more modest, yet hazardous role: deterring those who would act against American interests. On occasion, officials construed failures of extended deterrence as problems—challenges to be resolved quietly and diplomatically in due course. In his oft-quoted Farewell Address, Eisenhower urged his successor to treat challenges as problems, not crises that increase the risk of war.

Eisenhower's successors ignored his admonitions about the military-industrial-complex *and* about reckless crisis promotion. More often than not, due to a variety of personal, political, and strategic reasons, failures of deterrence were interpreted as crises: critical junctures demanding urgent actions that increase the danger of war, in many cases nuclear war. These crises were represented as inevitable responses to certain provocations—supposedly, decision-makers had no choice. However, to paraphrase an ancient philosopher, the world is not the source of our crises; it is our interpretation of the world. These episodes, in effect, provide a window (depending upon the availability of declassified documents) through which we witness decision-makers on the cusp between war and peace, agonizing about whether to reestablish the status quo ante through words or weapons.

Berlin

In 1948, the aftermath of World War II left Berlin within East Germany, although American forces controlled West Berlin. Moving to incorporate all of Berlin within their sphere of influence, the Soviets restricted Western access to Berlin and cut electric power—apparently, the Soviets were undeterred by the American nuclear monopoly. Truman construed the provocation as a problem to be resolved in due course. He responded with oblique threats: B-29s were sent to Great Britain and Germany; unbeknownst to the Soviets, none had nuclear weapons. Churchill and others urged an American nuclear attack, but no weapons were assembled, and, in any event, there were serious doubts about penetrating Soviet airspace. However, this early foray into "atomic diplomacy" may have pressured the Soviets into relenting.[44]

Rather than provoking a war—which probably wouldn't have mustered the support of a war-weary public, let alone American allies—a massive airlift supplied Berlin with essentials and nonessentials. If you would search for ironic incongruity, look no further than "Operation Gum Drop":

> Berlin Airlift pilots enjoyed their mission of flying into Germany to deliver food and supplies to the German people. It was a wonderful feeling to be delivering food and help, rather than delivering bombs. During one mission, pilot Lieutenant Gale S. Halverson decided to tour around the area of Germany where he landed each week. During his tour, he met lots of children who came out to watch him take pictures of the sites. Unlike most children, they did not beg money or candy from him, but just stood and watched. In a flash, an idea came to him. "You kids wait until tomorrow and I will drop you some candy from my airplane." The next day, Halverson kept his promise and dropped three small handkerchief parachutes of candy from the

plane. He used the flare chute in the bottom of the plane. From that first idea grew a daily effort to drop candy from the sky to the German children.[45]

The blockade ended after about ten months. However, this was not the last failure of deterrence involving Berlin; other episodes didn't end as sweetly. Khrushchev found Stalin's 1948 "appeasement" humiliating. In 1958, apparently relying upon the Soviet's newfound nuclear strength, he insisted that all of Berlin must come under Soviet control. Displaying considerable finesse, Eisenhower defined Khrushchev's demands as a problem, an issue to be deferred to a future conference, rather than a crisis demanding urgent resolution.[46] War hero Eisenhower had no need to prove himself by standing up to communism and by promoting a public crisis. To paraphrase Kissinger, Eisenhower hated war only the way an experienced military man could.

In 1961 the American nuclear arsenal didn't give Khrushchev second thoughts about provoking Kennedy with an ultimatum: *All* of Berlin must be controlled by the Soviet bloc. Given the dramatic increase in the Soviet nuclear arsenal, Khrushchev was, perhaps, emboldened to rely upon a compellence strategy of his own. Kennedy's response was guided by a policy of gradual escalation, the same strategy that would inform the Cuban missile crisis. McNamara escalated nuclear threats as American and Soviet tanks faced one another in Berlin.

In what presaged negotiations during the Cuban missile crisis, the president's brother met secretly with Soviet Ambassador Dobyrinin and offered to remove American tanks if the Soviet would do the same. They exchanged communiqués. Just as he would do the next year, Kennedy ignored belligerent messages and responded to more tractable guided missiles. The infamous Berlin Wall, a source of embarrassment to both sides, reestablished the status quo ante.

Kennedy set out to prove himself—to make a name for himself by confronting the Soviet challenge. Crises were not merely a concern; they were an obsession. Unfortunately, he never got the ones he wanted. Opposing Khrushchev over Berlin risked nuclear retaliation against the American homeland. He knowingly risked the lives of American citizens. Senator Mike Mansfield was disturbed by Kennedy's risk-taking—challenges irrelevant to safeguarding the American homeland. Referring to JFK's bravado during a Berlin crisis, he warned that

"[US policy] carries the ultimate implication to pledge the lives and fortunes of every man, woman, and American child in the nation to Berlin's defense."[47]

Cuba

One October day—it doesn't seem that long ago—American officials discovered a harrowing failure of extended deterrence. Soviet diplomats deceived American officials. U-2 reconnaissance revealed the surreptitious construction of a Soviet nuclear base in Cuba, a mere ninety miles from American shores. A prominent presidential advisor warned the base was a "quantum leap" in Soviet strategic capability. Department of Defense officials concurred.

This gloss on the all-but-forgotten Cienfuegos Bay episode of 1970 reveals the irony of the unforgettable 1962 Cuban missile crisis. Nuclear submarines operating out of Cienfuegos Bay posed a more formidable threat than the readily detectable, land-based missiles of 1962. Kissinger interpreted undetectable submarines as a quantum leap in the Soviet threat—a crisis demanding urgent attention and resolution.

It would seem that Nixon's defining moment was at hand—*the* once-in-a-lifetime opportunity to burnish his anticommunist credentials, the ultimate test of his mettle and his presidency. Nixon never tired of chastising Kennedy for vacillation and weakness in managing JFK's bravura crisis: Kennedy's "weak-kneed" response to the Cuban missile base put "the Atlantic alliance in disarray. Cuba is western Russia, and the rest of Latin America is in deadly peril."[48] Nixon vowed that *he* would have taught the Soviets an unforgettable lesson.

It was as if the Soviets invited Nixon to his defining crisis, if not the gravest crisis of the nuclear age. Much to Kissinger's dismay, Nixon found it inconvenient to attend.[49] He ordered his closest advisors, the Washington Strategic Action Group (WSAG), *not* to make a crisis move. According to Kissinger, the president was distracted by other matters, thought it unwise to promote a crisis close to the election (his motives might be suspect), and—again according to Kissinger—Nixon had his heart set on visiting the Mediterranean to watch the Six Fleet fire its guns.[50]

I don't doubt Kissinger's explanation; however, I suggest the president was distracted and inattentive because it wasn't a Nixon-style crisis. As Nixon revealed in *Six Crises* and subsequent responses—or lack of responses—to international challenges, his crises were venal and personal. Like Willy Loman in the low tragedy of *Death of a Salesman,* Nixon crises occurred when he wasn't "well-liked"—a frequent occurrence. Arthur Miller's synopsis of his play might well be Nixon's epitaph:

> It is the tragedy of a man who did believe that he alone was not meeting the qualifications laid down for mankind by those . . . new frontiersmen who inhabit the peaks of broadcasting and advertising offices. From those forests . . . he heard the thundering command to succeed as it ricochets down the newspaper-lined canyons of the city . . . not a human voice, but a wind of a voice to which no human reply in kind, except to stare into the mirror of failure.[51]

Nixon crises involved managing Nixon, not foreign affairs. *Six Crises,* for the most part, neglects the Korean War, the Soviet H-bomb, and the defeat of the French in Indochina. His crises include charges of misusing campaign funds (the Checkers Speech), having his car egged by South American "weirdoes," and exchanging insults with Khrushchev at an American appliance exhibit in the Kremlin.

Indifferent to the Soviet challenge in Cuba, Nixon vacationed as planned. However, before he departed, he permitted Kissinger to meet secretly with the Soviet ambassador to resolve the provocation secretly, quietly, and diplomatically. The Soviets dismantled the submarine base without alarm and fanfare. The prudent resolution of what might have become the gravest crisis of the nuclear age is all but forgotten—even among the participants themselves. Sometimes it's better to have Everyman in office rather than a would-be profile in courage.

Revisionist accounts of the 1962 Cuban missile crisis have gone mainstream. Initially, these accounts held the Soviets largely responsible, celebrated Kennedy's adroit crisis management—grace under pressures, and underplayed the danger of nuclear catastrophe. These accounts indicted the Soviets for lying to American authorities by surreptitiously deploying nuclear weapons just ninety miles from American shores. The president's response was narrated in superlatives. In what was, perhaps, the most influential mainstream take on Kennedy's response, Graham Allison wrote: "Here is one of the finest examples of diplomatic prudence, and perhaps the finest hour of the John F. Kennedy Presidency."[52] Considering the risks JFK hazarded, Chomsky called it "the lowest point in human history."[53]

Dean Acheson, the elder statesman who served as one of the president's advisors, was ridiculed by those closest to the president for urging that nuclear war was averted due to "plain dumb luck."[54] After praising the president's management as "brilliantly controlled and matchlessly calibrated," Kennedy confidant Ted Sorensen quipped: "Dean Acheson is right in crediting Kennedy with considerable good luck on this awesome occasion. . . . JFK was lucky in rejecting Acheson's reckless advice."[55] Kennedy wisely rejected the advice of hawks such as Acheson: He didn't launch an immediate attack on Cuba. He tried to give his adversary the time and incentive to back down. However, he feared his gradual escalation strategy would fail and prepared for full-scale nuclear warfare.

McNamara's revelations along with the declassification of American, Soviet, and Cuban documents lend credence to more disturbing, long-marginalized revisionist accounts of the crisis. Relying upon this material, Blight and Lang recount events that precipitated the crisis.[56] As they conclude: "It is now clear where the momentum begins toward the great crisis of 1962 the moment when an unsuspecting world would come closer than ever to . . . Armageddon. The moment, April 17, 1961."[57] The Bay of Pigs fiasco humiliated Kennedy and convinced Khrushchev that the Americans would stop at nothing to eliminate the Castro regime. The Soviets claim they knew of Operation Mongoose, what Blight and Lang call "terrorist" operations against Cuba. As the Church Committee revealed, Mongoose included attempts on Castro's life including assassination plans for October 1962.[58]

Concluding that Kennedy was inexperienced, weak, and indecisive, Khrushchev further humiliated the young president at the Vienna Conference. As we've seen, the Soviet ultimatum resulted in nuclear threats over the status of Berlin, and the infamous Berlin Wall. Apparently, in response, Kennedy hazarded a symbolic gesture: deploying obsolete nuclear missiles in Turkey across the Black Sea from the Soviet Union.

Journalist Norman Cousins recounted a conversation with Khrushchev as they gazed toward those missiles across the Black Sea. The bumptious Russian peasant vowed that Americans should get a dose of their own medicine; surely the Soviets had the right to respond quid pro quo.[59] In any case, the Soviets didn't promote a "Turkish missile crisis."

Somehow they learned to live surrounded by nuclear bases; Americans must learn to do the same.

Khrushchev, however, craved more than recognition and equality by deploying missiles in Cuba. He desperately wanted to preserve the Castro regime by deterring American clandestine actions and another invasion. Khrushchev believed that Kennedy would accept the defensive, deterrent nature of the deployment. (Critics aptly suggest that Khrushchev's Cuban deterrent strategy would have been less provocative had he simply increased Soviet military personnel in Cuba.) In any case, neither the formidable American arsenal nor Kennedy's vows deterred the Soviets from constructing and completing the base.

In response, Kennedy convened a panel of advisors known as the Ex-Comm (Executive Committee of the National Security Council). Ambassador Raymond Garthoff, an advisor to the Ex-Comm, generously shared his private communications with CIA Director John McCone, a member of the Ex-Comm. McCone's letter to Garthoff offers an insider's look at the deliberations:

> In the Ex-Comm deliberations we pursued many alternative courses of action ranging from presenting the case to the UN . . . or striking unilaterally as advocated by Dean Acheson. The committee reasoned that the UN could (and would) do little, and that military action would prompt an array of Soviet responses such as taking over Berlin, and acting violently elsewhere. Also it was noted that military action would spill quantities of Soviet blood, thus causing a most serious confrontation that probably would escalate into war. It was decided (by the president) that we should move positively, and always providing Khrushchev with an opportunity to retreat. For that reason military actions including a blockade (in itself an act of war) were temporarily set aside, and a program of a quarantine of Cuba was adopted. This was the first step, but if it was ineffective then military action would follow, and Khrushchev was so informed through channels that we knew he respected.[60]

The facts, of course, don't speak for themselves. Why did Kennedy publicly promote this failure of deterrence as a crisis in the first place? The incongruity between the president's public pronouncements regarding the missiles and his private assessment raises more troubling questions. In his October 22 address to the nation, Kennedy reiterated his solemn vow: Offensive weapons would not be tolerated in Cuba; such weapons dramatically increased the threat to the American homeland and beyond: "This urgent transformation of Cuba into an important strategic base—by the presence of these large, long-range, and clearly offensive weapons of sudden mass destruction—constitutes an explicit threat to the peace and security of all the Americas."[61]

Listening to the transcripts at the Kennedy Library of the president's deliberations with his closest advisors presents a different picture. At an October 16 meeting, the president allowed: "It doesn't make any difference if you get blown up from an ICBM flying from the Soviet Union or one that was ninety miles away. What difference does it make? They have enough missiles [within Soviet borders] to blow us up anyway."[62]

McNamara concurred. He urged that a missile's destination is significant, not its origins—"a missile is a missile." He continued, "As far as I'm concerned it [the Cuban missiles] made no difference. . . . The military balance wasn't changed."[63] Sorensen summarized the advisors' consensus: "It is generally agreed that these missiles, even when fully operational, do not significantly alter the balance of power—i.e., they do not increase the potential megatonnage capable of being unleashed on American soil."[64]

Nevertheless, as we've seen, Sorensen lauded Kennedy's willingness to risk nuclear war in order to remove missiles that didn't alter the balance of power as "brilliantly controlled and matchlessly calibrated." To be sure, the missiles were not totally insignificant. They posed a problem for Kennedy's international bargaining reputation and his career. However, the *crisis* was with himself—his dark night of the soul. In the aftermath of humiliating foreign policy defeats, he construed the missiles as the ultimate test of his authenticity—a crisis of identity. Would he be remembered as a Churchill or a Chamberlain? Kennedy struggled to be both—the crisis signifies the essence of *indecision*. Journalist James Reston recognized the irony: "Kennedy talked like Churchill and acted like Chamberlain."[65]

Talking like Churchill committed him to a perilous course of action he came to regret. In September he reiterated earlier vows: Offensive weapons would not be tolerated in Cuba—the gravest consequences would result. (Apparently his vows were made on the cheap, perhaps for political purposes: Most analysts agree that Kennedy simply couldn't believe that the Soviets would move nuclear weapons beyond their borders—the American deterrent was robust.) A month later Kennedy, at an early Ex-Comm meeting, lamented: "Last month I should have said that we don't care."[66]

While Kennedy resisted pressure to attack immediately, he pursued actions that he believed would likely culminate in worldwide thermonuclear war. In what was euphemistically termed quarantine, he committed acts of war by blockading the Soviet fleet and by violating Cuban airspace. (In what American officials claimed was an accident, a U-2 spy plane violated Soviet airspace; they made the same claim when Francis Gary Powers's U-2 violated Soviet airspace during the Eisenhower administration.) American forces were put on an unprecedented DEF-CON 2 alert—just short of full-scale nuclear war. Missiles were armed and readied for launching, and B-52s flew toward targets in fail-safe patterns.

Harrowing accidents occurred, and subordinates got out of control. Someone accidentally ran a war game program indicating Cuban missiles were about to hit Tampa, and missiles were tested despite orders to stand down.[67] Garthoff recounts an obscure but harrowing incident—an episode worthy of the ironic mockery of black comedy. Soviet authorities captured an American double agent, Oleg Penkovsky, on October 22, 1962, the day Kennedy spoke to the nation. Garthoff explained that, in the event of an imminent attack on the United States, Penkovsky was authorized to send a secret telephone signal to the CIA indicating the Soviets were about to launch a nuclear attack. This is precisely what he did prior to Kennedy's speech. As Garthoff explains:

> So when he was about to go down, he evidently decided to play Samson and bring the temple down on everyone else as well. . . . His Western intelligence handlers at the operational level, after weighing a dilemma of great responsibility, decided not to credit Penkovksy's final signal and suppressed it.[68]

These handlers should be regarded as an eleventh "profile in courage."

There was good news and bad news about the blockade: Soviet ships stopped, but work on the Cuban bases accelerated; the missiles became operational. (Later, it was learned that dozens of tactical nuclear weapons awaited American invaders.) Robert Kennedy recounts the apprehension: "I felt we were on a precipice with no way off. . . . President Kennedy had initiated a course of events, but he no longer had control over them."[69]

Perhaps out of desperation, in private, the president acted like Chamberlain. Writing about the feckless prime minister in *Why England Slept*, Kennedy allowed: "Appeasement did have some realism; it was the inevitable result of conditions that permitted no other decision."[70] As the crisis rapidly escalated and war seemed inevitable, Kennedy found himself in a "condition that permitted no other decision." According to Garthoff, charged with safeguarding Robert Kennedy's calendar, the president's brother met with the Soviet Ambassador almost every night of the crisis. The last fateful night, the Kennedy administration proposed what became known as the "Secret Deal." Khrushchev would publicly remove the Cuban missiles; Kennedy would secretly remove the Turkish missiles in April.

Heeding Disraeli's advice, the Kennedy brothers hoped for the best but expected the worst. They feared they pushed Khrushchev too far: seeming to appease an American president would be unthinkable. After proposing the Secret Deal, Robert Kennedy lamented:

> The president was not optimistic, nor was I. . . . He had not abandoned hope, but what hope there was now rested with Khrushchev revising his course within a few hours. It was a hope, not an expectation. The expectation was a military confrontation by Tuesday and possibly by tomorrow.[71]

Unexpectedly, Khrushchev accepted the Secret Deal—better red than dead. He kept it quiet as promised; scholars learned of it years later in Sorensen's account of the episode. In the words of one commentator: "Kennedy was thus salvaged for twenty-five years from the ignominy of having his eagerness to initiate a public swap known to most of his advisors."[72]

Existential Deterrence

During the Cuban missile crisis, both sides feared that adversaries might preempt rather than being the first to suffer a devastating blow. Had the Secret Deal failed, Soviet installations would have been attacked; no doubt a nuclear exchange would have followed. Plans for a nuclear attack on the Soviet Union were articulated in the Strategic Integrated Operational Plan (SIOP). The plan in place during the crisis, SIOP-62, orchestrated the greatest destruction of human life in all of history. There is little doubt that Soviet plans reciprocated. American authorities were armed and ready to operationalize the plan even though it meant the destruction of hundreds of millions of Soviet *and* American lives. After perusing recently declassified exchanges between Kennedy, Khrushchev, and Castro, Blight and Lang conclude: "A catastrophic nuclear war nearly happened in October 1962. We know it now because it is a matter of historical record. All three leaders came to believe, in October 1962, that they were staring down the gun barrel of a nuclear war."[73]

Based upon SIOP-62 American strategists planned:

- In the event of a warning about an imminent Soviet attack, American forces would preempt—3,200 nuclear weapons would hit 1,060 targets in the Soviet Union, China, and their allies.
- A retaliatory attack would deliver 1,706 nuclear weapons against 725 targets listed above. These targets include a minimum of 130 cities.

Certain officials expressed concern about overkill. For example, Nagasaki was destroyed by a 22-kiloton weapon. SIOP-62 targeted a city the size of Nagasaki with three 80-kiloton weapons. Given the overkill, there was concern that the fallout "can be a hazard to ourselves as well as our enemy."[74]

Planning to Kill our Friends

SIOP-62 in effect responded to strategist Albert Wohlstetter's concern discussed in his influential "Delicate Balance of Nuclear Terror" article published in *Foreign Affairs* in 1959. Wohlstetter was concerned because the American arsenal couldn't reliably kill half the Soviet population—the requisite number to properly titrate the balance of terror. Apparently SIOP-62 corrected this oversight. A puzzling question remains: What good would be served by annihilating tens of millions of Soviet citizens if deterrence fails? The Soviet people wouldn't be held responsible for such an act; Kremlin dictators would be blamed.

The Soviet people were not dehumanized; nevertheless, they were targeted for destruction. Every Cold War president had kind words for those behind the Iron Curtain. Eisenhower proclaimed: "No people on earth can be held, as a people, to be an enemy, for all humanity shares the common hunger for peace and fellowship."[75] Kennedy echoed this sentiment: "As Americans we find communism profoundly repugnant as a negation of personal freedom and dignity. But we can still hail the Russian people for their many achievements—in science and space, in economic and industrial growth, in culture and in acts of courage."[76] And Nixon praised the Soviet people by likening them to Americans: he found them warm and hospitable—they even laughed at his jokes. Imagine FDR expressing such warmth toward the Japanese. This sea change in the depiction of civilians in enemy lands goes largely unnoticed.

Those behind the Iron Curtain were praised and pitied, not dehumanized. Moviegoers and readers of popular magazines pitied Russians shivering in breadlines only to return to dismal apartments. Propagandists endlessly compared the barren shelves in the "workers paradise" with the bounty of the American consumer paradise. Movie critics suggest that early Cold War science fiction films symbolized the plight of the Soviet masses. In films such as *The Body Snatchers* people "just like us" were seized and denatured by alien forces—the obvious plight of victims of communism. As Andrey Shcherbenok suggests in "Cold War Cinema in the Soviet Union and the United States," the real shift in American Cold War cinema occurred in the mid-1960s:

> The Russians are humanized, while the American society splits not into foreign-sponsored Communists and freedom-loving people but into right-wing conservative hawks prone to start World War III at any moment and reasonable people who are free of anti-communist hysteria and are prepared to communicate with the Soviets.[77]

Films such as *Fail Safe* show that rational, morally sensitive dialog between American and Soviet leaders is essential for avoiding war amid crises. *Dr. Strangelove* famously satirizes the Cold War paranoia of Curtis LeMay's Strategic Air Command. And *The Russians Are Coming, the Russians Are Coming*, as Shcherbenok writes, "satirized American anticommunist hysteria and, in the same move, humanized the Russians."[78]

The Soviets (aka Russians) were humanized in presidential rhetoric and in popular culture, *and* targeted for destruction in a variety of SIOP scenarios. Stranger still, not even American civilians enjoyed noncombatant immunity; their own government contemplated their destruction. (FDR asked for sacrifice but never entertained the prospect of sacrificing millions of American civilians to a higher cause.)

Planning to Kill Americans

Awestruck by the fulminating mushroom cloud at the first atomic test, Oppenheimer famously quoted Krishna's doomsday rage in Hindu scripture:

> I remembered the line from the Hindu scripture, the *Bhagavad-Gita*. Vishnu is trying to persuade the Prince that he should do his duty and to impress him takes on his multi-armed form and says, Now I am become Death, the destroyer of worlds.[79]

Setting the quote in context reveals the prince's duty and the solemn duty of the nuclear strategists. Krishna (avatar of Vishnu, the Supreme Being) is enraged: Prince Arjuna is reluctant to do his duty; he must be compelled. Krishna becomes a ghastly, multi-armed visage, death personified—the destroyer of worlds. *But what was his duty?* Arjuna hesitated because he was ordered to kill his beloved family, friends, and teacher. A credible nuclear strategy must not hesitate to risk the lives of millions of Americans to deter aggression or to sacrifice these lives to survive and prevail in a nuclear war.

Duty trumps sentimentality as we learn from Krishna and from redoubtable Herman Kahn, who insists that we dutifully accept the prospect of sacrificing millions of our countrymen in the crusade against communism. In 1979 at the height of the Cold War, an official government agency, the Office of Technological Assessment, estimated that American casualties would range between 70 and 160 million. Subsequent deaths due to the destruction of the infrastructure were difficult to estimate.[80]

Kahn cautioned that we shouldn't get overly exercised by the prospect of fulfilling our sacrificial duty. In a work praised by officials such as Brent Scowcroft and Donald Rumsfeld, Kahn invites us to consider:

The possibility—both menacing and perversely comforting—that even if 300 million people were killed in a nuclear war, there would still be more than four billion left alive. . . . And a power that attains significant strategic superiority is likely to survive the war, perhaps even "win" by extending its hegemony—at least for a time—over much of the world. Reconstruction will begin, life will continue, and most survivors will not envy the dead.[81]

Thomas Schelling has no regrets about playing Russian roulette and pulling the trigger during the Cuban missile crisis: "The Cuban missile crisis was the best thing to happen to us since the Second World War. . . . Sometimes the gambles you take pay off."[82] President Kennedy wasn't as sanguine about risking the lives of American children. Both brothers doubted that the Soviets would accept the Secret Deal. Robert Kennedy explains:

The thought that disturbed him [JFK] the most, and that made the prospect of war much more fearful than it would otherwise have been, was the specter of the death of the children of this country, and all the world—the young people who had no say . . . but whose lives would be snuffed out like everyone else's.[83]

We'll never know the answer to a question that should never have been asked. In a posthumous coda that concludes Robert Kennedy's *Memoir*, Sorensen explains:

It was Senator Kennedy's intention to add a discussion of the basic ethical question involved: what, if any, circumstances or justifications give this government or any government the moral right to bring its people and possibly all people under the shadow of nuclear destruction?[84]

NUCLEAR TERROR AND WAR PREVENTION

It does not follow that war has been deterred solely by the nuclear threat. There are many, many other practical military, political, and economic factors which weigh against superpower conflict far more effectively than the incredible abstraction of nuclear deterrence.
—Admiral Eugene Carroll[85]

One does not enter the communion of mainstream discourse without acknowledging the blessings of deterrence. That the balance of nuclear terror deterred war remains, for the most part, an unthought, unquestioned truism. (These days since "terrorism" gets bad press, it's politically correct to refer to the venerable balance of power.) Unlike Admiral Carroll (in addition to his NATO post, he served as a Pentagon war-planner), mainstream accounts exclude the possibility that other factors contributed to the preservation of a tenuous peace.

While this is not the place to fully weigh other factors, it may be helpful to merely assert some possibilities. While those who eulogize deterrence seldom entertain such possibilities, they are generally aware of the difficulties inherent in deterrence doctrine. They grant that decision-makers could have had more in mind than deterrence: first-strike weaponry, atomic diplomacy, and grave risks during crises suggest that avoiding nuclear war was not always an overarching objective. Even if eulogizers admitted the possibility that deterrence is an ideology driven by economic interests, bureaucratic imperatives, and inter-service rivalry, such an admission would be irrelevant—it would miss the point, according to those who extol deterrence as a blessing in disguise. There is but one salient point: Unprecedented decades without a world war illustrate that despite—or because of—the worst of intentions, nuclear deterrence worked.

To paraphrase one influential celebrant of deterrence: The superpowers have unintentionally created a "nuclear weapons regime" that preserves the peace. In what resembles a variation of classical liberalism, eulogizers see an invisible hand at work. Regardless of elite intentions and fantasies, deterrence was astonishingly robust. Just as the unintended consequences of laissez-faire capitalism produce the best of all possible economies, laissez faire arms racing produced something even more wondrous—the best of all possible nuclear worlds. This salutary take on our nuclear predicament is based upon post hoc argumentation and unverifiable, counterfactual claims. [86]

The deterrence literature bestows privileged, uncontested status on the following argument; that the argument may commit a classic, post hoc fallacy is seldom considered:

- America has had a nuclear arsenal since 1945;
- No war occurred between the US and U.S.S.R. after 1945;
- Therefore, the arsenal deterred war.

Otherwise sophisticated analysts overlook the obvious: Correlation does not necessarily prove causation. I suspect that were it argued that the nuclear threats prevented war between the United States and Canada, these analysts would urge that salient variables are ignored. Save for long-ago unpleasantries during the War of 1812, there's no history of warfare between these nations. The same argument can be made about the superpowers. As President Kennedy observed: "Both the American and Soviet people abhor war. Almost unique among the major world powers, we have never been at war with each other."[87] (Evidently, the president overlooked the 1919 American invasion of Siberia.) In any case, this observation did not guide American strategy; Kennedy relied upon mutually assured destruction rather than the mutual abhorrence of war. Since there *is* a history of war between the United States and Germany, Italy, and Japan, why not argue that the nuclear arsenal prevented conflict with these powers? These examples, of course, are incommensurate—enmity became amity.

Those who extol deterrence rely upon counterfactual argumentation: If the American nuclear arsenal *had not* existed, war would have occurred between the superpowers. The status of counterfactual claims invites scrutiny. These arguments make sense in discussing law-like propositions. For example, if I lament that if I *had not* fallen off the roof, I wouldn't have been hurt (gravity—it's the law!). However, other counterfactuals don't make sense: "I shouldn't have left the slot machine because I was about to win a million dollars." (Alas, no law mandates that I must win.) Likewise, no law mandates that nuclear arsenals somehow *must* deter nuclear war.

To have a flair for the obvious, the deterrent power of nuclear weapons has not been tested by controlled experiments. Indeed, what conceivable experiment could demonstrate that *without* the American arsenal the United States and Soviet Union would have been locked in mortal combat? Such an experiment would demand a feat beyond the power of God—but not ideologues—rewriting history. Worse yet, it would be difficult to get a sabbatical—let alone a grant—to build a time machine, return to 1945, remove nuclear weapons from the scene, and witness the results.

Of course, with Aristotle, we should only demand proof and precision appropriate to the inquiry. There are, of course, lesser standards of evidence that might be somewhat convincing. Positivist standards of verification elude us, but is there no circumstantial evidence that suggests the efficacy of nuclear weapons in deterring World War III? If, for example, the period from 1917 to 1945 had been marked by frequent US/Soviet hostilities, and if these hostilities ceased with the advent of nuclear weapons, it would be reasonable to link the nuclear arsenal to war prevention. This is not the case. Save for that 1919 incident, no wars occurred. Indeed, there is reason to suspect that nuclear weapons were a provocation, not a deterrent.

According to doctrinal teaching, deterrence should have attained its apotheosis during the American atomic monopoly. Given the monopoly and the credible threat to use nuclear weapons (the destruction of Hiroshima and Nagasaki), the Soviets should have been extremely reluctant to provoke the West. However, this was the most adventurist period in Soviet foreign policy. To reiterate, the Soviets extended their hegemony, supported anti-colonial revolutions, and blockaded Berlin in the face of a perceived nuclear threat. Likewise, the monopoly didn't deter revolutions in China and Indochina.

Given the ill-defined, highly speculative nature of deterrence doctrine, we can construct contradictory narratives about the ultimate questions posed by a nuclear terror. Depending upon our mood and biases, we can argue that the arsenal deters war or that it provokes war. We can give license to our imagination and agendas because attempts to liken the arsenal to a deterrent or to a provocation can be neither confirmed nor disconfirmed.

CODA: RETIREMENT WISDOM

General Lee Butler, ex-commander of the Strategic Air Command, called for the elimination of all nuclear weapons at a National Press Club luncheon on December 4, 1996.[88]

Psychiatrist Robert J. Lifton coined "retirement wisdom" to refer to champions of nuclear endeavors who get second thoughts upon retirement. Examples are numerous but seldom publicized. In addition to Robert McNamara and Admiral Carroll, Eisenhower's Farewell Address comes to mind, as do Daniel Ellsberg's jeremiads. Herbert York, a Manhattan Project physicist and presidential science advisor, expressed his second thoughts about the arms race in *Race to Oblivion*.

However, given his years as supreme commander of American nuclear forces, General Butler provides the prime example:

> I made the long and arduous intellectual journey from staunch advocate of nuclear deterrence to public proponent of nuclear abolition. . . . We have yet to fully grasp the monstrous effects of these weapons, that the consequences of their use defy reason, transcending time and space, poisoning the earth and deforming its inhabitants. The general urges the United States to make unequivocal its commitment to the elimination of nuclear arsenals, and take the lead in setting an agenda for moving forthrightly toward that objective.

In effect, he advocates an end to nuclear irony: "We simply cannot resort to the very type of act we rightly abhor."[89]

NOTES

1. Quoted in "Minimum Nuclear Deterrence," SAIC Strategic Group, Washington, D.C., May 15, 2003.

2. George Orwell, *You and the Atomic Bomb*, accessed August 1, 2014, http://orwell.ru/library/articles/ABomb/english/e_abomb.

3. See, for example, John Lewis Gaddis, *We Now Know: Rethinking Cold War History* (Oxford: Oxford University Press, 1997).

4. See, for example, William Appleman Williams, *The Tragedy of American Diplomacy* (New York: W.W. Norton, 1959).

5. Quoted by Gregg Herken, *Counsels of War* (New York: Oxford University Press, 1987), 10.

6. Lewis Carroll, *Through the Looking-Glass and What Alice Found There* (Philadelphia: Henry Altemus Company, 1887), 46.

7. Cohn, 22.

8. See, for example, Peter Moss, "Rhetoric of Defense in the United States: Language, Myth, and Ideology," in *Language and the Nuclear Arms Debate: Nukespeak Today*, Paul Chilton, ed. (London: Frances Pinter, 1983).

9. Thomas C. Schelling, *The Strategy of Conflict* (New York: Oxford University Press, 1963), 207–9.

10. See my account of the Cuban missile crisis in *What If They Gave a Crisis and Nobody Came: Interpreting International Crises* (Westport: Praeger, 1997), 101–47. More recent studies conclude that Ex-Comm member Dean Acheson got it right: The world survived due to "plain dumb luck." McNamara stressed such luck in his last lecture on the crisis, and the peril comes through in painful clarity in the correspondence of Kennedy, Khrushchev, and Castro. See James G. Blight and Janet M. Lang in their *The Armageddon Letters: Kennedy/Khrushchev/Castro in the Cuban Missile Crisis* (Lanham: Rowman & Littlefield, 2012).

11. David Lilienthal, *Change, Hope, and the Bomb* (Princeton: Princeton University Press, 1963), 18–19.

12. Quoted by Robert Jay Lifton, *The Broken Connection* (New York: Simon & Schuster, 1979), 370.

13. Quoted by Peter Pringle and James Speigelman, in *The Nuclear Barons* (New York: Holt, Rinehart, & Winston, 1981), 49.

14. Quoted by Ibid., 51.

15. Quoted by Ibid., 39.

16. Quoted by Ibid., 89.

17. Quoted by Gregg Herken, "The Nuclear Gnostics," in Douglas MacLearn, ed., *The Security Question* (Totowas: Rowman & Allanheld, 1984), 1".

18. Herman Kahn, *On Escalation: Metaphors and Scenarios* (New York: Praeger, 1965), 281.

19. Solly Zuckerman, "Nuclear Fantasies" in *The New York Review of Books*, June 14, 1984, 28.

20. See, for example, Richard K. Betts, *Nuclear Blackmail and Nuclear Balance* (Washington, D.C.: The Brookings Institution, 1987).

21. For an account of these episodes, see Gregg Herken, "The Earthly Origin of Star Wars," in *The Bulletin of the Atomic Scientists*, October 1987, 114.

22. Betts, 118.

23. Ibid., 2.

24. Quoted by Fred Kaplan, *The Wizards of Armageddon* (New York: Simon & Schuster, 1983), 33.

25. See Richard Ned LeBow (2007) "Thucydides and Deterrence," *Security Studies*, 16:2, 163—88.

26. Carol Cohn poses this riddle in "Nuclear Language. . . .," 23.

27. Jonathan Schell, "Reflections," in the *New Yorker*, February 15, 1982, 45.

28. Interview with Rear Admiral Eugene Carroll Jr. at the Center for Defense Information, Washington, D.C., December 19, 1999.

29. Edward Luttwak, *Strategy: The Logic of War and Peace* (Cambridge: Harvard University Press, 1987), 3.

30. Quoted by John Canaday in *The Nuclear Muse* (Madison: University of Wisconsin Press, 2000), 222.

31. See Philip Green's discussion, in his *Deadly Logic: The Theory of Nuclear Deterrence* (New York: Schocken, 1969), 119–23.

32. Victor Turner, *Dramas, Fields, and Metaphors* (Ithaca: Cornell University Press, 1971), 38.

33. Herman Kahn, *On Escalation: Metaphors and Scenarios* (New York: Praeger, 1965), 81.

34. See Louis Beres's discussion of this episode in *Apocalypse* (Chicago: University of Chicago Press, 1980), 68–70.

35. Quoted by Green, 144.

36. Green, p. xi.

37. Herman Kahn, *Thinking About the Unthinkable in the 1980s* (New York: Simon & Schuster, 1984), 85.

38. Ibid., 56.

39. Ibid., 216.

40. Lawrence Freedman, *The Price of Peace* (New York: Henry Holt, 1986), 395.

41. Ibid., 1.

42. See my account of these and other eulogies in my *Massing the Tropes: The Metaphorical Construction of American Nuclear Strategy* (Praeger Security International, 2005), 86–88.

43. Quoted by Blight and Lang, 5.

44. See Betts's account of the incident, 23–30.

45. Accessed from the Truman Library, July 10, 2014, http://www.trumanlibrary.org/whistlestop/jc/jc5c.htm.

46. In his Farewell Address, Eisenhower famously warned of the danger of the "military-industrial complex." In an equally significant admonition, he warned his successors not to risk war by construing provocations as crises demanding urgent, reckless resolution; he suggested that challenges should be construed as problems to be negotiated quietly and diplomatically in due course.

47. Cited by Betts, 94.

48. Quoted by Stephen Ambrose, *Nixon*, vol. 2 (New York: Simon & Schuster, 1989), 9.

49. For more details, see my *What If They Gave a Crisis and Nobody Came?*, (Westport: Praeger, 1997), Chapter 4.

50. Henry Kissinger, *The White House Years* (Boston: Little Brown, 1979), 633–44. This was not the first time Nixon was preoccupied with vacationing rather than issues at hand. During a decisive time during the Alger Hiss investigation, Nixon chose to vacation rather than to remain in Washington. See Tom Wicker's discussion in *One of Us: Richard Nixon and the American Dream* (New York: Random House, 1992), 64.

51. Arthur Miller, "Introduction to Collected Plays," in *Willy Loman*, Harold Bloom, ed. (New York: Chelsea House, 1991), 39.

52. Graham Allison and Morton Halperin, "Bureaucratic Politics: A Paradigm and Some Policy Implications," in *Classics of International Relations*, John A. Vasquez, ed., 3rd. ed. (Upper Saddle River, N.J.: Prentice Hall, 1996), 39.

53. Noam Chomsky, "Interventionism and Nuclear War," in Michael Albert and David Delligner, eds., *Beyond Survival* (Boston: South End Press, 1983), 271.

54. Dean Acheson, "Homage to Plain Dumb Luck," in *The Cuban Missile Crisis*, Robert Divine, ed. (Chicago: Quadrangle Books, 1971), 207.

55. "Kennedy Vindicated," in Ibid., 209.

56. See Blight and M. Lang, *The Armageddon Letters*, for these letters along with the authors' glosses on this correspondence.

57. Ibid., 20.

58. Church Committee Report, accessed July 10, 2014, http://www.democracynow.org/2009/4/24/flashback.

59. See an account of the conversation, accessed July 10, 2014, http://globetrotter.berkeley.edu/conversations/Cousins/cousins3.html

60. Unpublished letter, McCone to Garthoff, September 22, 1987.

61. President John. F. Kennedy's October 22, 1962 address to the nation, accessed July 11, 2014, https://www.mtholyoke.edu/acad/intrel/kencuba.htm.

62. Transcript of the 6:30 p.m. Ex-Comm meeting of October 16, 1962, obtained from the Kennedy Library.

63. Ibid.

64. Quoted by Laurence Chang and Peter Kornbluh, eds., *The Cuban Missile Crisis, 1962* (New York: New Press, 1992), 114. This volume contains documents declassified by the authors' organization, The National Security Archive, Washington, D.C.

65. Quoted by Patrick Glynn in his *Closing Pandora's Box* (New York: Basic Books, 1992), 179.

66. Cited by Chang and Kornbluh, 103.

67. Scott Sagan described these and other incidents at the Institute on Global Conflict and Cooperation's Nuclear Proliferation Seminar at the University of California, Berkeley, April 12, 1996.

68. Raymond Garthoff, *Reflections on the Cuban Missile Crisis* (Washington: Brookings Institution, 1987), 57. Soviet Ambassador Anatoly Dobrynin confirmed Garthoff's account in his recollections in *In Confidence* (Seattle: University of Washington Press, 2001), 38.

69. Robert F. Kennedy, *Thirteen Days: A Memoir on the Cuban Missile Crisis* (New York: W.W. Norton, 1969), 70–71.

70. John F. Kennedy, *Why England Slept* (New York: Wilfred Funk, 1940), 192.

71. Robert Kennedy, *Memoir*, 109.

72. James A. Nathan, *The Cuban Missile Crisis Revisited* (New York: St. Martin's Press, 1992), 22.

73. Blight and Lang, 9.

74. "The Creation of SIOP-62: More Evidence on the Origins of Overkill," The National Security Archive, accessed July 15, 2014, http://www2.gwu.edu/NSAEBB/NSAEBB130/press.htm.

75. Quoted by Peter G. Filene, ed. *American View of Soviet Russia, 1917–1965* (Homewood, Ill.: Dorsey Press, 1968), 275.

76. Ibid., 387.

77. Andrey Shcherbenok, "Cold War Cinema in the Soviet Union and the United States," accessed July 16, 2014, http://www.units.muohio.edu/havighurstcenter/conferences/documents/shcherbenok.pdf.

78. Ibid.

79. Quoted in enWikinotes.org, accessed July 15, 2014.

80. Accessed July 16, 2014, http://hnn.us/article/129966#sthash.TTTS1hDn.dpuf.

81. Kahn, *Thinking About the Unthinkable in the 1980s*, 93.

82. Quoted by James G. Blight and David A. Welch, eds., *On The Brink: Americans and Soviets Reexamine the Cuban Missile Crisis* (New York: Hill and Wang, 1989), 104.

83. Robert Kennedy, *Thirteen Days*, 106.

84. Ibid., 128.

85. Eugene Carroll in "Nuclear Weapons and Deterrence," in *The Nuclear Crisis Reader*, Gwyn Prins, ed. (New York: Vintage, 1984), 4.

86. See Michael Mandelbaum's *The Nuclear Question* (Cambridge: Cambridge University Press, 1979), vii.

87. Quoted by Filene, 388.

88. General Lee Butler, USAF (Retired) National Press Club Remarks, December 4, 1996, PBS American Experience References, accessed August

16, 2014, http://www.pbs.org/wgbh/amex/bomb/filmmore/reference/primary/
leebutler.html.

    89. Ibid.

Chapter 3

GOODWILL TOWARD MEN *WITHOUT* PEACE ON EARTH

Have you noticed that it is the most civilized gentlemen who have been the subtlest slaughterers, to whom the Attilas . . . could not hold a candle? Now we do think bloodshed abominable and yet we engage in this abomination with more energy than ever.
—Dostoevsky's Underground Man[1]

There are marked differences between limited wars in Korea and Vietnam, and the total war known as World War II. Unlike Imperial Japan, none of these nations attacked the United States, and unlike Nazi Germany, they didn't pose a potential existential threat. None of these nations threatened vital interests. Indeed, preoccupied with Europe and China, American planners placed Korea outside the US sphere of influence.

And yet, there was continuity between World War II and those limited wars—something painfully familiar: the critics' operational definition of terrorism—carpet-bombing noncombatants with explosives and incendiaries. Despite the fact that the bombing surpassed World War II in these putatively limited, Third-World engagements, mainstream accounts don't refer to carpet-bombing in Korea and Vietnam as terrorism; "interdiction" is politically correct.

Critics such as Noam Chomksy,[2] Howard Zinn,[3] Daniel Ellsberg,[4] Chris Hedges,[5] Tom Engelhardt,[6] John Tirman,[7] and John Dower[8] reject politically correct labels and accuse the United States of resorting to terrorism in conducting these limited wars—bombing noncombatants. Although officials freely invoked "nuclear terror" in reference to deterring the Soviet Union, they didn't refer to Korean and Vietnamese air raids as terrorism. Apparently, "terrorism" was transitioning from an approved, if not laudable, notion to a pejorative.[9] Whether by accident or design, staggering numbers of noncombatants perished in these limited wars. They perished directly from ordnance and incendiaries or indirectly from the destruction of infrastructures that sustained life. Controversies about semantics and ethics don't matter to the dead and to those who managed to survive.

Obdurate facts of death matter, not evanescent abstractions. As Dower reminds us: "More noncombatants were killed in America's subsequent wars in Korea and Indochina than in the Allied bombing in World War II."[10] MIT political analyst John Tirman estimates that two to three million perished in the Korean War—at least half were noncombatants. McNamara regrets that good intentions, but errors in judgment, caused the deaths of perhaps a million Asian civilians.[11]

A WORLD WITHOUT ENEMIES

One of the most remarkable aspects of American wars is how little we discuss the victims who are not Americans. . . . As a nation that has long thought of itself as built on Christian ethics, even as an exceptionally compassionate people, the coldness is a puzzle.
                                                                    —John Tirman[12]

Puzzling indeed: World War II propagandists assumed that it was essential to dehumanize noncombatants in order to target them for destruction. It seems intuitive that the magnitude of the casualties in Korea and Vietnam would demand commensurate propaganda campaigns, massive, unrelenting efforts to dehumanize the inhabitants of these enemy lands. No campaigns occurred; the past wasn't prologue. Korean and Vietnamese civilians were depicted as hapless victims of communist aggression; even so, they perished in staggering numbers.

News of the puzzling irony didn't reach those concerned with the death of others. Koreans and Vietnamese were not dehumanized in massive campaigns; on the contrary, the public knew little and cared less about the death of Korean and Vietnamese civilians. On rare occasions when authorities mentioned these civilians, they portrayed them as honorary good guys, victims of cruel despots longing for regime change.

During World War II the public remembered Pearl Harbor and wanted to kill Japs. During the Korean and Vietnam wars, the public didn't care about the death of others—Koreans and Vietnamese never attacked the United States. A war-weary public was preoccupied with matters closer to home. World War II was about hot-blooded hatred; subsequent wars met with cold-blooded indifference.

Nevertheless, a commonplace, a truism, still resonates even among the most astute observers: Individuals must be dehumanized if they are targeted for destruction. To be sure, this claim is not without precedence: From time immemorial inhabitants of enemy lands were demonized and killed. Preeminent historians agree—the past is prologue. Fussell asserts: "For the war to be prosecuted at all, the enemy of course had to be severely dehumanized and demeaned."[13] Likewise, Dower claims, "stereotyped patterns of perception . . . toward the hated Japanese enemy in World War II also proved to be free-floating and easily transferred to the new enemies of the cold war."[14] The aftermath of World War II spins our moral compass. In revisiting these limited wars, we enter an epoch without precedence, a time of goodwill toward men without peace on earth.

Downsizing Enemies

World War II–style propaganda died with FDR. Such propaganda is as outmoded as a 1945 vinyl record. Civilians in enemy lands are no longer dehumanized—a sea change at once remarkable and overlooked. As we've seen, congressional resolutions urged Americans to pray for the well-being of the Soviet people—as they were targeted for destruction. Collective guilt was passé. Inhabitants of enemy lands were no longer painted with the brush that besmirched the Japanese. Even Japanese soldiers—once depicted as a vicious insect infestation—are rehabilitated in revisionist films such as Clint Eastwood's *Letters from Iwo Jima*. Viewers sympathize with unique individuals trapped in hopeless situations.

Professions of sympathy and friendship trump demonized caricatures of civilians in enemy lands. We've made a *human connection* with those in faraway places with strange-sounding names—or so it seems.

In the postwar world staggering numbers of noncombatants perished without bothering to dehumanize them. It won't do to disingenuously dismiss these deaths as "collateral damage." Every administration expressed affection for Koreans and Vietnamese as napalm rained down upon their villages and ordnance destroyed their life-sustaining infrastructure. In short, making that human connection didn't bestow noncombatant immunity.

Like much else in these United States, enemies are downsized. Belligerent, wartime propaganda is outsourced to zones of ethnic cleansing in areas such as Bosnia, Rwanda, and the Congo. America's enemies are drastically reduced from millions of civilians to a few celebrity evildoers—famous for being infamous. Only limited piecework remains for propagandists promoting limited wars: convincing those who still care that the enemy du jour is Hitler reincarnate.

Playing the Hitler Card

Customarily, the American military pictures celebrity evildoers on playing cards. The deck includes Joseph Stalin, Nikita Khrushchev, Mao Zedong, and Ho Chi Minh. Recent additions feature Saddam Hussein, Osama bin Laden, and Mahmoud Ahmadinejad. A glance at the cards reveals a strange visage. Like the Cheshire Cat, Hitler's image appears time and again.

The Austrian painter turned fuehrer became an immortal enemy reincarnated in America's latter-day enemies, real and imagined. He is *the* perfect enemy: powerful and murderous, a psychopath bereft of humanity—justly feared and hated. Both Bush administrations warned that Hussein was Hitler reincarnated, and lately we hear that the new Hitler speaks Farsi. Could it be that these visages justify killing our newfound friends in third-world countries? With friends like this who needs enemies?

As in World War II, this most formidable of all enemies must be vanquished by any means necessary. The lesson of Munich is indelible: Diplomacy and appeasement embolden enemies. It doesn't suffice merely to communicate with despots in the language of force; they must forcibly be eliminated by applied military power—airpower being the supreme American asset. Just as good Germans had to be killed in defeating evil incarnate, so good Koreans and Vietnamese had to perish.

Vanquishing Hitler avatars assures national security and liberates op-pressed people. When the Hitler card is played, it might be well to recall that Alice swallowed a magic pill, grew up, and put away childish things. No longer frightened by those Wonderland cards, she ex-claimed: "Who cares for you. You're nothing but a pack of cards!"[15]

HUBRIS: PROMOTING WHAT YOU WOULD PREVENT

Events have exposed as illusory American pretensions to having mas-tered war. Even today war is hardly more subject to human control than the tides or the weather.

—Andrew Bacevich[16]

If the real Hitler and his formidable juggernaut could be van-quished, surely his third-world surrogates could be utterly destroyed in a matter of weeks or months. And yet, in the aftermath of World War II, campaigns in Korea and Vietnam ended in stalemate and defeat. As Dower illustrates, American decision-makers—such as the neocons (neoconservatives) who initiated the "slam-dunk" Iraq War—reveled in their tactical brilliance only to be fouled-out by strategic imbecility. Grandiose plans to unify the Korean peninsula and crush Ho Chi Minh once again overestimated American power and resolve, and underesti-mated enemy strength and determination.

How much does it exaggerate to suggest that Korea and Vietnam were more about elite narcissists making a name for themselves, than about strategic exigencies? Before he was fired, MacArthur imagined reversing the tide of history and rolling back communism in China. Relying upon the gradual escalation policy, which Johnson and McNa-mara (at the time) believed resolved the Cuban missile crisis, they struggled—against their better judgment—to reinvent Vietnam as a bastion of anticommunism.

There was, of course, nothing new about the wishful thinking that drives folly. Heeding the call to work wonders in history is more American than apple pie. Prior to the fiascos that marked the mid-twentieth century, the arc of history seemed to bend toward an invin-cible, triumphant America. Providence destined the colonists to con-quer the New World, subdue the natives, and build that shining city on the hill. The colonists defeated the greatest power on earth and established a new republic. The new nation prevailed during the War of 1812 even as foes set the White House aflame.

Touring the new republic, de Tocqueville observed that Americans rarely wished for what they had; they yearned for more—fresh gratification.[17] The titles of nineteenth-century history texts reveal nationalistic bias: *British Imperialism* chronicles colonial conquests. The comparable American saga, titled *The Westward Movement*, sanctifies Manifest Destiny: It's as if the breath of the Almighty pushed the covered wagons toward Pacific shores. Americans won the West, and the Union survived the bloodiest challenge of all—civil war.

At the close of the century, historian Fredrick Jackson Turner famously lamented the closing of the frontier. Nevertheless, overseas frontiers loomed over the horizon. Teddy Roosevelt's manly imperialism led the way. America emerged from the Great War relatively unscathed and endured the Depression. The proudest memory (rightly so): vanquishing formidable Axis Powers. Surely the mischief of weak, third-world regimes was no match for the United States. LBJ couldn't imagine midgets wearing black pajamas defeating the United States.

In a secular age, naturalistic explanations justified America's postwar calling. Consummate realists such as George Kennan explained that, due to the demise of the British Empire, the free world faced a vacuum. Nature, of course, abhors a vacuum. It was only natural for a new, American Empire to fill the vacuum, and take its rightful place as the imperium destined to promote Pax Americana. National interest—real and imagined—trumped any remnant of Wilsonian idealism, let alone any passion to Christianize the pagan.

To be sure, these few paragraphs hazard a simplified gloss on centuries of American experience. Even so, I suspect that those who planned and executed mid-century wars embraced such a gloss on American destiny, i.e., *their* destiny. Looking backward to 1950, two things are clear: America never lost a war; and despite—or perhaps because of— its Soviet rival, America enjoyed overwhelming military superiority. Nevertheless, a curious dialectic emerged.

It's tempting to speculate. The mind-set of American elites presents the clinical picture of narcissism, progenitor of hubris. A fearful symmetry leads to tragic consequences: The greater the sense of grandiosity, the greater the anxious insecurity. No amount of narcissistic nutrients ever satisfies. Bored with merely making money, governing elites strive to make history—a fool's errand that seldom brings out the best in aspiring statesmen. These elites displayed the signature of the narcissistic character type: overreacting to minor challenges. Civil wars in Korea and Vietnam weren't comparable to the insults and challenges posed by Japan and Germany. Nevertheless, Truman, Johnson, and Nixon overreacted—their reputations were at stake.

The bombing in these "limited" wars surpassed the bombing in World War II. Why did Truman, Johnson, Nixon, and both Bush administrations resort to what their predecessors called terror bombing? These presidents vowed they wouldn't "cut and run"; they would not suffer the humiliation of losing a war to a third-world regime. Terror bombing might not guarantee victory, but in venues such as Korea it would avoid defeat.

Initially, of course, decision-makers assumed the forces that vanquished Hitler could utterly defeat the likes of Kim Il-Sung and Ho Chi Minh. Surely unrivaled American airpower could bring any foe to its knees. Despite massive bombardment, campaigns stalemated in Korea and failed in Vietnam.

KOREA: THE FORGOTTEN WAR

> *The three-year war in Korea took three million lives and ended in a stalemate, with the lines demarcating north from south nearly the same at the moment of cease-fire as they were at the moment of outbreak.*
>
> —John Tirman[18]

Those inclined to remember this "Forgotten War" rightly ask: How did the United States get involved in the costly, unprecedented stalemate called the Korean War? My question is more specific: Why did the United States once again practice strategic bombing? Unlike World War II, authorities didn't plan to rely upon strategic bombing; surely MacArthur's ground forces would triumph in a few months.

Secretary of State Dean Acheson spoke to the National Press Club in January 1950, and famously—or infamously—located Korea *outside* the US defense perimeter. Nevertheless, the Truman administration intervened when North Korea attacked on June 25, 1950. MacArthur promised American troops would be home for Christmas 1950. About 30,000 troops remain to this day.

Accounts of the conflict chronicle the ironies that American elites would rather forget—a bitter, three-year struggle called a mere "police action." The day after the destruction of Nagasaki, Americans (namely, Dean Rusk) drew an arbitrary line across the Korean peninsula: Soviet forces would occupy Korea above the 38th parallel; American forces would occupy below. Each occupying power established client regimes after they removed their forces in 1948: Kim Il-Sung ruled the North; Syngman Rhee ruled the South. Historians recount the draconian deeds of both dictators.[19]

The Soviets continued to back the North economically and militarily. Preoccupied with European affairs, and fearful that Rhee's bravado might foment conflict with the Soviets and the Chinese, the United States reduced its support. Frequent skirmishes and massacres occurred as both dictators sought control of the entire peninsula. Having de facto excluded Korea from the US sphere of influence, policymakers remained, for the most part, indifferent.

In early June 1950 Truman proclaimed the world was closer to peace than at any time in recent memory. And yet the CIA detected North Korean forces moving south but dismissed the maneuver as a defensive move. Once again, decision-makers underestimated Orientals due to racist bias: Just as the Japanese would not dare attack Pearl Harbor, so the North Koreans would not dare attack an American client. Such arrogance, complemented by faith in limitless American power, became the signature of the war, and of subsequent wars.

Much to the chagrin of leading Republicans such as Senator Taft, Truman didn't request a constitutionally mandated declaration of war: 1941 was the last time the imperial presidency bothered with such formalities. In Taft's words, the president had "no legal authority for what he has done."[20] Like his successors, Truman thought he faced exigent circumstances. Accordingly, he avoided a protracted congressional debate. (Moreover, Congress might lack enthusiasm for another war, especially a conflict beyond the pale of American interests.) Like his successors, Truman bypassed Congress and sought the imprimatur of the United Nations. The Soviets couldn't cast a veto.

Did Stalin appreciate the irony of *his* predicament? The Soviets began boycotting the UN in January 1950 due to its refusal to recognize

China. With no Soviet delegates present, the UN authorized the war. Forces fighting the North Koreans and Chinese were called UN forces—this designation bestowed the aura of legitimacy and international consensus. Since the United States supplied almost 90 percent of the personnel under US leadership, I refer to the combatants as US forces.

Another Red Scare

Devising an acceptable name for American intervention became critically important. Koreans attacked Koreans. Nevertheless, officialdom chastised those who called the conflict a civil war. The official interpretation—the North Korean attack was part and parcel of a communist conspiracy bent upon world domination—caused misery for tens of thousands of US soldiers and for hundreds of thousands of noncombatants. Like virtually every post–World War II conflict, officials drew tendentious historical analogies. The year 1939, not 1914, provided the template. It was 1939 again, and Hitler was reincarnated in Stalin. As Truman explained:

> Communism was acting in Korea, just as Hitler, Mussolini, and the Japanese had ten, fifteen, and twenty years earlier. I felt certain that if South Korea was allowed to fall, Communist leaders would be emboldened to override nations closer to our own shores. If the Communists were permitted to force their way into the Republic of Korea without opposition from the free world, no small nation would have the courage to resist threat and aggression by stronger Communist neighbors.[21]

Mere rhetoric? Did Truman actually subscribe to a domino theory that attributed evil designs to the Soviets? Those who suggest that Truman truly believed his justification point to a document drafted during his administration—National Security Council Document 68 (NSC-68). Rejecting Kennan's view that communism can simply be contained, the document claimed that:

> The Soviet Union, unlike previous aspirants to hegemony, is animated by a new fanatic faith, antithetical to our own, and seeks to impose its absolute authority over the rest of the world. Conflict has there-

fore become endemic and is waged, on the part of the Soviet Union, by violent or nonviolent methods in accordance with the dictates of expediency.[22]

In rhetoric, if not in reality, decision-makers saw Korea and Vietnam as the frontlines in the war against communist domination. Despite its victory over the Axis powers, America was losing its self-confidence. Communism was on the march. Dreams of an American Century vanished—the Soviets were a formidable nuclear power extending their hegemony into Eastern Europe, while supporting third-world revolutions. The Chinese Communists prevailed, and anti-colonial struggles occurred in places like Korea and Vietnam. Senator McCarthy found fifth-column communists in high places, not only in the State Department, but also in the Army and Bureau of Fish and Game. Even if certain officials believed the latest Red Scare was exaggerated, it would have been impolitic to say so. Other analysts give considerable weight to domestic politics: failing to respond to "third-world liberations movements" would be bad career moves both for Truman and his successors.

Given what was at stake domestically, and possibly internationally, Truman's efforts to underplay the invasion and the American response seem ironic. When a reporter asked whether it was correct "to call this [the US military response] a police action under the UN?" Truman replied, "This is exactly what it amounts to."[23] The term stuck.

In light of Truman's concern about provoking a wider war with the Soviets and Chinese, he tried to avoid war panic among a war-weary Congress and public. Perhaps General Omar Bradley said it best: Escalating the Korean War might provoke the Soviets and the Chinese, embroiling the United States "in the wrong war, at the wrong place, and the wrong time, and with the wrong enemy."[24] Truman resisted escalation until Chinese intervention overwhelmed American troops.

The mood during the first year was distinctly bipolar: Recapturing the South sparked near-manic enthusiasm: MacArthur's forces quickly pushed beyond the 38th parallel and neared the Chinese border. In arguably one of the worst disasters suffered by the American military, Chinese and North Korean forces overwhelmed the American Eighth Army, forcing it into a rapid and humiliating retreat—depressing indeed. Malaise set in during the next two years—in response to stalemated military campaigns and armistice negotiations. (On occasion,

however, Syngman Rhee's antics set off panic attacks.) A few salient
details reveal why Korea is the forgotten war.

The American Caesar

Tactical American naval and air power—Truman's initial response to
the invasion—didn't stop the well-disciplined North Korean army. The
enemy captured Seoul. Among the first to flee, Rhee burned bridges to
stop the invaders and to prevent his capture. An estimated 4,000 refugees perished as a result. But Rhee didn't burn bridges with the United
States. General Douglas MacArthur expressed supreme confidence. He
and his forces would quickly end North Korean aggression: "I can lick it
with one arm tied behind my back. . . . You'd see these fellows scuttle
up to the Manchurian border so quick."[25] Events vindicated his bravado—at first. American troops landed in Inchon under his command; the
enemy fled in ignominious retreat.

Uninhibited by the UN mandate to merely reestablish the status quo
ante, MacArthur, driven by acute success and chronic ambition, envi-
sioned pushing beyond the 38th parallel, uniting all Korea under Rhee's
regime, and (why not?) rolling back communism in China. The ebulli-
ent Truman administration joined MacArthur in dismissing British and
Indian proposals to settle for the status quo ante—a cease-fire at the
38th parallel. Zhou Enlai (China's foreign minister) warned that China
would enter the war if American troops crossed the parallel—surely a
bluff to gain advantage on the cheap. Acheson urged that it would be
"sheer madness" for China to attack (even though the Chinese placed
North Korea within *their* defense perimeter). The Chinese leadership,
according to the secretary, was preoccupied with internal political and
economic matters in the aftermath of protracted civil war.[26]

In his 1953 retrospective, General S. L. A. Marshall indicted such
manic optimism and recognized the ironic disparity between vainglori-
ous expectations and tragic results:

> Planners mistakenly calculated they were dealing with a gook army
> and an essentially craven people who would collapse as soon as mo-
> bile men and modern weapons blew a hot breath their way. But the
> play didn't follow the lines as written.[27]

As his victorious forces neared the 38th parallel, MacArthur cabled the Joint Chiefs: "There is no indication at present of entry into North Korea by major Soviet or Chinese forces." Secretary of Defense George Marshall gave MacArthur the green light: "We want you to feel unhampered tactically and strategically to proceed north of the 38th parallel."[28] General S. L. A. Marshall saw the irony: "[The] Communist enemy was being pursued to the Yalu River. Strategy was then at its wishful best; it was wishing out of existence a Red Chinese Army which was already over the border."[29]

Historian William Manchester offers a balanced portrait of MacArthur in *American Caesar*; the comparison seems apt until it breaks down at a crucial juncture. Caesar crossed the Rubicon and met with triumph. MacArthur crossed *his* Rubicon at the 38th parallel, ushering in a latter-day Greek tragedy. Korea and subsequent limited wars are studies in hubris. Time and again, not only did American planners fail to accomplish their objectives, but also their actions produced the predicaments they struggled to prevent. Out of desperation war-planners looked to the sky, but B-29s were no deus ex machina. Saturation bombing didn't bring foes to their knees nor exact the desired concessions.

In October, MacArthur captured Pyongyang, the North Korean capital. Americans boasted of a unique distinction. Bob Hope entertained the troops—in a liberated, communist capital.[30] More confident than ever, MacArthur predicted North Korean resistance would end by Thanksgiving. He assured Truman: "We are no longer fearful of their intervention. . . . If the Chinese tried to get down to Pyongyang there would be the greatest slaughter."[31] There was—just not the one the general expected.

Just after Thanksgiving, on November 28, 1950, Truman got the news: Two hundred thousand Chinese troops struck American forces. Undaunted, MacArthur reassured Washington that the Chinese were merely establishing a cordon sanitaire as his forces approached the Yalu River, the Chinese border. The attack continued, sending US forces into hasty retreat. General Marshall witnessed the attack and reminded his colleagues that the invaders forced the Eighth Army into the longest retreat in American history. Truman declared a national emergency.

Officials maligned the Chinese for committing unprovoked aggression. (One wonders how the United States might have responded to

Chinese troops crossing the Rio Grande.) James Reston's *New York Times* column conveyed the depth of the depression:

> Every official movement in the capital today, every official report . . . and every private estimate from well-informed men reflected a sense of emergency, and even a sense of alarm about the state of the UN army in Korea. Not even that fateful night twenty-three weeks ago when the Korean War started was the atmosphere more grim . . . [Senior military officials] now regard the immediate military situation with unrivaled anxiety.[32]

Once again enemy forces (North Korean and Chinese) pushed south. Enduring terrible losses, the demoralized US forces retreated south of the 38th parallel. The second evacuation of Seoul began. American forces eventually regained control and pushed the enemy north beyond the 38th parallel. A stalemate ensued both in the battle zone and at the bargaining table.

Admiral Turner Joy tried to bully his North Korean counterpart:

> Apparently you cannot comprehend that strong and proud free nations can make costly sacrifices for principles because they are strong, can be dignified in the face of abuse and deceit because they are proud, and can speak honestly because they are free and do not fear the truth.[33]

The North Koreans were not impressed. The stalemate persisted, and Truman feared that MacArthur's grandiose ambition would antagonize the Soviets, to say nothing of the Chinese. Accordingly, Truman rejected MacArthur's scheme to attack China by air and land. Perhaps Truman removed MacArthur because he feared the general's bravado would provoke nuclear war with the Soviets. In 1973 *Time* previewed a quote from Truman's pending publication *Plain Speaking*:

> I fired him [MacArthur] because he wouldn't respect the authority of the President. . . . I didn't fire him because he was a dumb son of a bitch, although he was, but that's not against the law for generals. If it was, half to three-quarters of them would be in jail.[34]

Truman's concern was not unfounded. MacArthur boasted that, had he not been stopped, "I would have dropped between thirty and fifty atomic bombs . . . strung out across the neck of Manchuria. No one could penetrate the radioactive wasteland."[35] Nevertheless, Truman and his advisors considered using tactical nuclear weapons. They did so out of desperation when conventional terror bombing failed to achieve desired enemy concessions.

Terror Bombing

> *The Chinese intervention in November 1950 signaled a new escalation in the Korean War and new responsibilities for bomber crews. Superfortresses hammered towns and cities all along the North Korean side of the Chinese border.*
>
> —Lt. General George E. Stratemeyer,
> author, official *USAF Fact Sheet*[36]

Unlike mainstream accounts, critics refer to hammering cities and towns as terrorism. As the armistice talks stalled, officials responded with their strongest suit: what *they* called terror bombing during World War II. Somehow, it's acceptable to refer to firebombing Tokyo as terrorism; it is not politically correct to refer to firebombing Pyongyang as terrorism.

Again, whether these actions fit one of the many contested definitions of terrorism distracts from what is salient: the deaths of hundreds of thousands of noncombatants. North Korea was bombed more extensively than the Pacific theater during this limited police action. According to official estimates, the United States dropped 503,000 tons of explosives in the Pacific theater during World War II, compared to 635,000 tons of explosives dropped on Korea—in addition to 32,557 tons of napalm.[37]

Strategists saw napalm as a wonder weapon: firestorms being more effective than explosives in destroying cities. The newfound enthusiasm was evident in official military journals. The titles speak for themselves: "They Don't Like Hell Bombs"; "Napalm Jelly Bombs Prove a Blazing Success in Korea"; and "Wonder Weapon: Napalm."[38] Conventional explosives, however, were used to demolish major dams in May of 1953 in order to destroy newly planted rice. Thousands perished in the ensuing floods and famine.

There is considerable debate regarding whether decision-makers actually intended to use tactical and strategic nuclear weapons during the war. The matter was certainly discussed and threats were made. At various press conferences Truman intimated that he had not ruled out nuclear weapons. During his campaign Eisenhower announced he would visit Korea and consider using nuclear weapons if necessary. In May 1953, Secretary of State Dulles threatened the Chinese: If the war were not resolved soon, the United States was prepared to use tactical nuclear weapons against Chinese forces.[39] Whether these threats would have been carried out is moot. However, Cumings claims that Truman actually signed orders to use nuclear weapons. The order was never sent due to the controversy and confusion in removing MacArthur. Nevertheless, nuclear weapons were readily available in Guam, and practice runs occurred over North Korea.[40] As Tirman comments: Truman and Eisenhower were amenable to using nuclear weapons against an adversary that didn't threaten the United States. This "speaks volumes about the attitude toward noncombatants."[41]

Tirman estimates that perhaps a million North Korean civilians died from the explosives and napalm dropped on their cities, and from drowning when dams were destroyed.[42] Nevertheless, the stalemate persisted on the ground and at the bargaining table. What some dubbed "Truman's War" didn't go according to plan. On March 29, 1952, Truman declared he wouldn't run for reelection. (Sixteen years later, LBJ bowed out after the apparent failure of Operation Rolling Thunder, his bombing campaign.)

Whether the bombing campaign broke the stalemate at the armistice negotiations is debatable. Some analysts cite the World War II *Strategic Bombing Survey,* which questions the efficacy of carpet-bombing. Others suggest that the death of Stalin broke the stalemate. Not surprisingly, Air Force officials credit their efforts with breaking the impasse: "Many features of the strategic air war in Korea pointed to USAF tactics of the future: the use of air power against sensitive enemy targets as a bargaining chip in negotiations."[43]

General Mark Clark lamented that he had the unenviable distinction of being the first US Army commander to sign an armistice without victory. His successors would have the same unenviable duty.

Selling the Korean War

During the 1950s and early 1960s, the first historians and political
scientists who wrote about the war reached the conclusion that Ko-
rea, because of its very nature, had been basically impossible to sell.
Americans, they insisted, only . . . embraced all-out crusades de-
signed to compel the unconditional surrender of the enemy.
                                                          —Steven Casey[44]

How was the Korean War sold to the public? It wasn't. Casey's
Selling the Korean War offers a detailed account of selling the war to
diverse elites: the United Nations, allies, domestic politicians, high-
ranking military men, and journalists. (However, as Casey notes, journalists lost interest during the stalemated malaise that marked the last
two years of the war.) As he and other historians note, a stalemated
conflict, a quagmire astride the 38th parallel, wasn't made for primetime.

Unlike World War II, no Office of War Information (OWI) mobilized massive propaganda. To be sure, Koreans were dehumanized in
boot camp and on the battlefield—like the Japanese they were "gooks."
The Korean War is notable for what was *absent* in plain sight—no
propaganda campaign to dehumanize the inhabitants of enemy territory.

Strategic bombing was easy to forget—no one remembered. Noncombatants were killed by the hundreds of thousands in Korea *without*
bothering to demonize them. Obviously, Koreans couldn't be demonized because the United States intervened to save the South Koreans
from Northern aggression. According to the official narrative, those in
the South valiantly fought Northern aggressors. (American commanders, however, were not impressed by the valor of South Korean troops.
GIs referred to Southern comrades as "HA"—hauling ass.)

World War II posters were variations on a theme—a buck-toothed,
Jap vermin, a caricature justifying extermination. Korean posters elicit
sympathy. Rare portrayals of Koreans depict aged, humbled peasants
beside their huts. Most posters feature a GI bravely flashing a smile as
he slogs through the mud, bayonet drawn.[45]

Listening to Korean War music is no trip down memory lane. Those
of us who are chronologically challenged recall 1950s rock 'n' roll and
American Bandstand. Korean War tunes are the stuff of obscure

archives. Patriotism, battle, religious faith, and emotional pain domi-
nate the genre. A rare tune can be found about discontent, but protest
music is virtually absent. Unlike World War II, there are no tunes
mocking, let alone demonizing, the Korean people, nothing comparable
to "Zap the Jap," no "Cap the Korean." A sample includes: "God Please
Protect America"; "Goodbye Maria: I'm off to Korea"; and "Thank God
for Victory in Korea" (issued prematurely). Two of those old vinyl discs
depart from the usual sentimentality. One sang the praises of extermi-
nating communists in a nuclear flash: "When They Drop the Atomic
Bomb Any Commies Left Will Be on the Run." Finally, "Korean Mud"
shamed those who didn't give blood to the Red Cross.[46]

For the most part, Hollywood produced escapist comedies, ro-
mances, and Westerns. Rare films about the Forgotten War are justly
forgotten, with few exceptions. Again, the contrast between the big-
budget, government-sanctioned World War II films and the output
during Korea is stark and seldom discussed. The Roosevelt administration deemed Hollywood participation essential to condone terror
bombing Japan. In the aftermath of World War II, terror bombing
became routine, part of the unnatural order of things. The strategy
required no more justification than building another strip mall or free-
way. Hollywood's services were no longer required.

Unlike World War II films, the Korean movies didn't depict civilians
as irredeemable evildoers. Chinese and North Korean soldiers were
seen as a mindless, savage horde. However, in rare images when Koreans were shown at all, they were seen as helpless peasants enslaved by
communism or fleeing Red invaders.

One film, however, is a notable exception—*Steel Helmet*. The film
portrayed a forlorn group of American soldiers trapped in an atrocity-
producing situation. Given their bias against Orientals, they disparaged
Koreans and killed a prisoner of war. Among the first Korean War films,
it was one of the first withdrawn from the theaters. The House Un-
American Activities Committee did not take kindly to Samuel Fuller's
painfully real story of moral dilemmas and racist bias.

A seemingly predictable wartime romance, *One Minute to Zero* depicts an unseemly incident celebrants of American intervention would
like to forget. To attenuate the plot: A brave American colonel saves a
woman as North Koreans attack Seoul—their bodies touch—he eventually gets the girl. The plot unfolds predictably as the colonel leads men

into combat. And yet, our hero commits a morally dubious, cowardly, act. Confronting refugees from the North, fearing communist infiltration, he orders *all* refugees shot. (According to historians mentioned above, such incidents occurred.)

Two postwar dramas symbolize the end of Eisenhower-era innocence—*M°A°S°H* and *The Manchurian Candidate*. Cynical and ironic, these productions scoff at those naïve enough to trust the government—they offer something to offend everyone. And yet, one subject is taboo—World War II–style terror bombing. These popular dramas are not the place to learn of the hundreds of thousands burned by napalm.

Sick humor and vulgar practical jokes inured Army surgeons Hawkeye and Hunnicut to the routine horror of American casualties. They ridicule colleagues who stick to protocol and lack the decency to be alienated: Major "Hot Lips" Houlihan is a frequent target. The TV show and subsequent movies are Sgt. Bilko for the cynical. [47]

Given its popularity, and the suspicion raised by *The Manchurian Candidate*, "Manchurian Candidate" became part of everyday language. As reviewer Roger Ebert explains, the term became "shorthand for a brainwashed sleeper, a subject who has been hypnotized and instructed to act when his controllers pull the psychological trigger." [48]

Raymond Shaw is the hapless American serviceman brainwashed by the Korean enemy and implanted with the posthypnotic suggestion to kill American officials. A secret agent, posing as an incarnation of the likes of Senator McCarthy, prepares to pull Shaw's psychological trigger.

The film provides fodder for conspiracy theorists confident that everyone they despise and fear, from Lee Harvey Oswald to Barack Obama, is a Manchurian Candidate. The film, as we'll see, provides the template for Obama's favorite show—*Homeland*. The film begins in conspiracy and ends in irony—no one's word is taken at face value.

Miracle on the Han River

South Korea has never been so prosperous, so gregarious, so hip—so much so that it seems as if the nation sneaked up on the world. . . . Now is South Korea's moment. And in that moment, it shines in such stark contrast to the sad state of North Korea—so impoverished its people literally stand a few inches shorter than their southern cousins. The peninsula's bipolar condition is reflected most aptly in its leading personalities. The stocky K-pop party rocker Psy spreads "Gangnam Style" to the world while the North's pudgy supreme leader, like his father and grandfather before him, spreads menace, Pyongyang style.[49]

The armistice took effect in the summer of 1953. It seemed woefully realistic, not cynical, to forecast a bleak future for South Korea. General S. L. A. Marshall wasn't optimistic. Either South Korea will become an international invalid—ever dependent upon American largesse, or ""eft a hopeless derelict . . . salvaged by Communist neighbors."[50] Amid the ravages of war, the nation suffered massive deaths and abject poverty. Even in better times, South Korea was an overpopulated nation bereft of resources and an industrial base.

The salutary irony continues to amaze: In a generation, a war-torn nation of third-world peasants transformed itself—with a little help from its friends—into a sophisticated, world-class economy. Bold innovation ushered in by a highly motivated, well-educated workforce drives South Korea's unanticipated success.

Historians, of course, consider the context. As Cumings writes: "Korea, after all, had no capitalists, no Protestants, no merchants, no money, no market, no resources, no get-up-and-go, let alone [any] discernible history of commerce, foreign trade, or industrial development." Nevertheless, South Korea prospered. Writing in a detailed research document, economists Harvie and Lee offer insight into South Korea's recovery.[51] No one, to be sure, suggests the war was a blessing in disguise. Nevertheless, the authors mention that the war destroyed class barriers and traditional mores, thereby facilitating the development of a modern industrial economy. Little growth continued under Syngman Rhee's dictatorship; US aid kept South Korea afloat. However, rigorous, albeit highly competitive, education provided an exemplary labor force vital for future developments, developments that began with the coup of Park Chung Hee.

Korean prosperity cannot be attributed solely to unfettered capitalism. Park's government invested national resources, encouraged the rise of highly efficient conglomerates, and fought corruption. His stress on "exports first" paid off: Korea supplied men and materiel for the nearby Vietnam War and for the booming construction occurring in the Middle East.

Electronics developed into a major industry, but as the authors point out: "The domestic sale of colour TVs was not allowed until 1980 . . . firms had to sell their products overseas." It is no surprise to owners of Korean automobiles, electronics, and appliances that exports became the source of newfound prosperity: "Exports increased rapidly rising from US$41 million in 1961 to US$1,333 in 1971 (an increase of almost 28 times)."[52]

Today, students show off the latest Samsung smartphones and computers upon their return from teaching English in Seoul. They buy Hyundais and wonder why the United States can't have an Internet like Seoul's.

VIETNAM: THE WAR WE CAN'T FORGET

In May of 1964, Senator Richard Russell told Johnson that Vietnam was "the damn worst mess I ever saw." LBJ replied, "That's the way I've been feelin' for six months." Shortly after, he told McGeorge Bundy . . . "The more I stayed awake last night thinking of this thing, the more . . . it looks to me like we're gettin' into another Korea. . . . I don't think it's worth fightin' for and I don't think we can get out. . . . What the hell is Vietnam worth to me? What is it worth to this country?"[53]

How did Lyndon Johnson come to find himself in a dilemma described by Woody Allen as a choice between disaster and catastrophe? He didn't choose wisely. The choice, as LBJ saw it, was between a disastrous career move (exiting Vietnam) and a momentous catastrophe (pursuing a foolish, unwinnable war). He wasn't the only one. As a former official of the Vietnam Pacification Program concludes: Those who planned the War committed "the most egregious error a country going to war can make: underestimating the adversary's capacity to prevail while overestimating one's own."[54]

Someday, perhaps, a latter-day Sophocles will adequately script the tragedy of Vietnam. I cannot. I merely call attention to classic, tragic elements—irony and hubris. What could be more incongruous: the nation that vanquished the Nazis—history's most formidable foe—defeated by Third World peasants. What could be more tragic: A million civilians perished along with almost 60,000 American servicemen. No dominoes fell, only American prestige.

The Vietnam War is unique—America lost what I call the first postmodern war. Most narratives stress the differences between World War II (the Good War), Korea (the Forgotten War), and Vietnam (the conflict my generation can't forget). The defining differences merit attention, so do neglected similarities.

A civilian in Hanoi during the Christmas season, 1972, had much in common with World War II residents of Warsaw, Chongquing, Dresden, and Tokyo, and inhabitants of Pyongyang—explosives and incendiaries dropped from the sky. It was no longer called terror bombing; the term had become pejorative. When all else failed, America resorted to its strongest suit—bombing civilians—call it what you will. In Vietnam, amid "Rolling Thunder," American forces redoubled their bombing even though they could barely recall their evanescent objectives.

The Pentagon Papers

The *Pentagon Papers* recount the history of the struggle from its origins in World War II to 1968. The initial similarities between Korea and Vietnam are striking. The Japanese surrender and negotiations with the Soviets resulted in artificial divisions within these nations between North and South. The consequent insurrections and civil wars were construed as the machinations of an international communist conspiracy—lack of evidence didn't matter. Acheson claimed that the State Department "has no evidence of direct links between Ho and Moscow, but assumes it exists." Indeed, the Department's Office of Intelligence Research found communist influence in Southeast Asia everywhere *except* Vietnam.[55] Nevertheless, McNamara claims that initially, he had good reason to believe that Ho and his forces were part of an international communist plan for world domination. Recalling the Korean calamity, he feared that an unrestrained American response might bring the Soviets and Chinese into the conflict.

Allied with America during World War II, Ho Chi Minh fought the Japanese occupiers and gave sanctuary to American flyers. Ho struggled to remain independent. The Vietnamese Declaration of Independence sounds familiar:

"All men are created equal. They are endowed by their Creator with certain inalienable rights, among these are Life, Liberty, and the pursuit of Happiness." This immortal statement was made in the Declaration of Independence of the United States of America in 1776. In a broader sense, this means: All the peoples on the earth are equal from birth; all the peoples have a right to live, to be happy and free.[56]

That Ho desired a Jeffersonian republic is, at best, arguable. Perhaps he intended to enamor his regime to America and its venerable, anticolonial ideals. One thing is beyond dispute, as the French and Americans would learn from bitter experience: Ho and his supporters (by most accounts, the majority of the Vietnamese) were fiercely nationalistic.

Despite the newly endorsed Atlantic Charter urging the right to self-determination, the United States supported the French as they reestablished colonial domination of Vietnam. Ho reignited the Vietnamese resistance. Following their defeat at Dien Bien Phu in 1954, the French left Vietnam. McNamara mentions Eisenhower's rhetoric about falling dominoes, but glosses over his decision—resisting pressure to intervene. Eisenhower believed that land wars in Asian jungles would end in a quagmire at a great loss of life and national treasure.

Nevertheless, covert American operations began with the introduction of CIA agents and other advisors. The Eisenhower administration established a client state in the southern portion of Vietnam governed by Bao Dai: a corrupt monarch who, according to Ike, enjoyed the spas of Europe more than fighting communism. Bao Dai was not the last of the corrupt leaders woefully unable to govern.

The Geneva Accords defined Vietnam as a unitary state, and established a cease-fire line at the 17th parallel. American authorities recruited Ngo Dinh Diem, a Vietnamese studying in the United States, to run against Bao Dai in an election in the South. Diem claimed he won by 98 percent. Much like Syngman Rhee, Diem ruthlessly oppressed opponents. Images of Buddhist monks set aflame made front-page news. The Vietcong emerged as part of the resistance to the corrupt, repressive regime.

The *Pentagon Papers* justify LBJ's apprehension; there were numerous variations on the theme "It looks to me like we're gettin' into another Korea. . . ." McNamara's advisors (most notably, Daniel Ellsberg) drafted these documents at his request. Perhaps he initiated the project to vindicate his newfound apprehensions about the war. According to the *Papers*, McNamara expressed his apprehension in his 1967 testimony to the Senate Armed Services Committee: There was "no basis to believe that any bombing campaign . . . would by itself force Ho Chi Minh's regime into submission."[57] McNamara resigned shortly thereafter.

Ellsberg, aware of his complicity in the "Credibility Gap," leaked the *Papers* to the *New York Times* and *Washington Post*. His gloss on the documents denies that he and his Pentagon colleagues were hapless pawns of the forces of history:

> To see the conflict and our part in it as a tragedy without villains, war crimes without criminals, lies without liars, espouses and promulgates a view of process, roles, and motives that is not only grossly mistaken but which underwrites deceits that have served a succession of Presidents.[58]

Many of the documents remain classified, and the authors lacked access to deliberations of the Joint Chiefs and the Executive. Nevertheless, the *Papers* narrate the events within McNamara's Department of Defense that led to his disillusion with the war and his resignation. The DOD didn't value candor, let alone concern for American and Asian lives. The Nixon administration failed to prevent publication. Much later, McNamara wrote a personal retrospective, contrite yet disingenuous.[59]

McNamara's introduction to *In Retrospect* offers insight into his character. During his campaign Kennedy claimed that Eisenhower and the Republicans didn't acknowledge a dangerous missile gap favoring Soviet forces. (Actually, Eisenhower didn't boast about the gap that actually *favored* the United States—such bravado might heighten the arms race.) Upon entering office, McNamara discovered: "There was a gap—it was in our favor!" He embarrassed JFK by informing the press of the truth. He apologized profusely for telling the truth: "Mr. President. I came down here to help . . . I've stimulated demands for your resignation. I'm fully prepared to resign." The President forgave and forgot "without the slightest hint of anger. . . . *I never forgot the generous way he forgave my stupidity.*" [Ital. mine.] A portentous comment indeed encapsulating McNamara's tenure as Secretary of Defense. It's a stupid, decidedly foolish career move to tell the truth; a boss who forgives scandalous truth-telling merits accolades.[60] (Subsequently, Kennedy aide Roswell Gilpatrick boasted about US *dominance* in the missile race. Could such bravado have prompted the Soviets to place missiles in Cuba?)

The Geneva Accords (tacitly supported but not officially endorsed by the United States) mandated countrywide elections for 1956. The elections were not held. According to Eisenhower: "It was generally conceded that had an election been held, Ho Chi Minh would have been elected Premier." Ho and his supporters throughout Vietnam felt betrayed and stepped up guerilla activity in the south. Eisenhower sent cadres of advisors and CIA agents in order to stabilize the situation. His efforts failed. McNamara reports that Eisenhower revealed his dilemma while consulting with the incoming Kennedy administration: He feared falling dominoes in Southeast Asia if Ho's forces prevailed, but he also feared the consequences of land war in Asian jungles.[61] (American leaders seldom recognize the tragic aspect of existence—not all problems have solutions.)

The young president, an enthusiastic student of counterinsurgency, vowed to "get the country moving again." McNamara allows that, like others in the new Kennedy administration, he lacked knowledge of Vietnam and hazarded simplistic assumptions. His reliance upon quantitative systems analysis led to such assumptions. In every metric, US forces outnumbered Vietnamese forces by several magnitudes; with sufficient resolve the United States could quickly triumph—whatever that meant. In retrospect, he laments that he lacked appreciation for Vietnamese history, language, culture, and values. In short, he claims he and other architects of the war were ill-informed—a disingenuous claim.

Charles De Gaulle—who likely knew more about Vietnam than he cared to—warned Kennedy that warfare in Vietnam would trap America in a "bottomless military and political swamp." And Eisenhower was not the only experienced military man who warned of the folly of war fighting in Asian jungles. French General Jacque LeClerc also knew more about Vietnam than he cared to. Not averse to invoking degrading images, he likened the Vietnamese to fleas who could never be extinguished; twenty-four million Vietnamese couldn't be subdued, let alone conquered. And MacArthur said it made his "blood boil" to think of Japanese troops used to fight America's war in Indochina.[62] In addition,

"Omar Bradley, and Mathew Ridgway . . . cautioned against ground combat involvement in wars on the Asian mainland."[63]

McNamara, to understate the case, found it difficult to work with Diem and his sister-in-law, Madam Nhu—an Asian Lucrezia Borgia. McNamara describes Diem as an inscrutable Oriental and Mdm. Nhu as a sorceress. In any case, the secretary and his colleagues decided that Diem had to go. He did in a November 1963 coup. The Kennedy administration's role in the coup remains controversial, but no tears were shed at Diem's demise.

McNamara claims that, had the president lived, American forces would have withdrawn. Others claim that, given JFK's enthusiasm for counterinsurgency, and fear of further humiliation after the Bay of Pigs and the Berlin Wall, he would have stayed the course and escalated the conflict. What we do know is that his key advisors planned policy during the Johnson administration.

McNamara's rational actor assumptions led to a gradual escalation strategy, the strategy—at the time—McNamara and the others believed successfully resolved the Cuban missile crisis. (As we saw in Chapter Two, he ultimately concluded that the crisis was resolved due to plain dumb luck.) To reiterate, the strategy presupposes that political actors think like accountants involved in noonday commerce engaged in cost/ risk/benefit analysis. As the pressure increased, Ho surely would realize he had everything to lose and nothing to gain by continuing the conflict. The United States enjoyed escalation dominance—it could prevail at any level of conflict. Moreover, gradual escalation would be less alarming to the Chinese and the Soviets. McNamara and his associates failed to recognize that the Vietnamese fought for national autonomy for centuries. Ironically, they embraced JFK's inaugural exhortation: They willingly paid any price, bore any burden—even if it wasn't cost effective.

Of course those in Hanoi had reason to question American prudence, rationality, and resolve. The United States failed to intervene to save a vital strategic asset—China. They didn't save the French colonialists in 1954, permitted the neutralization of Laos, and abandoned their allies at the Bay of Pigs. And during his campaign, LBJ vowed he'd never send American boys to do what Asian boys should be doing.[64]

The Gulf of Tonkin episode remains controversial. North Vietnamese attacked an American ship in international waters. Some claim US espionage and assaults provoked the attack; others claim the attack never occurred. In any case, the episode became a pretext for a congressional resolution giving LBJ carte blanche for attacking Vietnam. McNamara indicts LBJ—in retrospect—for misusing the authorization. Congress did not conceive of the resolution as "a declaration of war and did not intend it to be used, as it was, as authorization for an enormous expansion of US forces in Vietnam."

Vietnam was about dilemmas without solutions. As McNamara lamented: "Securing a declaration of war . . . might well have been impossible; not seeking it was certainly wrong."[65] Formalities aside, given the mind-set of American planners, withdrawing from Vietnam was impossible—political suicide; pursuing the war was foolhardy—strategic imbecility. General Maxwell Taylor offered a retrospective ignored by those promoting wars in Iraq and Afghanistan: "We didn't know our ally. . . . We knew even less about the enemy. And the last, most inexcusable mistake was not knowing our own people."[66]

Terrorizing Vietnam

Air Force jets sent their bombs down on the deserted ruins, scorching again the burned foundations of the houses and pulverizing for a second time the heaps of rubble, in the hope of collapsing tunnels too deep and well hidden for the bulldozers to crush—as though, having decided to destroy it, we were now bent on annihilating every possible indication that the village of Ben Suc had ever existed.
—Jonathan Schell[67]

Hundreds of thousands of young American invaders were thrown into an atrocity-producing situation—they committed atrocities. Efforts were made to cover up the My Lai massacre; the real cover-up, however, treats My Lai as the exception not the rule. As Nick Turse shows in *Kill Anything that Moves*, My Lai was the rule, not the exception.[68] Congressman Father Robert Drinan exposed the ultimate cover-up when he urged that Nixon should be impeached for breaking into Vietnam and Cambodia, not for a petty burglary.

Turse explains that he discovered My Lai was the rule while investigating post-traumatic stress disorder (PTSD) at the National Archives. In March 1968, Charlie Company massacred, tortured, and raped hundreds of villagers. A court-martial convicted Lt. William Calley of ordering the massacre. After three years of house arrest, Nixon pardoned him. Authorities never indicted bomber crews and their commanders who massacred with napalm, phosphor bombs, and high explosives.

Heroic stories emerge amid the atrocity. Several members of Charlie Company risked court-martial by disobeying orders—they didn't shoot. Warrant Officer Hugh Thompson landed his helicopter amid the massacre, pointed guns at Calley's troops, and ordered them to stop. He saved some and evacuated others. No good deed goes unpunished. Perhaps it wasn't mere coincidence that, following Thompson's actions:

> The army sent him out in increasingly dangerous situations. In an eleven-day period, Thompson's helicopters were shot down four times. The fifth time Thompson was shot down, during a mission from Da Nang to an airbase at Chu Lai, the fall broke his back and he narrowly escaped death from nearby Vietcong. In April, Thompson was awarded the Distinguished Flying Cross for his actions at My Lai, a document he threw away.[69]

The Archive's extensive Vietnam War crimes collection includes the "War Crimes Working Group" portfolio detailing over 300 allegations of massacres, torture, mutilations, and other atrocities documented by army investigators.[70] Despite Turse's frequent requests, the Army and Marines didn't provide information on the outcome of these cases. His account of other My Lai incidents raises a disturbing question broached by critics of American policy: What turned American kids into terrorists?

Men witnessing killing and mutilation crave revenge—payback. But Vietnam wasn't any war—postmodern may be the proper designation. Wars of modernity were about armies facing armies. World War II had identifiable boundaries, enemies, and objectives. The meaning was clear: avenging the Japanese attack on Pearl Harbor and defeating the Nazi destruction of civilization.

Postmodernism invokes suspicion of metanarratives—the ultimate story, the final answer. Sagas of fighting communism meant next to nothing for troops slogging through razor-sharp jungle grasses, hoping that, one day, they would make it home in one piece. "Don't mean nothin'" became the mantra in a conflict bereft of meaning. Too many died capturing tactically worthless "Hamburger Hills" for the benefit of news crews—film at eleven. Vietnam had no boundaries, no frontlines.

The ubiquitous enemy was everywhere and nowhere: in daylight ambushes, nighttime raids, whorehouses, thatched villages, and ornate temples—even in the American Embassy during the Tet Offensive. Trust no one—not even that street urchin selling gum. This was a quantum enemy akin to subatomic particles—invisible, unpredictable, and dangerous.

The ironic incongruity between public pronouncements and discussions in camera became the "Credibility Gap." American officials assured the public they were defeating communism by winning hearts and minds. The *Pentagon Papers* tell a different story, an immorality play about the perils of self-deception and grandiose plans:

> We lost our offensive . . . Search and Destroy operations can't build [required] momentum. We became mesmerized by statistics of known, doubtful validity, choosing to place our faith only in the ones that showed progress. . . . In short, our setbacks were due to wishful thinking.[71]

The *Papers* went on to argue that: "No ground strategy and no level of additional US forces alone could achieve an early end to the war." In responding to Senate hawks such as Senator Russell—who belatedly thought the Vietnam War was a good idea—McNamara concluded: There is "no basis to believe that any bombing campaign would by itself force Ho Chi Minh's regime into submission, short, that is, of the virtual annihilation of North Vietnam and its people."[72] Strategic bombing was the last resort.

The Last Resort

As in Korea, having failed on the ground, the United States resorted to airpower—Operation Rolling Thunder. Fearful that bombing the North would further antagonize the Chinese and the Soviets, strategists initially restricted bombing to the South. Nevertheless, US forces dropped massive amounts of ordnance and defoliants on a putative ally: about double the amount used by the United States in all World War II theaters. As in Korea, napalm set villages and villagers on fire. (Who can forget the image of the naked, scalded little girl fleeing her village?) While tactical airstrikes occurred in support of military operations, most of the strikes were "interdictions"—attacks on suspected enemy bases.[73]

The *Papers* reflect growing pessimism: "It will be difficult to convince critics that we are not simply destroying South Viet Nam in order to 'save' it and that we genuinely want peace talks."[74]

Pentagon strategists concluded that (once again) they underestimated Orientals: "Commanders have gravely underestimated the capacity of the enemy to absorb such punishment and to be still able to launch bold offensive operations."[75] John McNaughton, McNamara's deputy, declared, "70 percent of the US purpose in Vietnam was to avoid humiliating defeat." He continued, "The reasons we *went* into Vietnam . . . are now largely academic."[76]

Vietnam was not purely academic for LBJ. It was also a personal tragedy—an assault on his mental stability. According to Richard Goodwin, his special assistant, LBJ became mentally unbalanced if not paranoid. The president became unhinged as the calamity in Vietnam unfolded, protests in the streets mounted, and fellow Democrats defected from his ranks.

Goodwin and Press Secretary Bill Moyers were unnerved by LBJ's rants against the Kennedys and other "Communist sympathizers out to destroy him." At times, his entire staff was under suspicion. These LBJ confidants were so concerned that they reported the president's outbursts and delusions to three psychiatrists. The consultants concurred: LBJ's behavior "seemed to correspond to a textbook case of paranoid disintegration, the eruption of long-suppressed irrationalities." They suggested that the president's mental status would continue to deteriorate as the war worsened and remaining support crumbled. The once-ruthless pragmatist—the master of the Senate—inhabited an international and a mental realm beyond his control.

Of course, there was nothing delusional about realizing that Vietnam was beyond the control of the president and other decision-makers. Goodwin attended a staff meeting in which LBJ remarked:

> "But there's one thing you ought to know. Vietnam is like being in a plane without a parachute when all the engines go out. If you jump, you'll probably be killed, and if you stay in, you'll crash and probably burn. That's what it is." Then, without waiting for a response, the tall, slumped figure rose and left the room.[77]

Sixteen years—almost to the day—that Truman announced he wouldn't seek another term, LBJ announced that he too would not seek another term. The date was March 31, 1968.

Nixon inherited a steadily deteriorating situation in Vietnam and growing opposition at home. He campaigned on a "secret plan" to end the war—peace with honor. The plan coupled gradual troop withdrawal with intensified bombing of the North—along with Laos and Cambodia—to exact concessions. Nixon initiated Linebacker I: bombing North Vietnam and mining Haiphong harbor. As Kissinger remarked, "I can't believe that a fourth-rate power like North Vietnam doesn't have a breaking point."[78] An official Navy report to the Senate Foreign Relations Committee estimated the bombing caused 52,000 civilian deaths, and—ironically—hardened North Vietnamese resolve. According to an official document:

> There is no evidence to suggest that these hardships reduced to a critical level NVN's willingness or resolve to continue the conflict. On the contrary, the bombing may have hardened the attitude of the people and rallied them behind the government's programs.[79]

After rather Byzantine negotiations regarding the shape of the conference table, peace talks began. In early fall 1972 Kissinger negotiated a tentative agreement with his Vietnamese counterparts. Like the obstreperous Syngman Rhee, Nguyen Thieu (the American-backed leader in Saigon) rejected the tentative draft. Understandably, the Saigon regime feared the Americans were about to abandon them.

At the Paris Peace talks, Nixon and Kissinger offered a proposal initially rejected by both North and South regimes. They proposed to stop the bombing and withdraw American forces—*if* the viability of the Saigon regime could be assured. Privately, they believed the proposal would do no such thing. They would merely provide a "decent interval" that would allow the United States to withdraw without humiliation. When Ho's forces captured the entire nation—as they inevitably would—Nixon and Kissinger could blame Saigon's ineptitude. Historian Gideon Rose cites a White House tape:

> Nixon: South Vietnam probably is never gonna survive anyway. I'm just being perfectly candid. Can we have a viable foreign policy if . . . North Vietnam gobbles up South Vietnam?

Kissinger: We can have a viable foreign policy if it looks as if it's the result of South Vietnamese incompetence.[80]

Apparently, in order to placate Thieu and to prompt the North Vietnamese to return to the talks, Nixon initiated Linebacker II—massive air attacks on North Vietnamese cities, especially Hanoi. The Christmas bombing would not be terrorism-lite. As he reportedly told an aide: "The bastards have never been bombed like they're going to get bombed this time."[81] The raids began December 18, 1972, as 129 B-52s bombed Hanoi. In addition, the Air Force flew 729 sorties over North Vietnam. Attacks halted Christmas Day but resumed the next day, ending on December 29.[82]

Apparently, the bombing prompted the North Vietnamese to return to the talks. Nixon convinced the Saigon regime they wouldn't be abandoned. A peace agreement ended American involvement on January 23, 1973. As Kissinger aide John Negroponte quipped, "We bombed North Vietnam into accepting our concessions."[83] Communist forces were on the move—the administration abandoned the Saigon regime. Congress was in no mood to supply more troops or national treasure. On April 30, 1975, Ho's forces captured the entire nation; Saigon became Ho Chi Minh City.

Speaking at the United States Air Force Academy Harmon lecture (regarded by the academy as its most prestigious lecture), George Herring indicted the folly of the Vietnam War. The voice of Reinhold Niebuhr came through loud and clear as the speaker recognized the irony of American history played out in Vietnam:

> Failure in Vietnam challenged as perhaps nothing else has one of our most fundamental myths—the notion that we can accomplish anything we set our collective minds to—and partisans of many diverse points of view have sought in the aftermath to explain this profoundly traumatic experience.[84]

Protesting the Vietnam War

After the Tet Offensive, Walter Cronkite ("the most trusted man in America") denounced LBJ's policies and told millions of Americans that the war would end in a stalemate. "For it seems now more certain than ever that the bloody experience of Vietnam is to end in a stalemate." After watching Cronkite's broadcast, LBJ was quoted as saying, "That's it. If I've lost Cronkite, I've lost middle America."[85]

Mention Vietnam and antiwar protests come to mind, unique protests—at least in modern times. Only the Civil War matched the divisiveness of Vietnam and intensity of the protests. Like Vietnam, the Korean War seemed woefully misguided: the cause of tens of thousands of American deaths and hundreds of thousands of Asian deaths. But protests were minimal due to the war's comparatively brief duration and the lack of televised coverage. The draft, a decade of televised coverage, and proliferating reports of atrocities sparked opposition to the Vietnam War. Indeed, television turned Vietnam into "the living room war."

Morley Safer's August 1965 telecast departed from official reality and highlighted civilian casualties. Safer showed Marines lighting thatched roofs with Zippo lighters. The story angered LBJ who ordered a security check. Upon learning that Safer was merely a Canadian, not a communist, the president reportedly grumbled, "Well, I knew he wasn't an American."[86]

The protests began when students—mostly on elite campuses—engaged in teach-ins, occupied buildings, burned draft cards, and shut down campuses. At Berkeley, students blocked troop trains transporting soldiers to ships destined for Vietnam.[87] I was among the students who recognized the stark incongruity between the American ideals carefully taught in school and the destruction in Vietnam.

Likewise, members of faith-based communities also recognized the incongruity between their ideals and American policy. Michael Lerner (later ordained as a rabbi) was arrested in various protests, as were Catholic priests such as the Berrigan brothers, and Rev. William Sloan Coffin Jr., a Protestant activist. Another Protestant activist is particularly noteworthy—Rev. Martin Luther King Jr. Official memory sanitizes King. To be sure, he is rightly eulogized for his "I Have a Dream" speech and courageous activism. Few, however, recall his opposition to the war, opposition voiced in an April 1967 sermon, "Why I Am Opposed to the War in Vietnam," at Riverside Church in New York. He found it ironic that Negroes supposedly fought for human rights in Vietnam they didn't enjoy in America. And tragically, funds that should have been used fighting poverty and providing health care went to a needless, immoral war in Vietnam.[88]

The antiwar movement itself was not entirely free of racist bias. In May 1968 the highway patrol killed three black protestors in Orangeburg, South Carolina. Protests and press coverage were minimal. In May 1970 four white protestors died at Kent State, provoking massive coverage and protests. Friends predicted, "Years from now everyone will remember Kent State; Orangeburg will be forgotten." They were right.

The movement gained momentum following revelations of My Lai and the Tet Offensive. More clergy, politicians, and journalists joined student activists. By 1968, following McNamara's resignation, politicians such as Robert Kennedy and Eugene McCarthy opposed the war because it wasted American lives and treasure, and couldn't be won. Civilian casualties weren't an overarching concern.

Civilian casualties tormented combat veterans and haunted them for the rest of their lives. Thousands of antiwar veterans participated in Operation Rapid American Withdrawal (RAW): a reenactment of Vietnam combat in a small, New Jersey town. The vets posted flyers that read: "*A US infantry company just came through here.* If you had been Vietnamese, we might have burned your house . . . shot your dog . . . shot you."[89]

Unlike World War II and Korea, popular culture opposed the war, especially when the conflict seemed interminable. True, tunes such as Barry Sandler's "Ballad of the Green Berets" got airtime. But who would rank this patriotic hymn with Bob Dylan's "The Times They Are A-Changin'"? Nevertheless, even the jingoistic ballads are worth noting for what's left unsaid. During World War II, as we've seen, musicians burst into song about killing Japs, *all* Japs regardless of affiliation or locale. During the Vietnam War no one harmonized about killing Vietnamese. To be sure, soldiers called Vietnamese "gooks" in boot camp and in the combat zone, but such slurs never infected the mainstream press.

Likewise, John Wayne's *Green Berets* didn't merit the acclaim of Oliver Stone's *Platoon*. (Stone, unlike Wayne, served in Vietnam.) Nevertheless, Wayne's film is worth watching because it articulates the pretext for the war—preventing worldwide communist domination. A skeptical journalist embedded with the Green Berets soon learns the

truth about Vietnam—it's the frontline in the war against communism.
Unlike Wayne's World War II films that dehumanized the Japanese,
the Vietnamese are honorary good guys. American officers and South
Vietnamese officers are wartime buddies. And Vietnamese peasants are
innocent victims of the communist scourge. The irony is lost on those
who assume civilians must be demonized in order to be targeted for
destruction.

Those who condemn popular media for losing the war can't blame
Hollywood: *Green Berets* was the major studio's only production during
the war. After the war, highly critical postwar documentaries such as
Interviews with My Lai Veterans and *Hearts and Minds* won Academy
Awards. Even so, they didn't reach mass audiences. The bloody realism
of *Full Metal Jacket* engrossed large audiences. And *Coming Home*
disclosed a disconcerting truth: The war never ends for those suffering
PTSD. In the words of one critic, Hollywood's deferred response to the
war "portrays Vietnam as an indescribable hellhole to which young
American men are condemned and from which they cannot escape
intact."[90]

Those championing the war claim returning veterans were spat
upon. There is an instance: *Born on the Fourth of July*[91] was based
upon the plight and activism of a disabled combat veteran, Ron Kovic.
His organization, Vietnam Veterans Against the War, spoke out in
teach-ins and organized demonstrations. He and other disabled veterans interrupted Nixon's speech at the 1972 Republican convention.
Police forcibly removed them; delegates spat at them as they left.[92]

CODA: A LESSON FROM GRAND FENWICK

The comic satire, *The Mouse That Roared*, recounts an obscure fiefdom that deliberately loses a war with the United States. The leaders of
Grand Fenwick know that losers such as Japan and Germany enjoy the
postwar largesse of the United States—to lose is to prosper. Unfortunately, for Vietnam, they won. There were no reparations, no American
efforts to rebuild a shattered nation, no Marshall Plan. However, America established diplomatic relations and trade—after a decent interval.
Vietnam remains poor, but efforts are under way to promote tourism
and textiles.

During the War, the Vietnamese kept American prisoners of war in wretched confinement in what the prisoners called "the Hanoi Hilton"; guests included Senator John McCain. Today Hanoi boasts an actual Hilton and a Sheraton as well. Clothing is also manufactured and exported—such as the shirt I wear as I write. The indecipherable instructions for my new printer are printed in Vietnamese—a minor act of revenge? As post–World War II military fiascoes suggest, Americans should stick to what it does best: promoting popular culture and consumerism.

NOTES

1. Fyodor Dostoevsky, *Notes from Underground*, Walter Kaufman, ed. (New York: Penguin, 1963), 69–70.

2. Chomsky frequently makes this claim. See, for example, "Distorted Morality: America's War on Terror," Harvard University Lecture, February 2002; accessed May 1, 2014, http://www.chomsky.info/talks/200202.

3. See, for example, Howard Zinn, *Terrorism and War* (New York: Seven Stories Press, 2002).

4. See, for example, Daniel Ellsberg, "A Call to Mutiny," in Dan Smith and E. P. Thompson, eds., *Protest and Survive* (New York: Monthly Review Press, 1981).

5. See, for example, Chris Hedges and Laila Al-Arian, *Collateral Damage: America's War against Iraqi Civilians* (New York: Nation Books, 2008).

6. Tom Engelhardt, *The American Way of War* (Chicago: Haymarket Books, 2010).

7. John Tirman, *The Deaths of Others*, (New York: Oxford University Press, 2011).

8. John W. Dower, *Cultures of War: Pearl Harbor, Hiroshima, 9/11, Iraq* (New York: W. W. Norton, 2010).

9. A Google search of "Terror Bombing during the Korean War" reveals documents such as an Air Force Fact Sheet titled "Strategic Bombing: New Flexibility," accessed May 3, 2014, http://www.nationalmuseum.af.mil/factsheets/factsheet.asp?id=1933.

10. Dower, 222.

11. *The Vietnam War*, prepared for the United States Committee on Foreign Relations (Washington: US Government Printing Office, June 8, 1971). A recorded transcript of portions of the hearing is available at http://www.c-span.org/video/?181065-1/vietnam-war-hearing-1971. Robert McNa-

mara (a principal architect of the war) laments these deaths in *In Retrospect* (New York: Times Books, 1995), 43. "Air forces dropped over a million tons of bombs on the South, more than twice the tonnage dropped on the North. Fighting produced more and more civilian casualties. . . . The increasing destruction and misery brought on the country we were supposed to be helping troubled me greatly."

12. Tirman, Kindle locations 48–49.

13. Paul Fussell, *Wartime* (New York and Oxford: Oxford University Press, 1989), 116.

14. John Dower, *War Without Mercy* (New York: Pantheon, 1986), 14.

15. Lewis Carroll, *Alice's Adventures in Wonderland* (London: Macmillan, 1898), 116.

16. I am indebted to Andrew Bacevich's *The Limits of American Power: The End of American Exceptionalism* (New York: Metropolitan Books, 2008) for this gloss on American history.

17. Ibid., 186.

18. Tirman, Locations 994–95.

19. See, for example, Bruce Cumings, *The Korean War* (New York: Modern Library, 2010). Cumings claims the most heinous and persistent atrocities were committed by Rhee's regime in the South. Also see Steven Casey, *Selling the Korean War: Propaganda, Politics, and Public Opinion in the United States 1950–1953* (New York: Oxford University Press, 2008. Kindle edition); and Gideon Rose, *How Wars End: Why We Always Fight the Last Battle* (New York: Simon & Schuster, 2010. Kindle edition.)

20. Quoted by Casey, 33.

21. *The Autobiography of Harry S. Truman*, Robert H. Ferrell, ed. (Boulder: University of Colorado Press, 1980), 112.

22. NSC68-1950, US Department of State Office of the Historian, accessed May 5, 2014, https://history.state.gov/milestones/1945-1952/NSC68.

23. Quoted by Casey, 28.

24. Quoted by Rose, Kindle Locations 2744–47.

25. Quoted by Cumings, 14.

26. See Casey's discussion, 16.

27. See Brigadier General S. L. A. Marshall (Ret.), "Our Mistakes in Korea," in *Atlantic Monthly*, September 1953, 46–49.

28. Quoted by Tirman, 1479–84.

29. Marshall, 47.

30. See Casey's discussion, 101.

31. Quoted by Casey, 71.

32. Ibid., 137.

33. Quoted by Rose, 93.

34. "Giving Them More Hell," *Time*, December 3, 1973, 57.

35. Quoted by Tirman, 1534–36.

36. Accessed May 10, 2014, http://www.nationalmuseum.af.mil/factsheets/factsheet.asp?id=1933.

37. Cumings, 159.

38. Ibid., 153.

39. See Tirman's discussion, Location 1543–44.

40. See Cumings' discussion, 156–58.

41. Tirman, Location 1524.

42. See Tirman's discussion, Location 1736–68.

43. Lt. General George E. Stratemeyer; accessed May 12, 2014, http://www.nationalmuseum.af.mil/factsheets/factsheet.asp?id=1933.

44. Casey, 3.

45. An official Army document offers a collection of Korean War posters. Accessed May 13, 2014, https://www.flickr.com/photos/imcomkorea/sets/72157607808414225/ US Army Archive.

46. Accessed May 13, 2014, http://www.authentichistory.com/1946-1960/2-korea/3-music/.

47. See Roger Ebert's review, accessed May 13, 2014, http://www.rogerebert.com/reviews/mash-1970.

48. Accessed May 15, 2014, http://www.rogerebert.com/reviews/great-movie-the-manchurian-candidate-1962.

49. Scott Duke Harris, "South Korea: The little dynamo that sneaked up on the world," *Christian Science Monitor*, May 19, 2013.

50. S. L. A. Marshall, quoted by Cumings, 49.

51. Accessed May 15, 2014, http://ro.uow.edu.au/cgi/viewcontent.cgi?article=1066&context=commwkpapers.

52. Ibid., 4.

53. Quoted by Robert Dallek, "Three New Revelations About LBJ," in *The Atlantic Monthly*, April 1998, Vol. 281, #4, 42–44.

54. Jeffrey Record, *The Wrong War: Why We Lost in Vietnam* (Annapolis: Naval Institute Press, 1998), 37.

55. See the *Pentagon Papers*, 125–32.

56. Accessed May 15, 2014, http://www.unc.edu/courses/2009fall/hist/140/006/Documents/VietnameseDocs.pdf.

57. Department of Defense, *The Pentagon Papers—U.S. Vietnam Relations, 1945–1967* (Kindle Edition), Locations 44522–26.

58. Quoted by *Time*, "The Nation: Pentagon Papers: The Secret War," June 28, 1971, accessed May 8, 2014, content.time.com/time/magazine/article/0,9171,905234,00.html.

59. Robert S. McNamara, *In Retrospect: The Tragedy and Lessons of Vietnam* (New York: Times Books, 1995).

60. Ibid., 20–21.

61. Ibid., 33–34.

62. Robert Cottrell, *Vietnam: The 17th Parallel* (New York: Chelsea House, 2004), 59.

63. Record, 28.

64. See Record, 31.

65. McNamara, 127–28.

66. Quoted by Rose, 17.

67. Jonathan Schell, "The Village of Ben Suc," *New Yorker*, July 7, 1967, accessed August 17, 2014, http://www.newyorker.com/magazine/1967/07/15/the-village-of-ben-suc.

68. Nick Turse, *Kill Anything That Moves: The Real American War in Vietnam* (New York: Henry Holt and Co., 2013), Kindle edition.

69. "My Lai: A Half-Told Story," retrieved from: http://msu-web.montclair.edu/~furrg/Vietnam/mylailondontimesmag89.ptranscript./.

70. Turse, 14.

71. *Papers*, Locations 43541–45.

72. Ibid., 43773–75 and 4522–26.

73. See Raphael Littauer and Norman Uphoff, *The Air War in Indochina* (Ithaca: Cornell University Press, 1971), 62.

74. *Papers*, Locations 43692–95.

75. Ibid., Locations 44181–483.

76. Quoted by Record, 28.

77. Richard N. Goodwin, "President Lyndon Johnson: The War Within," *New York Times Magazine*, Aug. 21, 1988, accessed May 15, 2014, http://www.nytimes.com/1988/08/21/magazine/president-lyndon-johnson-the-war-within.html?src=pm&pagewanted=4.

78. Quoted by Rose, 30.

79. *Bombing: As A Policy Tool in Vietnam: Effectiveness, Study #5* (Washington: US Government Printing Office, 1962), 2.

80. Quoted by Rose, 193.

81. Quoted by Tirman, Location 2603.

82. Rebecca Kesby, "North Vietnam, 1972: The Christmas Bombing of Hanoi," *BBC Newsmagazine* (December 24, 2012), accessed May 15, 2014, bbc.com/news/magazine-20719382.

83. Quoted by Rose, 39.

84. George C. Herring, "Cold Blood: LBJ's Conduct of Limited War in Vietnam," United States Air Force Academy Harmon Memorial Lecture #33, accessed August 18, 2014, http://www.usafa.edu/df/dfh/docs/Harmon33.pdf.

85. "Reporting America at War." Walter Cronkite | PBS, accessed May 15, 2014, http://www.pbs.org/weta/reportingamericaatwar/reporters/cronkite/.

86. See "Reporting America at War. Morley Safer. The Burning of Cam Ne/ PBS," http://www.pbs.org/weta/reportingamericaatwar/reporters/safer/camne. html.

87. The University of California, Berkeley Library offers an online site listing critical junctures in the movement: http://www.lib.berkeley.edu/MRC/pacificaviet.html.

88. The King Center provides an online facsimile of the speech, accessed May 15, 2014, http://www.thekingcenter.org/archive/document/mlk-sermon-why-i-am-opposed-war-vietnam.

89. Tirman, Locations 3131–36.

90. Michael Griffin, "Media Images of War," in *Media, War, & Conflict*, 22, DOI: 10.1177175066352103568l3.

91. Ron Kovic, *Born on the Fourth of July* (New York: McGraw-Hill, 1976).

92. See Tim Gilmer's account in "Ron Kovic Reborn," *Alternet*, http://www.alternet.org/story/16214/ron_kovic_reborn.

Chapter 4

THE WAR ON TERROR

The "war on terror" has created a culture of fear. . . . Using the phrase actually undermined our ability to effectively confront the real challenges we face from fanatics who may use terrorism against us. The damage these three words have done—a classic self-inflicted wound—is infinitely greater than any wild dreams entertained by the fanatical perpetrators of the 9/11 attacks.

—Zbigniew Brzezinski[1]

As Brzezinski and others argue, the War on Terror answers bin Laden's prayers. But why a war on terror in the first place? Terrorism—long an exclusive nation-state prerogative—got bad press when non-state actors defied the state's monopoly on violence and threatened the state itself. They stood Thucydides's truism on its head: *The weak did what they had the power to do, and the strong must accept the consequences.* Conceptual vertigo threw governing elites off balance. States do not merely claim a monopoly on violence; the monopoly is their very signature, their *raison d'être*. As Weber explained "A state . . . claims the *monopoly of the legitimate use of physical force* within a given territory. . . . The state is considered the sole source of the 'right' to use violence."[2] Monopolists fight challenges to their exclusive franchises—none more so than the nation-state. Terrorism got bad press when non-state actors challenged the monopoly.

Two challenges stand out: September 5, 1972 and September 11, 2001. In the aftermath of the 1972 Munich massacre, cliques of experts arose investigating the history, nature, and threat posed by these non-state actors. After 9/11 the War on Terror was writ large in Iraq and writ small in drone strikes and other covert operations against the terrorist diaspora. Terrorism became the lingua franca of the political spectacle.

THE TRANSMUTATION OF TERRORISM

The shift in the meaning of "terrorism" . . . is clearly illustrated by a collection of over 250 definitions of the term collected recently. Practically every definition prior to 1972 refers primarily to state violence. But the definitions collected for 1972 and later either refer exclusively to insurgent violence or incorporate both insurgent and state violence . . . with very few referring primarily to state violence.

—Lisa Stampnitzky[3]

Sociologist Lisa Stampnitzky is among the few researchers investigating the conceptual shift, and attempts to frame terrorist studies as a distinct, legitimate, and viable discipline.[4] As she notes, prior to the 1972 Munich massacre American authorities defined airline hijackers, kidnappers, and various bandits and rebels as criminals, not terrorists.[5] (Today, of course, they would be terrorists.)

These felons of yesterday didn't challenge the state's monopoly. Their actions weren't made for primetime—even if they were, they couldn't be properly broadcast. In those bygone days before worldwide, 24/7 programming, "breaking news" didn't break into prerecorded shows by broadcasting the signature message of terrorism in real time— be afraid, be terribly afraid!

Munich and Its Aftermath

The massacre shocked a world accustomed to a secure, predictable environment safeguarded by nation-states. Palestinian members of Black September invaded the Israeli Olympic compound. Two unarmed Israelis died valiantly defending themselves and the athletes. As events unfolded, eight Palestinians held nine Israelis hostage. German sharpshooters attempted to save the hostages. Five Palestinians died along with the hostages.

Sean McManus was there and describes his father's (Jim McKay) sixteen-hour, continuous live broadcast. Millions stayed glued to the radio and television.

> He [Jim McKay] didn't realize—and nobody realized, I think—the impact this story would have on the American public. Terrorism was something that America just had not dealt with. The idea of masked gunmen kidnapping athletes was something that was so foreign to the consciousness. Now we are familiar with terrorism and kidnappings and bombings and massacres, but in those days it was just unheard of. So I don't think he realized how many people were watching him and what a huge, huge national event it was.[6]

What would happen next? Not only did Black September murder the innocent and demoralize the Olympics, it threatened the nation-states' cherished monopolies—an unforgivable offense. But why is the atrocity remembered as terrorism rather than a heinous crime? Cast in the perspective of those who controlled the post-Munich discourse, merely calling Black September's actions a crime—the initial response of some commentators—wouldn't do. "Crime" sounds venal—all-too-common perfidy. Criminals don't broadcast a message at once grandiose and horrifying to an entire nation, if not to the world. "Insurgency" wouldn't do (although many of the terrorism experts emerged from studies of insurgency). Insurgents don't necessarily commit the most heinous of deeds—deliberately harming noncombatants. And calling non-state actors' violence acts of war doesn't suffice. Wars are sustained efforts designed to seize and hold territory, and they can be just—especially to those who initiate them. "Just war" readily trips off the tongue; unlike the bad old days, terrorism no longer has favorable connotations. These days, "just terrorism" sounds like an oxymoron.

Post-Munich discourse went to extremes to express the rage and humiliation of being upstaged by non-state actors, actors who proved the nation-state could no longer safeguard its citizens. The official lexicon had an expression for violence taken to extremes—"terrorism." During World War II, facing a "supreme emergency," the Allies endorsed what I called "Just Terrorism Theory": They believed they were justified, if not obligated, in taking extreme measures to defeat the Axis powers. Accordingly, they inflicted the worst imaginable violence: terror bombing designed to kill, destroy, and demoralize. Terrorism expert Brian Jenkins got it right: Terrorism is theater. Terror bombing sent a message in the Asian and European theaters: Ordinary citizens were exquisitely vulnerable to horror visited by alien powers.

Turning to the Cold War, both American and Soviet officials hazarded extreme measures. American strategists didn't threaten the Soviets with crimes and misdemeanors, or with insurgency, or even with conventional war. These time-honored threats wouldn't do. Only the ultimate threat could deter the ultimate threat. Only nuclear terrorism had sufficient gravitas.

Prior to 1972 terrorism was acceptable to American planners—it was under *their* control: something they could do to others, sometimes with impunity, sometimes not. The strong do what they have the power to do, and the weak must accept the consequences: a natural and desirable state of affairs for Athenian *and* American elites.

Terrorism seemed like a good fit for "extremists" such as Black September and their progeny. However, a potentially embarrassing problem arose: The term had a time-honored pedigree. Prior to 1972, as we've seen, strategists argued about titrating the "delicate balance of nuclear terror."[7] When the Soviets launched Sputnik, newspaper headlines warned: "The Balance of Terror in Jeopardy"—not a good thing. Kennedy cast terrorism in a favorable light in his inaugural address: He described the United States and the Soviet Union, "both racing to alter that uncertain balance of terror that stays the hand of mankind's final war."[8]

Nuclear strategists didn't want to be caught dead with Black September terrorists. In order to avoid cognitive dissonance, an ironic and sudden shift in discourse occurred: It was no longer politically correct to extol the balance of nuclear terror. Just as the War Department became the Department of Defense as the Cold War began, the balance of terror became the venerable balance of power. Suddenly, "terrorism" only applied to foreign and domestic non-state actors. Officials worried about the terrorist diaspora mimicking state actors: engaging in nuclear terror with atomic diplomacy or actually detonating dirty bombs or primitive fission devices. American nuclear strategists absolved themselves of terrorism. Once an unequivocal reference to strategic bombing and nuclear strategy, terrorism morphed into the overused, equivocal pejorative that dominates discourse today. As Stampnitzky writes: Terrorism became "problematic—indefinable, infused with moral absolutism, and deeply politicized."[9]

Munich was not the last time non-state actors stole the show, committed mayhem, and terrified a captivated audience. It was only the beginning. Several episodes illustrate how terrorism became theater. In 1973 Black September struck again and kidnapped Cleo Noel, US ambassador to the Sudan. The kidnappers demanded the release of prisoners. The suspense ended tragically: Black September murdered the ambassador shortly after Nixon refused their demands. [10]

Various factions such as the Baader-Meinhof gang and other Red Brigades also gained notoriety by kidnapping officials. However, their wooden, ideological tracts weren't page-turners—"Rudy the Red" wouldn't do as James Bond's nemesis. Other terrorists, however, knew how to promote themselves in celebrity culture—they became famous for being infamous.

Terrorist entertainment debuted when a cause célèbre captivated public attention, a character definitely made for primetime—"Carlos the Jackal." Working with the Popular Front for the Liberation of Palestine, he hijacked an airliner with Joe Kennedy Jr. onboard. At a 1975 meeting of OPEC (Organization of Petroleum Exporting Countries) the Jackal took hostages—eleven prominent officials. (In the world according to nuclear strategists, only the United States and the Soviet Union were entitled to hold each other's civilians hostage.) The Jackal, of course, waited for television crews to arrive before parading his hostages. Enjoying his reputation as "the most dangerous man alive," he was your father's bin Laden: a self-promoter pandering a macho-psychotic image and a playboy lifestyle—James Bond's evil twin. Frederick Forsyth based his novel, *The Day of the Jackal*, on his exploits. Two films followed.

But who's a terrorist, and who's a principled revolutionary pursuing a just cause? The American New Left admired the Black Panthers. (This organization, prominent in the late 1960s and 1970s, should not be confused with the New Black Panthers, a racist cadre denounced by the original Panthers.) Like today's National Rifle Association, the Panthers armed for self-defense; unlike the NRA the Panthers denounced racism, militarism, and corporate profiteering.

J. Edgar Hoover didn't share the Left's admiration: He denounced the Panthers as the greatest terrorist threat to American internal security. Armed blacks ready to defend themselves were too much to bear. Authorities overreacted. The Chicago police raided Panther Headquarters as the inhabitants slept. A federal investigation disclosed that the Panthers fired one bullet while the police fired more than ninety.[11]

Speaking of Hoover, the official FBI retrospective on the Patty Hearst kidnapping reads like a script for *Law and Order*. In February 1974, the Symbionese Liberation Front kidnapped the newspaper heiress. According to the G-men: "Thus began one of the strangest cases in FBI history."[12] Unfolding events piqued suspense and mystery. Security cameras filmed Hearst, rifle in hand, robbing a bank with SLA comrades. She issued a tape praising the SLA while denouncing her heritage. The "talking heads" speculated: Was she a brainwashed victim of the Stockholm Syndrome or a true believer?

The FBI surrounded the SLA safe house; several members died in the shootout. Hearst escaped with a few comrades, prompting speculation about her whereabouts. After her capture, her brainwashing defense didn't persuade the jury. She served two years in prison before President Carter commuted her sentence. The *FBI Report* concludes with a bit of bravado: "We caught up with them all. The last two members were arrested in 1999 and 2002. Case closed."[13]

These incidents reveal American ambivalence regarding terrorism— dread alloyed with high drama. And in the aftermath of 9/11, Americans felt vulnerable as never before. Even so, as the popularity of shows such as *24* and *Homeland* illustrate, they just can't get enough terrorism. However, before turning to terrorism as entertainment in the next chapter, it's worth considering the new cadre of experts who take terrorism seriously.

Not surprisingly, proliferating terrorist activity spawned a growth industry—terrorism studies. As Stampnitzky's research reveals, prior to 1972, almost nothing was written regarding the terrorism of non-state actors. Terrorism was rarely found in the indices of the *New York Times* and *London Times*. However, by 1977 at least eleven catalogues emerged to track proliferating publications on terrorism. The author notes but one terrorism conference in 1972 and 591 in 1978.[14] Terrorism became au courant as a spate of new journals and books attest.

TERRORISM EXPERTS

Terrorism studies did not take shape as an ideal-typical discipline or intellectual field. The terrorism studies field remains a relatively weak, "undisciplined" one, and terrorism itself remains an unstable, "undisciplined" object of knowledge.

—Stampnitzky[15]

Stampnitzky investigates the history and nature of terrorism studies. This "invisible college" of experts piques her concern: a nexus of interests connecting academia with military, intelligence, government agencies, and the media. Who are these experts; what are their credentials? What sort of discipline emerged in the aftermath of Munich? She delineates boundaries.

These studies aren't comparable to traditional medicine with its demanding qualifications, standardized tests and curriculum, and ongoing certifications. There are no board-certified terrorism experts. Perhaps terrorism studies are akin to alternative medicine: an "undisciplined" field with self-proclaimed experts and porous boundaries. To be sure, some findings are worthwhile, others are dubious—it's not always easy to tell. The field is bereft of testable hypotheses, let alone tried-and-true theories. Nevertheless, much like the nuclear deterrence theorists of old, terrorism experts effect an authorial style reminiscent of well-established disciplines. My brief sampling of the field contrasts two academic experts—Bruce Hoffman and Noam Chomsky—along with two contrasting insiders—Richard Clarke and David Frum.

Hoffman's *Inside Terrorism* offers an influential contribution to traditional terrorism studies. This scholarly work analyzes the problem of defining terrorism; the history of terrorism; the role of popular media in—perhaps inadvertently—promoting terrorism; the causes of terrorism; and the novel challenges posed by al-Qaeda jihadists. To be sure, these contributions deserve attention—as does what's left unsaid. *Inside Terrorism* is a primer on how to avoid cognitive dissonance, especially the dissonance that undermines faith in American exceptionalism.

Political scientist Stephen Walt captures the faith in a single phrase: "The United States behaves better than other nations do."[16] Expert definitions of terrorism, such as the definition proffered by Hoffman, reinforce the faith and exonerate the United States from charges of terrorism. As Hoffman recognizes, hundreds of definitions vie for attention. His search for a definition begins with a history of terrorism, virtually a chronicle from Assassins to Zealots—albeit with notable omissions. What is left unsaid in order to avoid cognitive dissonance is telling. There is no mention of the terror visited upon Native Americans and African Americans. World War II terror bombing and the nuclear terror of the Cold War are ignored, as are wars in Korea and Vietnam.

Hoffman discusses changing definitions of terrorism at other times and places. However, there is no explicit account as to why these changes occur in recent American experience. Surely these changes are not natural phenomena occurring behind the backs and against the will of humans. Could it be that governing elites define terms in accord with their perceived interests?

On occasion, however, Hoffman implicitly recognizes the all-too-human motives in constructing concepts such as terrorism. He recognizes the self-serving agenda of Robespierre's definition of terrorism fashioned amid the reign of terror. He also recognizes bureaucratic politics when he sees it in State Department, Defense Department, and FBI definitions of terrorism.

However, the agenda for the post-Munich reframing of terrorism isn't considered. Why are state actors—save for American enemies—no longer practitioners of terrorism? Specifically, why does the author endorse this new mind-set? Like most mainstream terrorism studies, Hoffman accepts and promotes the national terrorism narrative, a narrative that bespeaks of American innocence and victimization.

Political scientists David Miller and Tom Mills offer a version of the post 9/11 narrative which I have modified:

> Non-state actors such as al-Qaeda initiated an unprovoked war against the United States and its allies. It is a war against cherished Western values, and (in effect) an advertisement for the power and destiny of jihadists. Not only do the jihadists deliberately kill civilians, they instill fear in the population. These fanatics—implacable and unscrupulous—are driven by hatred and religious dogmatism. Given the nature, scale, and persistence of the threat, the "terrorists" must be met with aggressive military action abroad and repressive policies at home.

This narrative is actor-based: The actor, not the action (such as a nation-state firebombing a village), determines whether an incident is

terrorism. Accordingly, by definition, only non-state actors are terrorists. As Miller and Mills conclude, the narrative plays an ideological role
in promoting a national consensus. Orthodox experts embrace this narrative in toto. Other experts also restrict terrorism to non-state actors,
but suggest that terrorists may be rational actors with grievances. Critical experts such as Chomsky argue that nation-states such as the United
States are the primary practitioners of terrorism. The orthodoxy, according to the authors, garners the most visibility. On rare occasions
when Chomsky is featured or cited, he is usually dismissed with derision. [17]

Hoffman acknowledges that government-backed death squads terrorized the citizens of El Salvador during the Reagan administration.
However, Hoffman doesn't want to accuse an American-backed regime
of terrorism. Accordingly, he proffers a curious distinction: The death
squads were guilty of "terror," not "terrorism." (Do victims of terror feel
better knowing they're not victims of terrorism?)

He does acknowledge that enemy governments resort to terrorism,
but not American allies. Accordingly, he indicts Colonel Gaddafi's Libya for engaging in terrorism. The Reagan administration responded by
bombing Gaddafi's compound, killing his stepdaughter and other noncombatants; this is "counterterrorism," not "terrorism." Despite making
exceptions for enemy states such as Libya, he concludes that terrorism
is "perpetrated by a subnational group or non-state entity."

Like other mainstream experts, Hoffman makes other exceptions to
support the national consensus. He rightly indicts terrorists for deliberately harming noncombatants. Even so, he defines attacks on American
military personnel as terrorism. He has attacks on Marines in Lebanon
and on the US *Cole* in mind. (Could it be that these days, terrorism
simply means violence you don't like?)

Hoffman aptly confronts linguistic problems in searching for a definition. And yet there is no reference to a renowned contemporary lin-
guist, a critical expert—Noam Chomsky. Chomsky is not ignored due to
his complex theoretical contributions to linguistics. He is marginalized
because he is not among the faithful; he doesn't hold that America is
the best-behaved nation. (Glenn Greenwald is writing a book analyzing
Chomsky's marginalization.) Chomsky detects considerable irony in
prevailing definitions that (appropriately enough) indict non-state, re-
tail terror while ignoring the wholesale terror visited by the United

States and other great powers. His account of terrorism is clear; he simply presses for logical consistency:

> I have been writing about international terrorism . . . [since] 1981. In doing so, I have kept to the official definitions of terrorism in US and British law and in army manuals. . . . Terrorism is "the calculated use of violence or threat of violence to attain goals that are political, religious, or ideological . . . through intimidation, coercion, or instilling fear."[18]

The definition encompasses state and non-state actors. Taking a cosmopolitan view, American lives aren't valued above others. Chomsky chronicles American actions that have killed and terrorized noncombatants. His indictments of American policy began with Vietnam and continued with criticisms of actions in Central and South America, and the Middle East, actions responsible for the deaths of hundreds of thousands of noncombatants.[19]

The salient issue is noncombatant casualties—call them what you will. Hoffman seems to endorse Chomsky when he allows that: "*National armed forces [such as those of the United States] have been responsible for far more death and destruction than terrorists might ever aspire to bring about.*" (Could it be that for every noncombatant killed by a terrorist a million have been killed by nation-states?) However, Hoffman quickly distances himself from Chomsky; he insists there is no moral equivalence between Americans and jihadists.

Unlike terrorists, Americans are guided by rules and accepted norms that prohibit certain weapons, and certain targets, and afford rights to POWs "in theory, if not always in practice."[20] Admittedly, "the armed forces . . . have been guilty of violating some of the same rules of war." Even so, we are reassured that perpetrators are held accountable; war crimes are punished.[21]

It would be helpful to see Hoffman's evidence; again, what's left *unsaid* is telling. There's no mention of World War II gratuitous terror bombing that occurred *after* the defeat of the Axis Powers appeared imminent, and no mention of Korean, Vietnamese, and Iraqi victims of napalm, phosphor weaponry, and cluster bombs—outlawed by treaty obligations. POWs, of course, are no longer prisoners of war; they are "enemy combatants" no longer protected by various Geneva Accords. And what of Robert McNamara who, as we've seen, claims he was a war criminal for orchestrating the firebombing of Tokyo? He also came to regret loss of civilian life in Vietnam. Nevertheless, he was not held accountable during his long—and perhaps troubled—retirement.

Mainstream experts such as Hoffman engage in considerable linguistic legerdemain to exonerate the United States from charges of terrorism. Simply put, Hoffman and other mainstream experts are preoccupied with what they do to us, not what we do to them.

POST-9/11 EXPERTISE

George W. Bush, who failed to act prior to September 11 on the threat from al Qaeda despite repeated warnings and then harvested a political windfall for taking obvious yet insufficient steps after the attacks; and who launched an unnecessary and costly war in Iraq that strengthened the fundamentalist, radical Islamic terrorist movements.

—Richard Clarke, principal advisor
on terrorism to three presidents.[22]

How could 9/11 happen? Unlike other nations, two great oceans separated America from Old World perfidy and Asian wickedness. The most formidable military the world had ever seen safeguarded American interests here and abroad. Surely the people of the world recognized that not only did America behave better than other nations, it selflessly aided the beleaguered and oppressed. Who could harbor hatred toward such a nation? Niebuhr questioned these assumptions in *The Irony of American History;* al-Qaeda demolished them along with the Trade Towers.

The End of Irony?

Pundits declared irony dead. They knew irony was sick—"the nihilistic shrug of an irritatingly shallow smart-ass"—it died with bodies plummeting from atop the World Trade Center. A refrain reverberated through the media: "Wipe that smirk off your face, young ironist, while terrorists are attacking us!"[23] True, there were no jokes, no double entendres, in the immediate aftermath of 9/11. The pundits, however, proffered a shallow, limited account of irony: irony is more than sarcasm and insincerity.

Irony as social criticism never died, but many wished for the death of ironists who brought the incongruity and hypocrisy of American policy into sharp focus. It is difficult to imagine an invective that *wasn't* hurled at Susan Sontag when, shortly after 9/11, she observed: "The disconnect between last Tuesday's monstrous dose of reality and the self-righteous drivel and outright deceptions being peddled by public figures and TV commentators is startling, depressing." Far from cowardly and unprovoked, she argued, the attack responded to American alliances and actions—such as killing hundreds of thousands of Iraqis.[24] Mayor Koch consigned Sontag to the ninth circle of hell.

Shortly thereafter, Bill Maher indicted the irony of American policy, bringing down the wrath of the White House. He wondered why nineteen hijackers who immolated themselves are derided as cowards while airmen who bomb civilians with impunity are not. Questioned about the president's response, Press Secretary Ari Fleischer warned: "It's a terrible thing to say. . . . Americans need to watch what they say, watch what they do, and this is not a time for remarks like that; there never is."[25]

The ironic outcome of actual policy-making—the chasm between expectations and results—is far more serious than incongruous criticism. 9/11 was the outcome of the administration's incompetence and hubris: Time and again, Bush and his advisors dismissed warnings about an imminent attack. Charged with managing America's initial response to 9/11, Clarke tells a familiar story, the same tale of hubris that led to Pearl Harbor, stalemate in Korea, and a quagmire in Vietnam: overestimating American prowess while underestimating adversaries.

According to Clarke, CIA Director George Tenet warned the president no less than forty times of the imminent al-Qaeda threat. Bush dismissed bin Laden as "that little man in Afghanistan"; he had "no interest in swatting flies." Clarke warned of al-Qaeda as soon as Bush assumed office; he called for an urgent meeting on January 25, 2001. "My message was stark: al-Qaeda is at war with us . . . it is clearly planning a major series of attacks against us; we must act decisively and quickly."[26]

The neo-conservatives dominating the Bush administration didn't take Clarke seriously. Iraq was their idée fixe. In 1998 these authors of the *Project for a New American Century*, officials such as Rumsfeld and Wolfowitz, urged Clinton to attack Iraq: "What is needed now is a comprehensive political and military strategy for bringing down Saddam and his regime."[27] Clinton wasn't receptive; Bush was.

Clarke laments the tragic irony:

> Nothing else could have so well negated all our other positive acts. . . . It was as if Usama bin Laden, hidden in some high mountain redoubt, were engaging in long-range mind control of George Bush, chanting "invade Iraq, you must invade Iraq."[28]

The administration finally acquiesced to Clarke's pleas and convened on September 4, 2001. Clarke recalls the meeting as a nonevent. I sense he felt like that unwelcomed relative one must invite to Thanksgiving dinner despite his annual conspiratorial diatribes. "Rumsfeld, who looked distracted . . . took the Wolfowitz line that there were other terrorist concerns, like Iraq."[29]

Given his newfound credibility, the principals of the Bush administration met with Clarke the day after the attack. He was stunned to learn that Rumsfeld and Wolfowitz exploited 9/11 as a pretext to attack Iraq. This made as much sense to Clarke as attacking Mexico in response to Pearl Harbor. Bush and the others urged Clarke to find evidence that Iraqis orchestrated the 9/11 attack, and that they possessed weapons of mass destruction. He found none. The 9/11 Commission drew the same conclusion.

Blowback

In narrating his tenure as the government's chief counterterrorism agent, Clarke discloses his role in events that inflamed jihadists. There's no mea culpa, just an unembellished account. In planning the first Iraq War, the first Bush administration feared Iraqi forces might attack Saudi Arabia. Accordingly, they sent a delegation headed by Clarke to persuade the Saudis to station American forces in their Kingdom. As he explains: Thousands of American soldiers and civilians profaned the sacred space of the Kingdom that hosted Islam's holiest shrines. Bin Laden took it personally. Not only did the Saudis appease the crusaders, but they also favored the infidels and rejected bin Laden's offer to safeguard the Kingdom.

Clarke mentions his involvement supporting Afghan jihadists in their battle against Soviet forces. Working with the Saudis, he reveals that Prince Turki, director of Saudi intelligence, relied upon one Usama bin Laden, to recruit, move, train, and indoctrinate the Arab volunteers in Afghanistan.[30]

Clarke didn't enamor himself to the Arab world by facilitating Israeli military advantage. In addition to supplying Israel with the latest weapons such as Patriot missiles, his negotiations enabled American personnel to operate out of Israel. As he observes—apparently without regret: "Closer relationship with Tel Aviv did over time inflame some Arab radicals and give them propaganda to help recruit terrorists to their anti-American cause."[31]

No Sympathy for the Devil

Bin Laden's complaints are not without merit. He accused the United States of doing what Clarke admits: occupying and profaning sacred space on the Arabian Peninsula, killing tens of thousands of Muslims, and enthusiastically supporting Israelis while ignoring the plight of Palestinians. Any attempt to recognize, let alone to understand, these grievances was sacrilegious in the aftermath of 9/11. As Stampnitzky notes, subsequent discussions of terrorism degenerated into theological debates about the nature of evil. She concurs with experts such as Brian Jenkins: Officials struggled to understand the Nazis; the same efforts are essential to understand jihadists.[32]

Jenkins's intellectual efforts get C-Span coverage and academic references. Celebrity experts such as David Frum—credited with coining the phrase "Axis of Evil"—enjoy a wider audience. In addition to appearances on network TV, he's often the token right-wing celebrity on the popular, left-leaning Bill Maher show. Frum—Bush's speechwriter—attributes 9/11 to al-Qaeda's irredeemable evil, an evil to be destroyed, not understood. Invading Iraq would begin the creative destruction and create a democratic ally—a harbinger of better days in the Middle East.

Frum's well-publicized, coauthored (Richard Perle) Manichean narrative, *An End to Evil: How to Win the War on Terror,* far outsells the works of the traditional experts.[33] The authors stress American innocence and idealism. They commend Americans for their initial resolve in eradicating terrorism, but they fear such resolve is flagging. Worse yet, the War on Terror—waged in Iraq as it must be—has become a partisan issue. Evidently, Democrats would rather win elections than win the War on Terror.

The authors insist that trying to understand terrorism is worse than futile—no light emerges from such a black hole—it verges on blasphemy if not treason. Stampnitzky calls this sensibility "anti-knowledge"; I call it cognitive insolence. Those who would understand what makes terrorists tick have sympathy for the devil. Unspeakable evil cannot be understood, let alone contained: "End this evil before it strikes again and on a genocidal scale . . . It is victory or holocaust."[34] Indeed, the only thing to understand is that, like Hitler, due to some unfathomable evil, Islamic terrorists are bent upon destruction and world domination.

Promoting the president's view, the authors insist that Iraq is *the* enemy in the War on Terror. Given his clever, diabolic nature, Hussein has hidden weapons of mass destruction and concealed his alliance with bin Laden. (Shortly after the book appeared, the Bush administration reluctantly endorsed Clarke's intelligence assessment, along with the conclusions of the 9/11 Commission: There were no WMDs, and Hussein and bin Laden were not allies—Iraq had no connection with 9/11.) According to the authors, the partisan pessimists don't appreciate the stunning overthrow of the Hussein regime; they dwell on a few "dead-enders"—at worst, a minor nuisance as Iraq emerges as a fragile democracy. Just as things were "a bit messy" after the American Revolution, things were bound to be a bit "untidy" after overthrowing Hussein. Writing in 2003, the authors find much to celebrate: "We liberated an entire nation, opening the way to a humane, decent society . . . and to reform of the ideological and moral climate of the whole Middle East."[35]

The authors foresaw a long, but not endless, war. Like former CIA Director James Woolsey, Frum and Perle, in effect, advocated World War IV. According to Woolsey, the Cold War was World War III. "[The] new war is actually against three enemies: the religious rulers of Iran, the 'fascists' of Iraq and Syria, and Islamic extremists like al-Qaeda." Woolsey added that World War IV should make the Egyptians and Saudis nervous—they could be next.[36] The democracy the oppressed people of the Middle East desire can and must be imposed by force. (After all, wasn't American democracy created by force of arms?) Dreams of a peaceful world, if they ever come true, will be ushered in and defended by American armed might.[37]

Are Responses to 9/11 Overwrought?

> *Dear foreign policy therapist. I want to be safe. I want safety. But I have a terrible problem. . . . I lost several thousand loved ones to a horrible crime. I feel an overwhelming need to apprehend and punish those who committed this unbearably cruel act, but they designed their crime in such a diabolical fashion that I cannot do so, because they arranged to be killed themselves while committing the crime, and they are now all dead.*
>
> —Wallace Shawn[38]

Have the "foreign policy therapists" created a safer homeland? How have Clarke's successors fared? It appears they've done very well indeed. As of this writing, nothing comparable to 9/11 has occurred. Initially, American officials and the public construed 9/11 as a harbinger—the worst was yet to come. The question was not "What?" but "When?" Happily—as of this writing—all's quiet on the American front.

What accounts for such apparent success? According to the widely accepted view, 9/11 got the government's attention. Officials put a vast, highly efficient security apparatus in place; there hasn't been another 9/11 or anything comparable in the United States. Is this prima facie evidence of Homeland Security's effectiveness? Perhaps. The official story could be correct. That said, alternative explanations are worth entertaining.

Writing in *International Security*, analysts Mueller and Stewart suggest another explanation: bin Laden got lucky; 9/11 was an aberration—his best shot and only shot. Just as enemies can be grossly underestimated, they can be grossly overestimated—often at their first signs of success. "It seems increasingly likely that the . . . reaction to the terrorist attack of September 11, 2001, has been substantially deluded—massively disproportionate to the threat that al-Qaida has ever actually presented . . . as an international menace."[39]

The authors cite Glenn Carle, a former CIA intelligence officer, who claims the post-9/11 terrorist threat is greatly exaggerated: "Americans have become victims of delusion displaying a quality defined as a persistent false belief in the face of strong contradictory evidence."[40] Indeed, there is an inverse relationship between the number of terrorist attacks and the amount of alarmist rhetoric. The evidence is found in the authors' glosses on fifty post-9/11 threats to American citizens, unsuccessful threats perpetrated by the likes of shoe bombers and underwear bombers. The authors are not in awe of such would-be terrorists.[41]

Anxious moments regarding terrorism seem out of proportion. The authors are right. Based upon the past thirteen years, the chances of death by terrorism—within American borders—are about the same as being struck by lightning or drowning in the bathtub. The National Consortium for the Study of Terrorism and Responses to Terrorism concludes that terrorist attacks and attempted attacks in the United States have become less frequent since the 1970s—though September 11 was a tragic exception. An American citizen has a 1 in 20 million chance of perishing at the hands of a terrorist both here and overseas. However, in recounting this study, the *Washington Post* suggests that "terrorist attacks obviously loom much larger in our collective consciousness—not least because they're designed to horrify. So, understandably, they get much more attention."[42]

And yet, the United States remains exquisitely vulnerable to those who would harm the homeland. The authors are dismissive regarding the prospect of non-state actors constructing nuclear weapons. The Kennedy School's Graham Allison is not. In a jeremiad titled *Nuclear Terrorism*, he argues that such a threat is a real—albeit preventable—possibility.[43] Ruminations regarding future threats are speculative. What's not: The seemingly endless Iraq War—the frontline of Bush's War on Terror—foments newfound enemies.

IRAQ: A NEVER-ENDING STORY

I think for us to get American military personnel involved in a civil war inside Iraq would literally be a quagmire. Once we got into Baghdad, what would we do? Who would we put in power? . . . I do not think the United States wants to have US military forces accept

*casualties and accept the responsibility or try to govern Iraq. I think
it makes no sense at all.*
—Dick Cheney's 1991 admonition about deposing
Hussein and occupying Iraq[44]

Dick Cheney sometimes undergoes a change of heart. Currently, the
Iraq War enters its fourth phase, and it's not going as planned, in part
because Cheney didn't heed his own admonition. Many factors drive
the war—how could it be otherwise? Even so, a relentless passion informs each phase—reaffirming Thucydides's truism, standing things
aright. No longer would the likes of weak Koreans, Vietnamese, Iraqi,
and non-state actors do what they can and make the United States
suffer the consequences. The time was long overdue for the United
States to impose *its* will.

Other responses were logically possible following the 9/11 attack,
but what were the real, historical possibilities? The attack could have
been construed as a tragedy: nothing to be done—the perpetrators
died. The attack could have been construed as a heinous crime: The
British saw IRA bombing in London as such a crime; they pursued the
perpetrators rather than bombing Belfast. Likewise, US authorities
could have covertly pursued the planners with special forces—as they
eventually did in assassinating bin Laden. It would, however, have been
political suicide for the Bush administration to do nothing. The public
demanded a massive display of revenge.

In October 2001 the Bush administration invaded Afghanistan to
depose the Taliban regime. They claimed the regime provided sanctuary for al-Qaeda and its notorious leader, bin Laden. Allied with certain
tribes, the United States quickly deposed the Taliban but failed to capture bin Laden. By 2003, despite the ensuing chaos, Afghanistan faded
into an afterthought. The administration's unrequited passion lay with
regime change in Iraq.

True to his campaign promise, Obama renewed American efforts in
Afghanistan with a surge of 30,000 troops and additional aid. There are,
to be sure, differences between the conflicts in Iraq and Afghanistan.
Even so, there's a common denominator: overestimating American
strength and underestimating enemy prowess in borderless conflicts
with evanescent enemies. Once again, expectations didn't match results. The ironic outcome, provoking what you intend to prevent, applies to both cases.

The Iraq War began in 1991 when the first Bush administration drove Iraqi forces out of Kuwait—making the desert fiefdom safe for feudalism. The Clinton administration imposed harsh sanctions coupled with sporadic cruise missile attacks. The latter-day Bush administration invaded Iraq in 2003, granting the neocons' long-requited wishes. In spring 2014, following American withdrawal, Sunni jihadists captured major cities along with oil-producing facilities. Each phase, in its own way, reaffirms the tragic irony of American policy.

In this context, I cannot do justice to the complexities of a conflict that, thus far, has lasted five times longer than US involvement in World War II. Once again, Prometheus stopped mortals from foreseeing doom by sowing in them blind hope. Redolent with ironic twists, the ongoing war mocks its perpetrators. Saddam Hussein, a beneficiary of American largesse during the Reagan administration, became "Hitler incarnate" during the Bush administrations. Both Bush administrations expressed affection and respect for the Iraqi people; even so, they perished in staggering numbers. The first Iraq War became a *casus belli* for jihadists. The second, meant to express irrepressible American might, displayed American limitation in no uncertain terms. I am not the first to note the irony of George W. Bush's May 2003 choreographed landing on that aircraft carrier just off San Diego: theater for a somewhat premature declaration—"Mission Accomplished."

The First Gulf War

> Forty-three successive days of bombardment by US manned bombers, cruise missiles, and laser-guided explosives decimated Iraq's civilian infrastructure, much as Anglo-American forces had done in the air war against Germany and Japan.
>
> —John Dower[45]

Why was there a Gulf War in the first place? Hussein's grievances were not patently unreasonable. Recognizing that, in the aftermath of World War I, the British arbitrarily carved up the Middle East, Hussein argued that Kuwait rightly belonged to Iraq, a nineteenth province—it was part of the Basra *vilayet* during the Ottoman Empire. More significant, Hussein, with American backing, acquired onerous debts in fighting Iran. In his view, the prosperous Kuwaitis didn't pay their share. Worse yet, they siphoned oil from Iraqi reserves.

It appears that Ambassador April Glaspie gave Hussein the green light to invade Kuwait. After apologizing for unfavorable coverage of the dictator in American media, the ambassador famously allowed: "We have no opinion on the Arab-Arab conflicts, like your border disagreement with Kuwait."[46] In fall 1990 the Iraqis invaded Kuwait, an invasion that cost thousands of Kuwaiti lives. The Bush administration issued an ultimatum: withdraw or face American forces.

Critics of American policy, especially leftists and pacifists, claim the war was about oil—"No blood for oil!" The first Bush administration insisted policy was driven by ideals: punishing and redressing the violation of Kuwaiti sovereignty. A US Army document, drafted by their official historian, supports the leftist and pacifist perspective:

> For the American government and President George H. W. Bush, the first priority [of Desert Shield and Desert Storm] quickly became the defense of Saudi Arabia. Disruption of Kuwaiti oil supplies was damaging enough to the global economy; disruption of Saudi oil supplies could be disastrous. The Saudis shared Bush's view, and their leadership overcame an established national antipathy toward allowing foreign troops into their kingdom.[47]

Strategically, Iraq was little more than a filling station, but one administered by an unscrupulous manager who might gouge and manipulate the world's supply. Kuwaiti oil and financial assets made the dictator a formidable regional force. Unable to control their former ally, US elites feared Hussein might have designs on Saudi Arabia if not other Gulf monarchies. In short, he couldn't be trusted.

The conflict was also about overcoming the Vietnam Syndrome: "Never again will the United States gradually tiptoe into questionable wars without a clear-cut objective, overwhelming military force, an endgame strategy and, most important, the support of Congress and the American people."[48] Of course, once the president drew a line in the sand and proclaimed: "This shall not stand," the conflict was also about Bush's persona, and American credibility and bargaining reputation.

Despite repeated threats Hussein refused to withdraw. Bush launched Operation Desert Storm in January 1991. He overcame the Vietnam Syndrome not simply by projecting military might, but by avoiding mistakes that led to folly in Vietnam, mistakes such as gradual escalation, mistakes that permitted relatively uncensored press coverage. The Powell Doctrine mandated a full-fledged air and ground response, a response that rapidly deployed approximately 500,000 troops to Saudi Arabia and Kuwait. And unlike Vietnam, Bush got the imprimatur of the UN. Negotiations and financial incentives persuaded other nations to contribute token forces to an American operation.

General Norman Schwarzkopf commanded the operation:

> Soldiers, sailors, airmen, and Marines of the United States Central Command, this morning at 0300, we launched Operation DESERT STORM, an offensive campaign that will enforce the United Nations' resolutions that Iraq must cease its rape and pillage of its weaker neighbor and withdraw its forces from Kuwait. My confidence in you is total. Our cause is just! Now you must be the thunder and lightning of Desert Storm. May God be with you, your loved ones at home, and our Country. [49]

The campaign began with aerial bombardment summarized in an official Air Force document highlighting air superiority that destroyed "the strategic industrial and military targets which keep a military running. Electricity, oil, communications, supply depots and transportation modes are vital to any nation's ability to use military power." The Air Force launched 65,000 sorties. B-52s delivered over 25,700 tons of munitions. The campaign introduced smart weapons: "7,400 tons of precision munitions with the ability to precisely kill military targets while minimizing civilian casualties." Based upon this performance, the Air Force concludes it's the best in the world: "From the early hours over Baghdad to the final minutes in Kuwait City, the United States Air Force proved it is the world's best." [50]

Not to be outflanked, the US Army celebrated its victory—a hundred-hour rout of Iraqi forces. Army historian Jeffrey Clarke claims the Army overcame the Vietnam Syndrome. Desert Storm provided absolution: Victorious troops would "show the world how effective, and needed, it was. The United States would send the best-prepared force America had ever deployed in response to naked aggression in the Persian Gulf." [51]

Civilian casualties are briefly noted amid extended accounts of maneuvers and battles. Hapless citizens unknowingly put themselves in harm's way as they fled Kuwait City to avoid the massive US assault. Pilots gunning in the turkey shoot on the "Highway of Death":

> Could see hundreds of burning and exploding vehicles, including civilian automobiles, buses, and trucks. Hundreds more raced west out of Kuwait City to unknowingly join the deadly traffic jam. Here and there, knots of drivers, Iraqi soldiers, and refugees fled into the desert because of the inferno of bombs, rockets, and tank fires.[52]

On this side of the Atlantic, who—other than a few critics—cared? Critics insisted that Desert Storm and its aftermath fit their operational definition of terrorism: hundreds of thousands of Iraqis perished due to the destruction of the infrastructure and sanctions. However, for the war planners and most of their constituents, the stunningly quick victory proved that, at last, war is good clean fun. Good because the mission was accomplished. Clean because, supposedly, careful targeting and precision weapons limited civilian casualties. Fun? TV coverage beat any video game.

The popular media readily acquiesced to de facto government censorship: Press pools restricted access to the war's brutality. Journalist John MacArthur's account of the unprecedented censorship quotes Joseph Lelyveld, *New York Times* managing editor: "The First Amendment gives us the right to publish just about anything. It doesn't give us the right to go anywhere."[53] The press did what it was told with little protest.

Perhaps censorship was unnecessary. Entertainment trumped news and analysis. The networks spent considerable sums on animation, graphics, and music to attract viewers—and sponsors. Few were dismayed although "Some editorial writers asked if dazzling graphics and upbeat soundtracks had given war the ambience of football playoffs and African adventure movies."[54]

Media promoting Desert Storm relied upon the newfound popularity of video games: "Never before had carefully designed imagery so dominated the coverage. . . . The imagery harmonized perfectly with the Pentagon's plans to hide the killing."[55] Schwarzkopf's press conferences featured video games—Lawrence of Arabia in *Star Wars*. Glued to our student union's new big screen, viewers shrieked approval as smart bombs flashed down chimneys, demolished tanks, and severed bridges—much cooler than *Super Mario*.

Rightly and wrongly, the generals of World War II evoked solemnity and respect. In an ironic age of kitsch, "Schwarzkopf" became a designer brand *and* a foil for amusement. The extended title of an op-ed piece says it all: "The Lines Are Formin' For Norman. Everyone Wants This All-Star Gem Of A Four-Star General, For Ads, Lectures, TV, Books, Movies. All The Witty And Winning Norman Schwarzkopf Has To Do Is Put Them In His Game Plan." The commentator foresaw a prosperous future for "Stormin' Norman." "Everything's positive," gushed one publicity honcho. "It's all clean! The guy just won big-time in Iraq. What more could an ad exec, or book publisher, or lecture agent, or Hollywood producer ask for? Beverly Hills agent Irving 'Swifty' Lazar had already written Schwarzkopf, offering him a $4 million book deal."[56]

War, ever-profitable, became a laughing matter. Times were good for Schwarzkopf impersonators and who better than his doppelganger, comedian Jonathan Winters. Decked out as the General, Winters boasted of "Air Superiority"—for America West Airlines:

> Comedian Jonathan Winters parodies Gen. Norman Schwarzkopf in an ad aimed at drumming up more business for financially troubled America West Airlines. The new marketing scheme is one of the first to do a comic spoof on the Persian Gulf War, raising questions about whether Americans are ready yet for the playful potshots.[57]

Americans were certainly ready for a reaffirmation of their virility. Desert Storm wasn't about effeminate diplomacy, negotiation, and compromise; it was a tough, hardened, masculine response. Sports metaphors showed what a full court press could do—a slam-dunk. No one blinked, let alone withdrew, when Hussein threatened "the mother of all battles." But all was not well. War-planners attained their anticipated climax, but they didn't respect themselves the morning after.

Sic Transit Gloria

Schwarzkopf wasn't so tough after all. He didn't go all the way by conquering Baghdad and deposing Hussein. Frum and Perle put it succinctly: "Saddam had survived; therefore we had lost." In what may be grist for the Freudian mill, George W. Bush vowed: "Dad made a mistake not going into Iraq when he had an approval rating in the nineties. If I'm ever in that situation, I'll use it—I'll spend my political capital."[58]

Celebrations didn't last long. Officials had second thoughts. Desert Storm became a Pyrrhic victory—Hussein remained in power. War-planners preferred to forget that they encouraged, but failed to support, Shia and Kurd rebellions, insurrections crushed by weapons Schwarz-kopf allowed Hussein to keep. And they'd rather not think about how the war became a *casus belli* for jihadists such as bin Laden.

Bin Laden remembered Desert Storm when he told a *Frontline* reporter: "They kill and murder our brothers. They compromise our honor and our dignity and dare we utter a single word of protest against the injustice, we are called terrorists." Bin Laden deeply resented infi-del forces in the sacred spaces of Saudi Arabia. (Catholics would not take kindly to Muslim contingents occupying Vatican City.)[59] To be sure, these grievances don't justify killing 3,000 innocent civilians on 9/11. What justifies killing hundreds of thousands of Iraqis by destroying their infrastructure and by imposing Draconian sanctions?

The Aftermath

The Air Force flew 65,000 sorties and dropped over 33,000 tons of explosives, in part, to destroy the military value of "electricity, oil, com-munications, supply depots, and transportation." What's left unsaid: These assets were indispensable for sustaining civilian life and well-being. Infrastructure destruction led to starvation and disease. Clinton administration sanctions compounded the suffering.

Desert Storm"s impact on civilians got minimum coverage in the United States. However, it left an indelible impression in the Middle East. *PBS Frontline* estimated that three million Iraqis escaped to neighboring countries. "Children died from typhoid, dehydration, and dysentery. Some refugees were blown up by land mines. At one point in 1991, an estimated 2,000 Kurds were dying every day. The UN High Commissioner for Refugees called the exodus the largest in its forty-year history."[60]

Hussein had some culpability for the disaster that befell the Iraqis; however, appropriate weight must be given to the actions—or inac-tions—of the United States and the United Nations. They deliberately neglected their responsibilities in the "Food for Oil" program. As Tir-man explains: Hussein's tactics were minor compared to American actions including denying vaccines and other medicines. "Tactics of delay and obstruction practiced by the United States led to successive UN chiefs in Baghdad and other UN officials resigning in protest." Tirman quotes UN official Denis Halliday: "We are . . . destroying an entire society. I had been instructed to implement a policy that satisfies the definition of genocide: a deliberate policy that has effectively killed well over a million individuals."[61]

Estimates of Iraqi casualties precipitated by infrastructure destruction and sanctions vary. However, by all accounts, Iraqis faced a catastrophe of Biblical proportions. Just after the war, the Harvard School of Public Health estimated that 170,000 Iraqi children would perish due to the destruction of the Iraqi infrastructure.[62] By 2000, UNICEF estimated that 500,000 children under five years of age had died due to malnutrition and lack of medicine.[63]

Clinton's UN ambassador, Madeleine Albright, acknowledged American responsibility for the suffering that befell Iraqis. Interviewing Albright on *60 Minutes* (May 12, 1996), Lesley Stahl questioned the morality of US sanctions: "We have heard that a half million children have died. I mean, that's more children than died in Hiroshima. And, you know, is the price worth it?" Secretary Albright responded: "I think this is a very hard choice, but the price—we think the price is worth it."[64]

Andrew Bacevich is not persuaded:

> [Her] response once again expressed a perspective that enjoyed wide currency and that still remains central to the Washington consensus. American purposes are by definition enlightened. The pursuit of exalted ends empowers the United States to employ whatever means it deems necessary. If US-enforced sanctions had indeed caused the deaths of 500,000 Iraqi children, at least those children had died in a worthy cause. . . . It was conviction encased in an implacable sense of righteousness.[65]

As the Army document suggests, this sense of righteousness prompted a return to Iraq to settle scores: a "return to the Persian Gulf region in force to settle, once and for all, with Hussein."[66]

The Second Gulf War

The supreme irony, of course, is that a military action aimed to awing the world degenerated quickly into an embarrassing advertisement of the limits of US conventional military supremacy and of the persistence of American public intolerance of protracted warfare against irregular enemies. The Iraq War's primary strategic beneficiaries have been al-Qaeda, Iran, and China, not Iraq or the United States.
—Jeffrey Record, Strategist, US Air War College[67]

Record urges that Americans deserve an explanation as to why the United States got embroiled in a war against a country that posed no significant threat. "It still isn't possible to be sure—and this remains the most remarkable thing about the Iraq War."[68] While he lists plausible reasons, he's unnerved by uncertainty, uncertainty shared by analysts such as John Mearsheimer and Stephen Walt:

The decision to overthrow Saddam Hussein even now seems difficult to fathom. . . . In the aftermath of 9/11, when one would have expected the United States to be focusing laser-like on al-Qaeda, the Bush administration chose to invade a deteriorating country that had nothing to do with the attacks on the World Trade Center and the Pentagon and was already effectively contained. From this perspective, it *is* a deeply puzzling decision.[69]

It's as if Bush is likened to Meursault—the anti-hero in Camus's *The Stranger* who kills an Arab for no apparent reason. Or, more charitably, to Sir Edmund Hillary, who famously quipped that he conquered Mount Everest because "it was there." As Record quips: Perhaps Iraqi Freedom "was just something people wanted to do." As the *Project for a New American Century Report* indicates, it *was* something people just wanted to do ever since 1998.

I admire such candor. And to be sure, a comprehensive, fully satisfying account of the war eludes us—there's nothing comparable to the *Pentagon Papers*. That said, we're not completely in the dark. Ironists know there are always very good reasons for war—and the real reasons. These analysts recognize the speciousness of Bush's very good reasons: No weapons of mass destruction were found, and Iraq bore no responsibility for 9/11. (Bin Laden and Hussein were mortal enemies.) It's curious, however, that these analysts fail to recognize several real rea-

THE WAR ON TERROR

sons that informed Iraqi Freedom—oil and geopolitics. While the war cannot be reduced to these factors, they must be given appropriate weight.

We can take it on high authority that the war, in large measure, is about oil. It's obvious to General John Abizaid, former head of Military Operations in Iraq. "Of course it's about oil; we can't really deny that." Alan Greenspan, former Federal Reserve Chairman concurs: "I am saddened that it is politically inconvenient to acknowledge what everyone knows: The Iraq war is largely about oil." Defense Secretary Chuck Hagel said the same thing in 2007: "People say we're not fighting for oil. Of course we are."[70]

The US Embassy in Baghdad literally and figuratively represents the role of geopolitics—a permanent American presence in the center of the Middle East. It is by far the nation's largest, most heavily fortified diplomatic outpost, housing thousands of personnel. It provides the security of Fort Knox, the consumer attractions of an all-American shopping center, and many of the amenities of a Club Med. (The buffet's dessert table does look tempting.) A sense of probity prevails: fearing perhaps that personnel might curse their predicament in Iraq, a sign warns, "This is a profanity free establishment."[71]

Oil is not listed as one of Record's plausible possibilities. However, he makes oblique reference to geopolitical concerns when he suggests that the 2003 invasion enhanced the Israeli sense of security and bolstered Iraq as a countervailing force against neighboring Iran. In addition, Record and the others recognize the neo-conservative (neocon) obsession with Iraq and the shame of unfinished business—settling scores.

Hussein allegedly conspired to assassinate the first President Bush during his visit to Kuwait. And of course Hussein's rhetoric along with violations of the US-imposed no-fly zones were neuralgic points. Regime change was long overdue. The change would be quick, decisive, and easy. Compared to the Iranian and North Korean regimes rotating 'round the Axis of Evil, Iraq was the easiest to grab. Those other rogue states would get the message—counterterrorism is also the propaganda of the deed.

Blinded by Hope

The neocon's grandiosity merits further attention; their dreams were not fueled by oil alone. Confidently improvising their dreams assured that irony would never die. Neocon intellectuals such as Francis Fukuyama dispelled any doubts by bestowing blind hope. War-planners weren't bound by the usual historical circumstances; they recognized and embraced a new zeitgeist. History was at an end; indeed, it had an end—American-style corporate liberalism. Contests between ideologies were over—America won:

> What we may be witnessing is not just the end of the Cold War, or the passing of a particular period of post-war history, but the end of history as such: that is, the end point of mankind's ideological evolution and the universalization of Western liberal democracy as the final form of human government.[72]

Not only must America get on the right side of post-history, it must not forswear its democratizing ideals. Perhaps more significant, Uncle Sam must not betray his gender—so historian Robert Kagan implied in his essay "Americans Are from Mars, Europeans Are from Venus."[73] Hitting below the belt, Kagan derived his title from a popular book contrasting masculine and feminine traits. Effete, testosterone-challenged Europeans refused to support robust, preventive wars. Given French criticism of the coming invasion, the congressional restaurant acted decisively: French fries became "freedom fries." (Given that "algebra" is an Arabic term, perhaps it should have been changed to "freedom math." And what of Arabic numerals?)

A manly America would usher in Fukuyama's world beyond history. If America fulfilled its destiny, the captives of Middle Eastern tyrants would soon enjoy regimes with an American accent—if only America would act, not ruminate about al-Qaeda's motives and the history of imperialism. Rather than paralysis induced by weakness and passivity, a "masculine response, the natural riposte of heroes, was to go to war; and go to war against the savage."[74]

Cheney knew the Iraqis would welcome such manly liberators:

> They're going to welcome us. It will be like the American army going through the streets of Paris. They're sitting there ready to form a new

government. The people will be so happy with their freedoms that we'll probably back ourselves out of there within a month or two.[75]

It takes a flair for the obvious to recognize the irony—although Cheney remains unapologetic. Two neglected ironies invite further scrutiny:

1. Officials predicted the occupation of Iraq would emulate the successful occupation of Japan; what went wrong?
2. Both Bush administrations expressed affection for the Iraqi people; why do we always hurt the one we love?

The Occupation

> *To invoke Japan as some sort of assurance that the United States could easily win the peace once it had been victorious . . . was to engage in false analogy and magical thinking.*
>   —John Dower[76]

Operation Iraqi Freedom is notable for its lack of postwar planning. Cheney and the others apparently believed their own ideology: Some semblance of American-style liberal democracy—free elections *and* free markets—would inevitably follow a quick regime change. In accord with Fukuyama's arc of historical progress, democracy somehow automatically follows the demise of tyranny. Another hundred-hour rout would set the stage for a fledgling democracy—and a new American ally—in the midst of the Arab world. Doubts were grounds for dismissal. Military men who knew more about war, and the Middle East, than they cared to were skeptical. General Eric Shinseki got fired for suggesting 100,000 troops were essential for an inevitably chaotic occupation.[77]

Iraq fell apart; the center no longer held. Nevertheless, reluctant to admit their misjudgments, the neocons proclaimed the occupation a blessing in disguise. Postwar Japan proved that democracy could flourish in exotic climes, so could Iraq. Inspired by a shining city in the desert, Iraq's neighbors would follow suit.

Tempting historical analogies are the stuff of wishful thinking: they highlight similarities between events while concealing differences. Officials usually deal with temptation by giving in. To be sure, there were similarities. Imperial Japan and Iraq were non-Western, brutally authoritarian, militarist regimes subject to massive US intervention. But much was left unsaid.

We won't be buying products "Made in Iraq" any time soon. Dower directs attention to the differences between Japan 1945 and Iraq 2003. The United States enjoyed uncontested legitimacy—even Soviet approval—in occupying Japan. Images of MacArthur towering over the emperor pleased Japan's neighbors—feckless victims of Japanese aggression. The Bush Doctrine of preventive war deeply troubled American allies, especially the French and Germans. Save for Israel, Iraq's neighbors resented US intrusion in the Middle East: Another round of killing Muslims didn't win favor. Any residual legitimacy evaporated in the absence of weapons of mass destruction and fictions about the role of Hussein in 9/11.

American officials wisely kept the emperor and the Japanese bureaucracy in place. Shock and Awe replaced Iraqi leadership with inexperienced Americans. Concerned primarily with quantitative calculations of troops, aircraft, and ordnance, planners were indifferent to soft subjects such as history and anthropology. Japan was a homogenous culture with a venerated heritage. As Bush would learn, the British created Iraq ad hoc out of three Ottoman provinces. The Turks realized there was nothing new about animosity between these provinces, animosity traced back to the seventh century. The Turks, and Saddam Hussein, kept the Shia, Sunni, and Kurds at bay. The Americans would also learn of tribal, clan, and familial animosity unleashed with the demise of the Hussein regime. American actions in Iraq destroyed the leadership, bureaucracy, and much of civil society. Unlike Japan, Iraq had no revered leader exhorting citizens to honor the occupiers. In a final touch of irony, al-Qaeda took advantage of Hussein's demise and infiltrated Iraq's porous borders.

Why Do We Always Hurt The One We Love?

> We come to Iraq with respect for its citizens, for their great civilization and for the religious faith they practice. We have no ambition in Iraq, except to remove a threat and restore control of that country to its own people.
>
> —George W. Bush

Like the war, the irony never ends. The Bush White House continually expressed respect and admiration for Iraqi citizens and their faith and civilization—inconceivable during World War II. (Imagine FDR inviting Japanese clerics and officials to the White House to celebrate their holidays and glorious contributions to civilization.) Unlike Clinton, who succumbed to pressure from his own party, Bush celebrated occasions such as Ramadan, Eid (a post-Ramadan festival), and *Iftars* (dinner parties) with Muslims. Just after 9/11 he reminded Americans

> that most Muslims in their midst are hardworking, loyal American citizens. After lauding Muslim charity and generosity, he declared that "Islam brings hope and comfort to millions of people in my country, and to more than a billion people worldwide . . . Islam gave birth to a rich civilization of learning that has benefited mankind . . . Laura joins me in sending our best wishes to Muslims across America, and throughout the world."[78]

The incongruity between amiable rhetoric and cruel reality is puzzling: Why did the Bush administration praise Iraqis while launching an invasion that directly and indirectly caused hundreds of thousands of deaths? The contrast between a festive White House evening and torture at Abu Ghraib stands out in stark relief. There's something incongruous about effusive expressions of goodwill and "Shock and Awe."

Shock and Awe

As journalist George Packer observes: "America's capacity for mistakes and crimes . . . [is] proportionate to its innocence and self-righteousness."[79] Had bin Laden called his operation "Shock and Awe," it would have been roundly condemned as terrorism. The same designation is not applied to Bush's operation. Once again, critics are politically incorrect: Shock and Awe fits their operational definition of terrorism.

Shock and Awe began with a massive air attack: the destruction of the infrastructure began anew along with predictable civilian casualties. Those who defend American actions point out that, unlike the war against Japan, steps were taken to reduce noncombatant casualties. The United States didn't use every weapon at its disposal (such as nuclear weapons) nor engage in a campaign of total extermination. Precision guided weapons may also have reduced casualties. Despite these restraints, occupation forces randomly raided homes, arrested Iraqis, demolished buildings, and indiscriminately killed in "free fire zones."

According to Air Force documents, US aircraft flew 24,000 sorties during the first six weeks of the war. Apparently, the biggest role of the air campaign occurred in 2007 (twice the number of sorties as the previous year, about 18,000). An air assault to recapture Fallujah relied upon napalm and phosphor weapons—"everything but nuclear weapons."[80] In addition to strategic bombing, airpower played a tactical role in supporting ground operations. However, the majority of civilian casualties resulted from infrastructure destruction, civil war, and combat with American troops.

By and large, the occupation was not welcome relief from the Hussein regime. For those who didn't openly oppose the old regime, life was considerably better compared to surrounding regimes; Iraqis enjoyed a relatively high standard of living. Resentment built as services such as water, electricity, and police protection were no longer taken for granted.[81] An official Rand report to the US Army understates the obvious: Planning for a "free and prosperous post-war Iraq" was not as rigorous and detailed as planning for combat.[82]

Military men lament what might have been had Hussein remained in power. Record speculates:

> How different the world might look now had Bush pocketed his enormous victory of coercing Saddam into accepting an occupation of his country by an inspection regime, an occupation that would have precluded the necessity for a US invasion and made a laughing-stock of Saddam's pretensions on the world stage! It seems that the White House's obsession with removing the Iraqi dictator blocked recognition of its stunning diplomatic triumph.[83]

We don't know what Iraq and the world would be like had Hussein remained in power. He might have become an ally once again in US disputes with Iran, or he might have promoted Sunni insurgency. What we *do* know from the *Lancet* study is that the Iraqi death rate increased dramatically after the US invasion.

Some died amid the Shia/Sunni conflict. Hussein's brutality kept the lid on these perennial antagonists. Hussein kept his enemies close and engaged in brutal purges. He also kept enemies such as al-Qaeda distant. Borders vanished with Hussein's demise. Al-Qaeda established a

franchise—al-Qaeda Iraq. What's the culpability of the Bush administration for opening the lid by deposing Hussein? I can't recommend a
suitable moral metric, nor can I excuse the administration for what they
claim are unintended consequences—they were warned (in 1992) by
authorities such as Cheney, Scowcroft, and by George H. W. Bush
himself. Sometimes it also pays to heed an enemy's warning. Al-Qaeda
gloated over the American Iraqi dilemma: If you stay, you will bleed to
death; if you withdraw, you'll lose everything.[84]

American soldiers bore responsibility for a significant amount of the
suffering; how much is unknowable. As General Tommy Franks allowed, "We don't keep body counts." However, I assign primary responsibility to the war-planners who threw young Americans into an atrocity-producing situation that turned them into "victims and execution-
ers"—to borrow from Camus once again. Those who planned the war
didn't fight; and those who fought didn't plan. Indeed, most of the
planners never fought.

The military bestowed life and death power on eighteen-year-olds
deemed too immature to drink a bottle of beer. Like those before them
in Vietnam, they faced an enemy likened to a quantum particle—invisible, unpredictable, and dangerous. Violence took many forms: a tribal
dispute; atrocities at a Sunni mosque; death squads marauding the city
and countryside; honor killings; road blocks; and house-to-house
searches. Unlike traditional wars, there were no fronts, no trenches, and
no set-pieces to move about a war-gaming board—no way to connect
evanescent dots that were always in motion.[85]

As journalists Hedges and Al-Arian conclude from interviews with
Iraqi combatants: "The campaign against a mostly invisible enemy . . .
has given rise to a culture of terror."[86] It was war against all Iraqis.
Soldiers followed Dick Cheney's 1 percent dictum: only a slight possibility an Iraqi meant harm meant another Iraqi death. Shoot first; no
questions asked later: "Most veterans speak of a world so brutally dangerous and chaotic that it is deemed more prudent to shoot Iraqis who
appear to be a threat."[87]

Death sometimes resulted from misunderstanding. For an American
soldier, an open hand means Stop! For Iraqis it means come closer. A
nodding head means one thing in American culture, and the opposite in
many Arab cultures. Some soldiers appreciated Iraqi frustration and
anger: "If you were in Washington and basically everybody had an AK-

47, and no one had picked up the sewage and waste in six months . . . people would get pretty upset."[88] Even so, nothing this captain could do could remedy the situation. It was "me or them."

It seemed foolhardy to take chances: Any vehicle that looked suspicious or approached too fast got targeted. Unsurprisingly, tragic breakdowns in communication occurred. In order to minimize such breakdowns, the United States devised two-stage checkpoints that would, in theory, minimize casualties. Like Iraqi policy in general, what worked in theory failed in practice. At the first stage, Iraqi soldiers would warn civilians to stop or be shot at the second point operated by Americans. Unfortunately, lax Iraqi soldiers often didn't do their job and waved civilians through. They got shot when they failed to stop at the second point. Veterans regarded these shootings as routine.[89] Many of the American deaths are attributed to attacks on convoys with improvised explosive devices (IEDs). Survivors craved payback and often opened fire on anything in the surroundings. One veteran noted that more IEDs appeared just after US nighttime raids on Iraqi homes.[90]

Secretary of Defense Rumsfeld seemed indifferent to both American and Iraqi casualties. During a visit to Iraq several troops complained about the poor quality of their Humvees, especially vulnerability to IEDs. The Secretary responded: "As you know, you go to war with the army you have, not the army you might want or wish to have at a later time."[91] Rumsfeld and his colleagues didn't get the war they wanted or wished to have at a later time.

The Death of Others

John Tirman, executive director of the Center for International Studies at MIT, believes "The dead of war have something to tell us. The way that wars are fought leaves a signature, a pattern of destruction on the societies where they occur." He became involved in the 2006 *Lancet* study of Iraqi deaths.[92]

The study, conducted by the Johns Hopkins School of Public Health and published in *Lancet* (the premier British science journal) compared death rates before and after the US invasion, and held the invasion directly and indirectly responsible for approximately 655,000 deaths. Relying upon a comparable inquiry, the *New England Journal of Medicine* estimated 400,000 excess deaths. Wikileaks revelations corroborate these figures. The US military provided a much lower estimate—77,000.[93]

The Hopkins study took into account the "general attributes of the society as a whole—geographically, urban/rural, ethnic, and sectarian." The research determined prewar death and postwar death rates in select households. The initial inquiry, conducted after the first seventeen months of warfare, estimated 98,000 additional deaths due to the invasion. The 2006 survey, analyzed by statisticians at several universities, estimated 655,000 additional deaths during the first forty months of war due to the invasion.[94] *Lancet*, of course, peer-reviewed methods and findings prior to publication.

Would Pentagon estimates of 77,000 deaths legitimize Operation Iraqi Freedom? Is the difference between 77,000 and 650,000 merely quantitative, or is it a qualitative difference? No authoritative tribunal exists to provide answers to everyone's satisfaction. Justifying the death of others is self-confessional: It reveals the moral sensibility of the advocate, not an objective state of affairs. In any case, Tirman urges that those who perished deserve representation—the magnitude of the tragedy is not to be ignored. Tirman expresses a wistful hope: Emphasizing the magnitude of the deaths could conceivably chasten war-planners and the American public—but he's pessimistic.

His lamentation brings to mind Camus's anti-hero once again: "I may not have been sure about what really did interest me, but I was absolutely sure about what didn't." During World War II Americans took an enthusiastic interest in the death of Japanese noncombatants. However, as Niall Ferguson quips, "By 1945, it was time for the West to lay down its arms and pick up its shopping bags—to take off its uniform and put on its blue jeans."[95] Ever since then, the death of others became a matter of profound indifference. It occurs under the radar like the cruise missiles that attack enemy lands. Understandably, ordinary Americans are concerned with matters closer to home: family, jobs, finances, and—if they're prosperous—spectacles and commodities.

Rare images of civilian casualties in enemy lands pale beside sensationalized, choreographed violence of primetime entertainment. Even real-time firsthand experiences of actual violence cannot compete with the unreality of virtual, mediated violence. Long ago an attacker killed Kitty Genovese as her neighbors watched from their apartments. No one called the police, let alone intervened. Today we passively watch the destruction of our neighbors in other lands numbed by cold-blooded indifference.

Tirman finds governing elites and their constituents uninterested in hundreds of thousands of refugees who fled Iraq, let alone in the death of a like number of Iraqis. A content analysis reveals of the more than 1,800 stories on six networks (NBC, ABC, CBS, CNN, Fox, and Al-Jazeera) at the war's outset, only seventy-three stories mentioned Iraqi casualties.[96] Would 1,800 accounts of casualties make a difference? As widely lamented voter apathy suggests, ordinary Americans believe they are powerless to effect change—not an unreasonable belief considering the national venue. Sociologist C. Wright Mills said it best long ago: "[Americans] feel that they live in a time of big decisions; they know that they are not making any."[97]

Virginia Woolf believed—or furtively hoped—that widely distributed, shocking pictures of grisly atrocities of World War I and the Spanish Civil War would unite people against war. Today, grisly images are widespread—they no longer shock. As Sontag quips in her account of Woolf's struggle, "Shock has term limits." In her apt metaphor, just as an overexposed photograph fogs out, violence rapidly fades from reality through overexposure.[98] In a torrent of images that Woolf could never imagine, gory scenes—at once entertaining and desensitizing—flash across our high-resolution screens, macho-psychotic video games, and slasher movies. Woolf warned that those not pained by such images can neither grasp reality nor feel empathy—but who's afraid of Virginia Woolf?

The public fears boredom, nor reprobation. Life without an iPhone or the Internet would be unbearable. No problem Googling information about the death of others, but statistics regarding real atrocities are *boring*—statistics don't bleed. Like all else in a culture of spectacles and commodities, violent spectacles are judged in terms of their entertainment value, not their verisimilitude or morality.

At the risk of generalizing from my experience, those of us who traffic in studies of violence cannot do so without what psychiatrist Robert Jay Lifton calls "psychic numbing. . . . How is one to comprehend dimensions of destruction that . . . have little to anything to do with the mind has previously confronted?"[99] Leaders depict the "Other" in surprisingly human terms, leaving us dehumanized, bereft of feelings. Psychic numbing is a cognitive and effective strategy for psychological survival in the world we no longer comprehend or trust.

American officials and their constituents ignore or rationalize Iraqi deaths; jihadists do not. Tirman cites an official US intelligence assessment: "The Iraq conflict has become the cause célèbre for jihadists, breeding a deep resentment of US involvement in the Muslim world and cultivating supporters for the global jihadist movement." The involvement is an answer to a jihadist's prayer. [100]

DRONES: TERRORISM-LITE

Drones hover twenty-four hours a day over communities in northwest Pakistan, striking homes, vehicles, and public spaces; their presence terrorizes men, women, and children, giving rise to anxiety and psychological trauma among civilian communities.
—Stanford/NYU Human Rights Study [101]

Seeking a serious, balanced introduction to the US drone program, I watched the *Frontline* documentary *Rise of the Drones* on Netflix. [102] Naturally, I expected the inimitable voice-over of Will Lyman. As Sean Woods quipped in *Rolling Stone*, "Lyman could read the phone book and make it feel like it's important to the country." [103] The medium—to be entirely unoriginal—is the message. Lyman's ominous inflections mean: Stay tuned for a serious, balanced documentary.

I didn't hear Lyman. Did I accidentally download the latest *Star Wars*? Did Netflix mislabel *Return of the Jedi*? The breathless voice-over suited kid's science fiction; the musical score promised high adventure ahead—in outer space! Drones—as wondrous as Jedi weapons—were replacing old-fashioned fighter pilots and spy planes. No worries about another incident like the U-2 shot down over the Soviet Union. (Khrushchev didn't forgive; he enjoyed a "propaganda field day" and hurled "every invective in the book.") The documentary (sponsored by Lockheed) featured a rogues' gallery of bad guys, such as al-Awalki, killed by drones—no mention of his American citizenship.

The film celebrated the American entrepreneurial spirit. Much like the daring Apple pioneers, Abe Karem invested $18,000 of his own money, and invented the first drone in his garage about thirty years ago. Although the Department of Defense soon supported his efforts, he hoped drones would be used for peaceful purposes. However, according to the voice-over, undeclared air wars in perhaps a score of Middle Eastern and African countries kill with drones.

Drones are the latest technological fix for an intractable problem—managing history. Barack Obama lauds theologian Reinhold Niebuhr as his favorite philosopher. And yet, he ignores the theologian's jeremiads. Even great powers are subject to forces they cannot fully understand, let alone control; they are "caught in a web of history in which many desires, hopes, wills, and ambitions, other than their own, are operative. . . . The recalcitrant forces in the historical drama have a power and persistence beyond our reckoning."[104]

Chastened by policy failures in Iraq and Afghanistan, Obama sought a new approach. Apparently, in order to distance himself from his predecessor, he abandoned the "War on Terror" rubric in favor of a "Contingency Plan." The plan doesn't abandon American hegemonic aspirations; it simply offers a more streamlined, less obtrusive approach. And like previous plans, it gives short shrift to diplomacy, let alone to addressing enemy grievances. Rather than protracted, massive invasions of nation-states such as Iraq and Afghanistan, the plan involves covert operations—"a light footprint." Drones are the centerpiece of the Obama Doctrine.

The documentary mentions *Terminator* films portraying autonomous killer drones commanded by a heartless computer—the signature of a totally administered, surveillance society. Asked about whether such weapons exist, a Department of Defense official responds that they do not, "but we should be so lucky!" At the moment those who manage the American arsenal must settle for the Reaper drone guided by a remote operator.

The Reaper fires Hellfire missiles and drops 500-pound bombs. Operated from virtually anywhere on the globe, it can stay aloft for up to 22 hours at altitudes above 20,000 feet. The Obama administration authorized the use of such a device to assassinate three American citizens in Yemen in 2011.

The assassination of American and foreign nationals presents legal and moral controversies that cannot be resolved to everyone's satisfaction. Like the academic debates regarding the definition of terrorism, the drone program is subject to filigreed discussions of legalities and contesting moral perspectives. Responses to these legal and moral issues reveal what commentators can tolerate, if not applaud. With the exception of those who romanticize chivalrous, medieval combat, enthusiasts this side of the Atlantic laud the drone program for keeping Americans out of harm's way. In this not-so-brave new world: "They only face danger when they [drone operators] leave the job: a sign . . . warns a pilot to 'drive carefully' because this is 'the most dangerous part of your day.'"[105]

However, a surprising number of insiders find the debates about legality and morality impurely academic and distracting; they're concerned with short-term and long-term consequences. For example, Hungju Koh, legal advisor to the US Department of State, quipped: "Sometimes a policy proposal is lawful but awful." A state action may constitute a legal act, but its negative repercussions may outweigh any potential benefit derived from following that course of action."[106]

Practical, potentially resolvable inquiry weighs the results, the possible consequences, of drone policy. It would not be the first time results betrayed expectations. Drones may not be the long-awaited deus ex machina appearing on the world stage just in time to bring order out of chaos in the empire's hinterlands. Seeking yet another technological fix may bring blowback and hubris.

In response to these issues, General John Abizaid and Rosa Brooks authored a *Drone Task Force Report*, a study better balanced and more nuanced than Lockheed's *Frontline* documentary. Other high-ranking military and government officials and members of the intelligence and scientific communities contributed to the report conducted under the auspices of the Stimson Center. The findings endorse official accounts of the short-term consequences of the drone program: al-Qaeda commanders and others bent on harming the homeland were killed, and nefarious plots were disrupted. [107] There is considerable apprehension, however, regarding long-term consequences. Even relatively few civilian casualties "can anger whole communities, increase anti-US sentiment, and become potent recruiting tools for terrorist organizations."[108]

A Stanford/NYU study shares the apprehension. It estimates that, during a fourteen-month period, in Pakistan alone, drones killed 474 civilians, including 176 children; many more may have perished. Official estimates are much lower; the Obama administration asserts that such casualties are "extremely rare." However, the study stresses that even conservative think tanks present higher estimates. The Stanford/

NYU study alludes to a recent exposé in the *New York Times* that partially explains the White House's low estimates. In procedures comparable to Vietcong body counts, the Obama administration considers "all military-age males [killed] in a strike zone to be 'combatants.'"[109]

The Stimson Center report criticizes the current administration for assigning priority to technological fixes rather than seeking venues such as new alliances, diplomacy, and negotiations. The authors fear the precedence: Will other powers feel emboldened to violate national sovereignty with lethal drones; will the reliance on drones foment an arms race, a destabilized world patrolled by ever-more dangerous drones? The center shares a concern of other drone critics who ask troubling questions: Will reliance on drones increase the temptation to conduct secret wars and other covert operations?

In any case, there is reason to fear the long-term consequences of the drone program; it may prove to be an effective recruiting tool for jihadists. Anthropologist Akbar Ahmed's indictment of the drone program seems applicable to every post-World War II campaign: "It is difficult to escape the conclusion that the United States has been fighting the wrong war, with the wrong tactics, against the wrong enemy, and therefore the results can be nothing but wrong."[110]

NOTES

1. Zbigniew Brzezinski, "Terrorized by 'War on Terror,'" *Washington Post*, March 25, 2007, accessed August 1, 2014; http://www.washingtonpost.com/wdyn/content/article/2007/03/23/AR2007032301613.html.

2. Max Weber, *Politics-as-a-Vocation*, quoted and accessed August 1, 2014, http://anthroposlab.net/wp/wp-content/uploads/2011/12/Weber-Politics-as-a-Vocation.pdf.

3. Stampnitzky, Lisa. *Disciplining Terror* (Cambridge: Cambridge University Press, 2013), Kindle Edition, Locations 171–73.

4. Other researchers include Remi Brulin, "Defining Terrorism: The 1972 General Assembly debates on International terrorism and their coverage by the *New York Times*," September 30, 2013, accessed August 1, 2014, www.NYTExaminer.com/2013/09/defining-terrorism/.

5. Stampnitzky, Locations 171–73; also see Remi Brulin, *If It Was Not for Terrorism: Crisis, Compromise, and Elite Discourse in the Age of War on Terror*, Chapter 1, accessed August 2, 2014, in www.NYT.com/203/09/defin-

ing-terrorism; and Glenn Greenwald, "The Sham 'terrorism' expert industry," accessed August 2, 2014, www.salon.com/2012/08/15/the_sham_terrorism_expert_industry/.

6. Sean McManus, "How My Dad Covered the Munich Massacre," *The Hollywood Reporter*, July 27, 2012, accessed August 3, 2014, http://www.hollywoodreporter.com/news/olympics-2012-cbs-sports-sean-mcmanus-munich-massacre-353669>.

7. Albert Wohlstetter, "The Delicate Balance of Nuclear Terror," *Foreign Affairs*, vol. 37, no. 2 (1959), 211–34.

8. See an account of this address accessed August 3, 2014, http://www.bartleby.com/124/pres56.html.

9. Stampnitzky, 252–54.

10. See David A. Korn's account of the incident in his *Assassination in Khartoum* (Bloomington: Indiana University Press, 1993).

11. See for an account of this incident, accessed August 3, 2014, http://www.chicagotribune.com/news/politics/chi-chicagodays-pantherraid-story,0,3414208.story.

12. *FBI Report: Patty Hearst Kidnapping*, accessed August 8, 2014, http://www.fbi.gov/about-us/history/famous-cases/patty-hearst-kidnapping.

13. Ibid.

14. Stampnitzky, Locations 540–50.

15. Ibid., 3642–45.

16. Stephen Walt, "The Myth of American Exceptionalism," in *Foreign Policy*, October 11, 2011, accessed August 8, 2014, http://www.foreignpolicy.com/articles/2011/10/11/the_myth_of_american_exceptionalism.

17. David Miller and Tom Mills, "The terror experts and the mainstream media: the expert nexus and its domination in the news media," *Critical Studies on Terrorism*, Vol. 2, No.3 (2009): 414–37.

18. Noam Chomsky, "The evil scourge of terrorism: Reality, construction, remedy" (Erich Fromm Lecture 2010), Stuttgart, Germany, March 23, 2012, accessed August 8, 2014, http://www.chomsky.info/talks/20100323.htm.

19. Chomsky's works are voluminous. A compendium is found in James Peck, ed., *The Chomsky Reader* (New York: Pantheon, 1987).

20. Bruce Hoffman, *Inside Terrorism* (New York: Columbia University Press, 2006), Kindle Edition. Locations 738–49.

21. Ibid., Locations 766–69.

22. Richard A. Clarke, *Against All Enemies: Inside America's War on Terror* (New York: Simon and Schuster, 2004), Kindle Edition.

23. David Beers defends post-9/11 irony in "Irony is dead! Long live irony!", *Salon.com*, September 25, 2001, accessed August 4, 2014, http://www.salon.com/2001/09/25/irony_lives/.

24. Susan Sontag, *The New Yorker*, September 24, 2001, accessed August 3, 2014, http://www.newyorker.com/magazine/2001/09/24/1256341.

25. Ari Fleischer, September 26, 2001 Press Conference, *Washington Post* transcript, accessed August 4, 2014, http://www.washingtonpost.com/wpsrv/nation/specials/attacked/transcripts/fleischrtext_092601.html.

26. Ibid., 227.

27. Donald Rumsfeld, Paul Wolfowitz, et. al "Open Letter to the President, February 19, 1998," accessed August, 8, 2014, http://www.iraqwatch.org/perspectives/rumsfeld-openletter.htm.

28. Clarke, 247.

29. Ibid., 237–38.

30. Ibid., 246.

31. Ibid., 247.

32. Ibid., Locations 4385–87.

33. David Frum and Richard Perle, *An End to Evil: How to Win the War on Terror* (New York: Random House, 2003), Kindle Edition, Locations 583–85. An early advocate of the invasion of Iraq, Frum currently expresses second thoughts.

34. Ibid., Location 115.

35. Ibid., Location 382.

36. Quoted by Charles Feldman and Stan Wilson, "Ex-CIA Director: U.S. Face World War IV," CNN.com, April 3, 2003, accessed August 4, 2014, http://www.cnn.com/2003/US/04/03/sprj.irq.woolsey.world.war/.

37. Frum and Perle, Location 3487.

38. Wallace Shawn, "The Foreign Policy Therapist," in *A Just Response* (Katrina Vanden Heuvel, ed.) (New York: Nation Books, 2002), 296.

39. John Mueller and Mark Stewart, "The Terrorism Delusion," *International Security*, Vol. 37, No. 1: 95.

40. Ibid., 82.

41. Ibid., 88.

42. Brad Plumer, "Eight facts about terrorism in the United States," Washington Post, April 6, 2003, http://www.washingtonpost.com/blogs/wonkblog/wp/2013/04/16/eight-facts-about-terrorism-in-the-united-states/.

43. Graham Allison: *Nuclear Terrorism: The Ultimate Preventable Catastrophe* (New York: Holt, 2005).

44. Mary Ann Akers, "The Untold Story of the Cheney 'Quagmire' Video" accessed August 8, 2014, voices.washingtonpost.com/.../the_untold_story_of...; the video of Cheney's admonition is available on this site.

45. John W. Dower, *Cultures of War* (New York: W.W. Norton, 2010), 88.

46. "Excerpts From Iraqi Document on Meeting with U.S. Envoy," *New York Times International*, September 23, 1990, 2.

47. Jeffrey J. Clarke, *War in the Persian Gulf: Operations Desert Shield and Desert Storm August 1990-March 1991*, May 2010, accessed August 5, 2014, http://www.history.army.mil/html/books/070/70-117-1/CMH_70-117-1.pdf.

48. Marvin Kalb, "It's Called the Vietnam Syndrome, and It's Back," accessed August 5, 2014, www.brookings.edu/blogs/up-front/posts/2013/01/22-obama-foreign-policy-kalb. The return of the syndrome in the aftermath of the second Gulf War might be called "Gulf War Syndrome."

49. Naval History and Heritage, "General H. Norman Schwartzkopf, USA Commander-in-Chief U.S. Central Command, message, January 16, 1991," accessed August 5, 2014, http://www.history.navy.mil/wars/dstorm/ds5.htm.

50. *White Paper-Air Force Performance in Desert Storm*, Department of the Air Force, April 19, 2003, accessed August 9, 2014, http://www.pbs.org/wgbh/pages/frontline/gulf/appendix/whitepaper.html.

51. Jeffrey C. Clarke, 2.

52. Ibid., 67.

53. Quoted by John A. MacArthur in *Second Front: Censorship and Propaganda in the Gulf War* (New York: Hill and Wang, 1992), 35.

54. Ibid., 80.

55. Ibid.

56. Sandy Bauers, "The Lines Are Formin' For Norman. . . ." *Philadelphia Inquirer*, March 18, 1991, accessed August 5, 2014, http://articles.philly.com/1991-0318/news/25791428_1_norman-schwarzkopf-million-book-deal-war-heroes.

57. Anon. *Deseret News* "Stormin' At Norman," March 9, 1991, accessed August 9, 2014, http://www.deseretnews.com/article/161289/.

58. Quoted by Robert Draper, *Dead Certain: The Presidency of George W. Bush* (New York: Free Press, 2007), 173.

59. John Miller, *Frontline* interview with bin Laden, May 1998, accessed August 9, 2014, http://www.pbs.org/wgbh/pages/frontline/shows/binladen/who/interview.html.

60. Quoted by Tirman, Locations 3569–74.

61. Tirman, Locations 3662–85.

62. The Harvard University School of Public Health estimated that 170,000 Iraqi children would perish from famine and disease due to the destruction of the infrastructure during the 1991 Gulf War and the subsequent sanctions. See Sam Fulwood III and Nick B. Williams Jr., "170,000 Iraqi Children Face Death, Health Study Finds," *Los Angeles Times*, May 21, 1991.

63. Tirman, Locations 3650–52.

64. See "Madeleine K. Albright," Center for Media and Democracy, accessed August 9, 2014, http://www.sourcewatch.org/index.php/Madeleine_K._Albright.

65. Andrew J. Bacevich, *Washington Rules: America's Path to Permanent War* (New York: Metropolitan Books, 2010), 143.

66. James C. Clarke, 4.

67. Jeffrey Record, "Why the Bush Administration Invaded Iraq," *Strategic Studies Quarterly*, Vol. 2, No. 2, (2008): 87.

68. Record, 64.

69. John J. Mearsheimer and Stephen M. Walt, *The Israel Lobby and U.S. Foreign Policy* (New York: Farrar, Straus and Giroux, 2007), 229.

70. Antonia Juhasz, "Special to CNN: Why the war in Iraq was fought for Big Oil," accessed August 11, 2014, http://www.cnn.com/2013/03/19/opinion/iraq-war-oil-juhasz/.

71. "A Look Inside the American Embassy in Baghdad," *New York Times*, February 7, 2009, accessed August 12, 2014, http://www.nytimes.com/slideshow/2012/02/07/world/middleeast/20120208-BAGHDAD-8.html.

72. Francis Fukuyama, "The End of History?" *The National Interest*, Summer 1989, accessed August 12, 2014, http://ps321.community.uaf.edu/files/2012/10/Fukuyama-End-of-history-article.pdf. Initially enthusiastic about the Iraq War, Fukuyama subsequently claimed he was mistaken.

73. See a European critique of Kagan's argument at: accessed August 12, 2014, http://www.telegraph.co.uk/news/worldnews/northamerica/usa/1423535/Americans-are-from-Mars-Europeans-from-Venus.html.

74. Tirman, Locations 3800–3804.

75. Quoted by Robert Draper, *Dead Certain: The Presidency of George W. Bush* (New York: Free Press, 2007), 178.

76. Dower, *Cultures*, 314.

77. Tirman, Locations 3955–57.

78. *Muslim Republicans*, "Welcome All Muslim Republicans," February 2, 2006), accessed August 13, 2014, http//www.muslimrepublicans.net/article.asp?ID=163http.

79. George Packer, *The Assassins' Gate: America in Iraq* (New York; Farrar, Straus and Giroux, 2005), 89.

80. *Air Force Historical Studies Office*, accessed August 13, 2014, http://www.afhso.af.mil.

81. Tirman, Locations 4075–77.

82. Nora Bensahel et al. *After Saddam: Prewar Planning and the Occupation of Iraq*, accessed August, 13, 2013, http://www.rand.org/pubs/monographs/MG642.html.

83. Record, 64.

84. Walter Pincus, "Al-Qa'ida Releases Tape Predicting U.S. Defeat," *Washington Post*, September 10, 2004. Quoted by Hoffman, 399.

85. See Tirman's account, Locations 4342–46.

86. Chris Hedges and Laila Al-Arian, *Collateral Damage: America's War Against Iraqi Civilians* (New York: Nation Books, 2008), xxv.

87. Ibid., 96.

88. Ibid., 97.

89. Ibid., 30.

90. Ibid., 84.

91. "Troops Question Secretary of Defense Rumsfeld About Armor," *PBS Newshour*, December 9, 2004, accessed August 13, 2014, http://www.pbs.org/newshour/bb/military-july-dec04-armor_12-9/.

92. Tirman, Locations 6395–96.

93. Ibid., Locations 5544–47.

94. Ibid., Locations 5730–32.

95. Niall Ferguson, quoted by David Bromwich, "The Disappointed Lover of the West," *The New York Review of Books*, December 8, 2011, Vol. LVIII, #19, 21.

96. Tirman, Locations 3095–96.

97. C. Wright Mills, *The Power Elite* (New York: Oxford University Press, 1957), 5.

98. Susan Sontag offers an account of Woolf's project in *Regarding the Pain of Others* (New York: Farrar, Straus and Giroux, 2003), 7–17.

99. Harry Kriesler, *Robert Jay Lifton Interview: Conversations with History*; Institute of International Studies, UC Berkeley, accessed August 14, 2014, http://globetrotter.berkeley.edu/people/Lifton/lifton-con3.htmlrelationship.

100. See Tirman, Locations 7768–71. Also see Office of the Director of National Intelligence, "Declassified Key Judgments of the National Intelligence Estimate. Trends in Global Terrorism: Implications for the United States," April 2006, accessed 14, 2014, http://www.dni.gov/press_releases/Declassified_NIE_Key_Judgments.pdf.

101. *Living Under Drones: Death, Injury and Trauma to Civilians from US Drone Practices in Pakistan*, Stanford Human Right and Conflict Resolution Clinic & New York University School of Law, accessed August 14, 2014, http://www.livingunderdrones.org/download-report/.

102. The documentary was originally aired January 23, 2003.

103. Sean Woods, "The Voice, Will Lyman Frontline," *Rolling Stone*, January 3, 2010, accessed August 14, 2014, http://www.rollingstone.com/culture/pictures/fall-tv-special-20100903/the-voice-will-lyman-frontline-37621712#ixzz38bVSAsgv.

104. Quoted by Andrew J. Bacevich, "Illusions of Managing History: The Enduring Relevance of Reinhold Niebuhr," *Bill Moyer's Journal*, August 15, 2008, accessed August 8, 2014, http://www.pbs.org/moyers/journal/08152008/profile.html.

105. Tom Engelhardt, *The American Way of War: How Bush's Wars Became Obama's* (New York: Perseus, 2010), 87.

106. Quoted by Cheri Kramer, "The Legality of Targeted Drone Attacks as U.S. Policy," 9 Santa Clara J. Int'l L. 375 (2011), accessed August 14, 2014, http://digitalcommons.law.scu.edu/scujil/vol9/iss2/4.

107. General John P. Abizaid and Rosa Brooks, *Recommendation and Report of The Task Force on US Drone Policy* (Washington: Stimson Center, 2014), accessed August 14, 2014, http://news.genius.com/Task-force-on-us-drone-policy-executive-summary-annotated.

108. Ibid.

109. Stanford/NYU study, 2.

110. Akbar Ahmed, quoted in "Terror the Hidden Source," in *New York Review of Books*, Vol. LX, No. 16, October 24, 2013, 23.

Chapter 5

TERRORISM AS ENTERTAINMENT

According to the *New York Times*, the president confided in [Damian] Lewis: "While Michelle and the two girls go play tennis on Saturday afternoon, I go in the Oval Office, pretend I'm going to work, and then switch on *Homeland*." [1]

Terrorism provides rich and varied post-9/11 entertainment. It's worth viewing the background before turning to Obama's guilty pleasure. Consider his predecessor: When no weapons of mass destruction were found, George W. Bush didn't dissemble or apologize—"Shock and Awe" became "Aw Shucks."

At first, Bush and his advisors didn't get it. They deemed deception essential in promoting the Iraq War: They assumed their audience cared about the truth—their claims had cognitive content. Accordingly, in March 2003, as a pretext for war, the president claimed Hussein had weapons of mass destruction. American forces invading Iraq became the avant-garde in Bush's War on Terror. Absent WMDs—the pretext vanished. Surely, with its limitless resources, the administration could have planted and "discovered" such weapons amid a media frenzy, thereby avoiding cognitive dissonance and charges of duplicity. But could it be that truth is overrated?

In April 2003, I interviewed a member of the Congressional Armed Services Committee who wishes to remain anonymous. He predicted an "October surprise." The administration didn't bother to counterfeit images of WMDs. There's no need to avoid cognitive dissonance in a culture that promotes cognitive insolence: Truth isn't merely ignored, it's ridiculed. Bush and his advisors finally got it. They realized that their audience *could* handle the truth because no one cares. When entertainment becomes the métier of discourse, it's not merely a means to propagandize; entertainment becomes an end in itself.

SHOCK AND AWE BECOMES AW SHUCKS!

Anyone who looks with anguish on evils so great, so repulsive, so savage, must acknowledge the tragedy of it all; and if anyone experiences them or even looks on them without anguish, his condition is even more tragic, since he remains serene by losing his humanity.

—St. Augustine[2]

The Bush administration determined that Americans no longer inhabit a reality-based culture. What happens in Vegas *doesn't stay* in Vegas. Cognitive insolence debuted in high places as we learn from revisiting the 2004 White House Correspondents' Dinner. The terror suffered by Iraqi citizens and American troops became a laughing matter as Bush pretended to look for those pretend weapons of mass destruction.

Bush was the life of the party. A high-tech, big-screen production featured a forlorn Bush gazing out a White House window with a plaintive sigh: "Those weapons of mass destruction have *got* to be somewhere." Bush clowned amid the laughter of politicians and media celebrities. He looked behind curtains, peered under a desk, and checked cabinet drawers—all in good fun.[3]

Nation editor David Corn (from whom I've drawn this account) found such antics arrogant and callous—to say nothing of tasteless. However, the mainstream press found a certain charm in the chief executive's self-deprecating antics. For the pundits at the major networks and cable channels, mocking the rationale for a war that already cost thousands of lives and untold misery was amusing—nothing more. As early as 2004, CBS anchor Julie Chen found bad news about Iraq tiresome. As she explained the day after Bush's performance:

"At least someone's making jokes about it [the Iraq War] other than the late-night talk show hosts." The performances even got favorable reviews from Bush critics at the *Washington Post*. Ceci Connolly complimented Bush's comic gifts: "You know, trying to be funny at these things is so difficult, and he is quite good at it. I mean, he really is very good at self-deprecating humor. The pictures were funny. I laughed at the photos. I mean, he looks goofy, and he's got that great deadpan delivery."[4]

Nevertheless, a few poor sports who lost sons and daughters in Iraq failed to see the humor. Laughter may be the best medicine for the Beltway elite; ordinary folks can also have fun. Even as the smoldering Trade Center ruins cooled, Bush urged his countrymen to visit Disney World, shop at the mall—enjoy life. As Andrew Bacevich quips: "Bush certainly wanted citizens to support his war—he just wasn't going to require them actually to do anything."[5] Self-sacrifice might spoil the fun.

DAYDREAMING IN THE AFTERMATH OF 9/11

"Everything has changed" was our insta-bite mantra recited in lieu of insight. Our media chatted on about the death of irony . . . without ever getting close to the birth of comprehension.
—Susan Faludi[6]

Journalist Susan Faludi depicts a stunned America reverting to collective daydreams in the aftermath of the 9/11 nightmare. The apparent hysteria of five young girls—unable to swallow—provides interpretive metaphors. 9/11 was just too much to swallow; and it couldn't be given voice—at least initially. Faludi argues that regressing to the engrossing myths of the 1950s—when men were men and women were women—made tragedy digestible. The humiliating anxiety visited upon America was easier to swallow by recapturing puerile innocence. As she explains: "We reacted to our trauma . . . not by interrogating it but by cocooning ourselves in the celluloid chrysalis of the baby boomer's childhood."[7]

The chrysalis offered comfort food for the soul: cinematic images imbibed with stale popcorn and sugary drinks at those long-ago Saturday matinees. Ironists such as Susan Faludi recognized the incongruity in language—rhetoric depicting George W. Bush and Donald Rumsfeld as incarnations of John Wayne. She cites *Wall Street Journal* columnist and former Republican speechwriter Peggy Noonan, who almost literally expected Bush to "tear open his shirt and reveal the big 'S' on his chest." UPI's national political analyst, Peter Roff, said Bush's post-9/11 rhetoric reminded him of Batman, Bulletman, and the Shadow—a resemblance he applauded. "This is just the kind of hero America needs right now," Roff wrote, because comic book language "rallies the nation to even greater accomplishments and sacrifice, bringing forth great leaders to rescue the country." *Time* dubbed Bush our "Lone Ranger." *Newsweek* called him America's "dragon slayer." Such hyperboles didn't resonate deep in the Iraqi quagmire.[8] To paraphrase dialog from Brecht's *Galileo*: Woe to the land that has no heroes. No! Woe to the land that *needs* heroes.

No Creel Committee or Office of War Information devised and coordinated propaganda—no need. The popular media and many public intellectuals eagerly spun the administration's thrilling saga of the War on Terror. However, on several occasions, the Bush administration hired Hollywood producers to craft documentaries lionizing their struggle against evil. *The Spirit of America*, a rapid-fire montage of heroic imagery, celebrated macho cowboys—reluctant avengers who never threw the first punch. Showtime produced *DC 9/11: Time of Crisis*, a paean to Bush's response to 9/11. Richard Clarke, his counterterrorism expert and, in effect, first-responder to 9/11, was not to be seen. And Cheney faded into the setting—lest anyone conclude he ran the show. *DC 9/11* showed no more originality and insight than a typical Saturday matinee Western: A virile, resolute "cowboy-in-chief" took charge and set out to right wrongs.[9] Bush, of course, entertained by playing the part in public proclaiming that bin Laden was wanted dead or alive; he'd smoke 'em out!

Traditional heroes simply couldn't compete with sensational, post-9/11 entertainment. Comics and video games proliferated based upon the 9/11 incident. Even Superman got chastised, "Where were *you* on 9/11?" New York City police and firefighters became the new heroes, along with Mayor Giuliani. The regression to comfort zones harkened back to 1890s melodramas. Most victims of the tragedy were men. Nevertheless, iconic images of uniformed men rescuing hapless women, carrying them out of harm's way on their broad shoulders, prevailed.[10]

Few memorable films emerged from the 9/11 tragedy and the frustrations of the Iraq War. Even the apparent antiwar message of films such as *Jarhead* and *Blackhawk Down* got lost in what Stacy Takacs calls the "noble grunt" narrative.[11] The distinction between ethics and morality is salient. Ethics refers to the normative structure of an entire culture: its principles, rules, and mores. Ethics are public matters. Morality is a private concern, a matter of individual choices. World War II films such as *Why We Fight* argued for time-honored ethical principles of just war. Entertainment was a means, a vehicle for carrying the message.

Post-9/11 filmmakers realized that entertainment, not argumentation, engages the public. Their morality plays narrated a soldier's personal dilemmas, not timeless collective principles. Individuals found themselves in novel situations in which they had to choose amid uncertainty. These harrowing dilemmas are more gripping and entertaining than didactic rationales for just wars. As Takacs concludes: War became a "moral proving ground in which Americans demonstrated bravery, loyalty and discipline, and self-sacrifice." In effect, despite sporadic antiwar sentiments, the genre extolled military virtues.[12] Perhaps. But could it be these graphic depictions of war were popular simply because they were entertaining? To paraphrase William James: Indicting the horror of war is useless; the horror is the main attraction.

Bush stopped promoting the war during his second term, and the Obama administration promised to end hostilities—after a decent interval. Apparently, Hollywood producers thought Americans wanted to forget Middle Eastern debacles. Reinvented with new verve, Marvel comic book characters became heroic once again, as blue aliens on a distant planet came out of the screen in 3D.

THE PRESENT IS A FOREIGN COUNTRY

Americans no longer talk to each other, they entertain each other. They do not exchange ideas; they exchange images. They do not argue with propositions; they argue with good looks, celebrities, and commercials.

—Neil Postman [13]

Al Gore recognized that, like many products, truth is seldom produced in the United States: "Many people in both parties . . . have the uneasy feeling that there is something deeply troubling about President

Bush's relationship to reason [and] his disdain for facts. He has in effect outsourced the truth."[14] Not exactly. Entertainment, not truth, is manufactured and outsourced. Bush personified the new, anti-intellectualism—cognitive insolence. He and the neocons didn't deny the facts of death in Iraq, Afghanistan, and the terrorist diaspora. They dismissed the facts with disdain. No wonder communication theorist Neil Postman longed for the day when the printed word and sustained argument meant something: "Our politics, religion, news, athletics, education, and commerce have been transformed into congenial adjuncts of show business." He doesn't merely suggest that entertainment undermines or taints venues such as politics, religion, and news; he urges that these venues are denatured—*reduced* to entertainment. "We are a people on the verge of amusing ourselves to death."[15]

Pundits lauded Bill Clinton's rousing speech at the 2012 Democratic Convention—a bravura performance. It must have been. It equaled the ratings of *Here Comes Honey Boo Boo*, TLC's foray into hillbilly Appalachia. (Mitt Romney's speech didn't fare as well; the hillbilly show got higher ratings.) Reviewers couldn't believe that a network that—without irony—dubs itself "The Learning Channel"—reached new lows in vulgarity. One reviewer, however, was grateful for a minor improvement: "The show returned to our lives . . . with less flatulence and more conflict." Another reviewer allowed some might be genuinely entertained, "without realizing how awful and soul-crushing it is. Others— let" say this is you—watch it because . . . it's the green light to laugh at rednecks and fat people."[16] Perhaps the show entertains because it thrives on humiliation and mocks the underclass. Or maybe the show is nothing more than frivolous entertainment. In any case, for whatever reason, when entertainment is the métier of discourse, even carefully scripted discourse delivered by a consummate communicator barely competes with trash-talk.[17]

This postmodern anti-intellectualism ain't your daddy's anti-intellectualism incisively analyzed by Richard Hofstadter.[18] Hofstadter's anti-intellectuals cared enough about the truth to censor or persecute those who spoke the truth, and to lie when necessary. True, some still pay dearly for telling the truth. However, as Postman quipped, there's no need to burn books when no one reads them. Intellectuals—such as ironists attentive to incongruities in thought and action—are ignored, mocked, or dismissed as "elitist."

Ronald Reagan knew that politics is show business—image is every-thing. There's nothing new about impression management—an over-arching concern of the Kennedy administration. Impressions aren't about truth-claims; they're neither true nor false. Either you like the impression or you don't. Movie star-handsome JFK, along with an at-tractive wife, manufactured a likeable impression portraying himself and his advisors as the best and the brightest—brilliant, charismatic, yet practical. He was idolized and still is: *the* image of what we wished we could be. George W. Bush promoted a different brand: He's "one of us"—who wouldn't enjoy a beer with a regular guy like W?

Only snobs and elitists wouldn't. No wonder those unamused—or bemused—by his swaggering showmanship met with derision. Journal-ist Ron Suskind reports a confrontation with Mark McKinnon, a senior Bush advisor, who reminded Suskind that ordinary Americans don't read elite papers such as the *New York Times* or *Washington Post*. Real Americans "like the way he [Bush] walks and the way he points, the way he exudes self-confidence." McKinnon explained that attacks on Bush's malapropisms and jumbled syntax are good for the administration. "Be-cause you know what those folks don't like? They don't like you! But folks in the Red States *do* like Bush; as they say, 'He's one of us.'"[19]

Suskind just didn't get it. He thought he lived in a reality-based community—a milieu that assumes solutions emerge from scrutinizing empirical reality. Bush's claims aren't judged on their veracity.

> It doesn't work that way. We're an empire now, and when we act, we create our own reality. And while you're studying that reality . . . we'll act again, creating other new realities. We're history's actors . . . and you, all of you, will be left to just study what we do.[20]

Iraq became an improvisation: History's actors made it up as they went along, inventing subjective realities. Unfortunately—for the Bush ad-ministration, and for the rest of us—the war occurred in reality, a world Bush couldn't control, an objective world that "objected" to unbridled wishful thinking. General Daniel Bolger, a commander of troops in Iraq and Afghanistan, didn't have the luxury of creating his own reality; he found himself in an objective world of lost causes:

> I am a United States Army general, and I lost the "global war on terror." It's like Alcoholics Anonymous: Step one is admitting you

have a problem. Well, I have a problem. So do my peers. And thanks to our problem, now all of America has a problem, to wit: two lost campaigns and a war gone awry. [21]

THE SACRED AND THE PROFANE

All that is solid melts into air; all that is holy is profaned, and man is at last compelled to face with sober senses his real conditions of life, and his relations with his kind.

—Karl Marx [22]

Marx foresaw commodity culture, a time bereft of sacred spaces, a time when even the most hallowed events become just another item bought and sold in the marketplace. (I am probably not the first to note the profanation of the birth of Christ.) I want to discuss the profanation of the ultimate terror weapon, commemoration as a source of entertainment. I also lament profaning the 9/11 tragedy: turning it into a pretext for yet another tawdry gift shop.

Picnicking in the Shadow of the Bomb [23]

Once, there was a time when the atomic bomb evoked awe and reverence, especially among its creators. Unleashing the power that binds the firmament wasn't merely an explosion; it was redolent with symbolic power—wholly other. "It beggared description." Those witnessing the blinding flash at Trinity, those who weren't left speechless, conjured images of Vishnu destroying worlds and the rapture ushering in Christ's second coming.

The day before Kim Jong Il boasted about his first nuclear test, I witnessed festivities at the site of the first American test: the Trinity Test Site—a national monument on the highway the Spaniards called *"Jornada del Muetro"* (the official literature didn't mention the English translation—"Journey of Death"). As I strolled between the picnickers and souvenir stands at America's original Ground Zero, I witnessed (with apologies to Hannah Arendt) the evil of banality: the world's first nuclear blast—a portent of destruction that spewed radiation over a wide swath of America—reduced to just another tourist attraction. Marx's aphorism popped into my mind as I munched fabled New Mexico green chili burritos and marveled at slogans emblazoned on t-shirts: "Trinity Test Site: I Glow in the Dark!"

This sojourn on the *Jornada del Muetro* culminated the University of New Mexico's Conference on the Early History of the Atomic Bomb. I expected that the atom bomb would be credited with ending World War II and preserving a fragile peace during the Cold War: Speakers from military contractors such as Sandia and the Los Alamos National Laboratory didn't disappoint. However, I didn't anticipate the commercialized vulgarity at the official museums—it gave kitsch a bad name. Predictably, Albuquerque's Atomic Museum (funded by a variety of military contractors) highlighted mock-ups of Fat Man, Little Boy, and an assortment of latter-day nukes. But, like much else in American culture, weapons of mass destruction were a laughing matter. The exhibit highlighting the Bikini Test (which forever contaminated the Marshall Islands) featured a scant bikini swimsuit draped over a map of the ill-fated archipelago. And, like any museum worthy of its name, a gift shop displayed T-shirts, atomic shot glasses, and bottled atomic firewater. The worst, however, was yet to come: the offspring of an unnatural act between Dr. Strangelove and Chuck E. Cheese. A gaily colored banner, just around the corner from the weapons of mass destruction, beckoned the Birthday Party Room: "An exciting spot for fun, games, cake and ice cream." They called it the "Zoom Zone," and it hyped "hands-on" activities. Imagine what "fair and balanced" Fox News would say about junior jihadists celebrating birthdays amid weapons of mass destruction at camp al-Qaeda.

An ominous sky of thickening clouds marked our pilgrimage in the Alamogordo wilderness. Robert Oppenheimer named the test site "Trinity" in honor of very dark verses penned by metaphysical poet John Donne. The site is only opened to the public two days every year. An anthropologist observing our October visit from afar might conclude that we were on a religious pilgrimage. Hundreds of visitors in cars, SUVs, and tour buses drove through miles of desolation that begs description. (Signs warned that no weapons were permitted at the site—irony is not the strongest suit of the military mind.) Visitors trekked some distance to an obelisk where the plutonium bomb vaporized a steel tower on July 16, 1945 at 5:30 in the morning. A blind girl 100 miles distant, we were told, somehow experienced the flash. It was felt at distances surpassing 160 miles, according to the official literature—the day the sun rose twice over New Mexico.

Like the trace of remaining radiation (we were told not to worry), a residue of the sacred endured. Our security agent explained that the ashes of a recently departed Manhattan Project physicist (whose name could not be revealed) would be scattered at Ground Zero after the site closed to the public. Death was the last thing on the mind of the boisterous, picture-taking public. Like Cinderella's Disneyland castle, the obelisk provided a backdrop for vacation snapshots. After the digital cameras clicked, the throng moved along a cyclone fence, counterclockwise, in an orderly fashion gazing upon icons—pictures of the fulminating atomic blast. Our anthropologist might have likened the procession to veneration of the Stations of the Cross. He or she would have missed the point, or maybe there was no point to miss.

The site was simply famous for being famous. In addition to the black obelisk, the curious could visit a nearby ranch house where scientists assembled the plutonium implosion mechanism. The dilapidated structure looked like an ideal spot for a Manson Family reunion. The scientists' scrawl on the door remained: "Wipe your feet!" I entered the plutonium assembly room with clean feet, but I still felt dirty and disappointed. (Indeed, a few years after the blast and destruction of Japanese cities, a contrite Oppenheimer would tell Truman, "I have blood on my hands.") Just as getting that celebrity autograph is often disillusioning, the Trinity adventure was a letdown bereft of the solemnity it deserved, let alone of the adrenaline-driven thrills befitting any self-respecting tourist attraction.

Is Nothing Sacred?

A *Washington Post* headline says it all: "Families infuriated by 'crass commercialism' of 9/11 Museum gift shop." Giggling teenagers taking "selfies" were not. The *New York Post* called the Museum the "Little Shop of Horrors." 9/11 became a commodity hours after Bush had his finest hour consecrating the new Ground Zero as sacred space. Briefly, for the observant, the new Ground Zero became hallowed ground—wholly other, far-removed from the mundane distractions of ordinary life and noonday commerce. It evoked reverence, confrontation with the mysteries of life and death, and for too many—the dark night of the soul. The commercialization of Christmas took centuries; Ground Zero was commercialized in a matter of weeks. Beginning in late September 2001, nearby stores sold commemorative T-shirts complemented by the usual kitsch.

The museum houses the burial vaults of what remains of the 9/11 victims. Kurt and Diane Horning, founders of WTC Families for Proper Burial, sued New York City for the right to properly bury remains. They objected to the remains used as a "programmatic element" in a tourist attraction, what they called a "three-ringed circus." In the words of one visitor whose son perished on 9/11: "It's crass commercialism on a literally sacred site. . . . It's a burial ground." A museum official claimed gift shop items were carefully selected. Victims' families remained unconvinced. They didn't appreciate memorabilia such as dark tower tote bags picturing the towers askance amid ominous darkness. However, for the lighthearted there's a bag imprinted with "I Love New York Even More!" And kids might enjoy hoodies picturing the towers, toy trucks, and badges. There are, of course, doggie vests for the family pet. No wonder a survivor exclaimed: They're "making money off my dead son."[24]

CAN'T GET ENOUGH TERRORISM

We had no idea that there was still an appetite to . . . talk about the war on terror, to talk about how America was protecting its power overseas. Were people exhausted, was there fatigue? After bin Laden was killed, we were like, "Well now everyone is really going to tune out."

—Alex Gansa, co-creator of *Homeland* [25]

Homeland merits special attention: Millions watch the president's favorite show. Previously, the show's creators—Alex Gansa and Howard Gordon—produced *24*, a decidedly predictable celebration of the War on Terror. Counterterrorist Jack Bauer races against the clock—you can almost hear the time bombs ticking—to foil the plots of swarthy jihadists. After Gansa and Gordon caught the Israeli show *Hatufim* ("Prisoners of War"), they created *Homeland*—*24* for grown-ups.

The show departs from the usual, formulaic script—perhaps its main attraction. Nicholas Brody (played by Damian Lewis) returns to America after long imprisonment by jihadists. He witnessed scores of children killed by US drones, including Issa, a boy he befriended. The trauma, coupled with Stockholm syndrome, turns him into a latter-day Manchurian candidate—an all-American Marine turned closet terrorist.

CIA agent Carrie Mathison (Claire Danes), the show's protagonist, suffers from bipolar disorder; due to her illness, she's not taken seriously. She's mentored by her CIA boss, Saul Berenson (Mandy Patinkin). She loves and hates Brody, as she suspects that he is a jihadist agent who converted to Islam during his captivity. The award-winning show is so captivating that viewers are warned to watch responsibly and not to binge. President Obama, evidently, doesn't heed the warning. In addition to his guilty Saturday afternoon pleasure, he ordered copies of his favorite episodes. Lewis gave the president autographed copies at a state dinner—"from one Muslim to another."

The CIA entertained their fictional counterparts. Dane's Yale roommate attended—she works for the CIA. Is it possible that Dick Cheney is also a *Homeland* fan? In one episode, we learn that the fictional vice president who ordered those drone attacks has a pacemaker to manage heart disease. The jihadists successfully plot to send signals disabling the pacemaker. Shortly thereafter, Dick Cheney sought advanced protection for *his* pacemaker. A *Washington Post* headline confirms that truth is at least as strange as fiction: "Yes, terrorists could have hacked Cheney's heart."

> On *60 Minutes* this Sunday, former Vice President Dick Cheney revealed that his doctor ordered the wireless functionality of his heart implant disabled due to fears it might be hacked in an assassination attempt. And despite literally being a scenario from Homeland, that's a pretty valid fear.[26]

Homeland, wrought with ambiguity, invites self-confessional interpretations. These interpretations probably reveal more about the reviewer than the show. The interpretive spectrum includes accounts of the show as an Israeli Jewish conspiracy, captivating propaganda-lite, and simply well-crafted entertainment.

An Israeli Jewish Plot?

A well-credentialed academic, Joseph Massad (Columbia University associate professor of modern Arab politics), offers a conspiratorial take on *Homeland*. He detects an Israeli Jewish influence that debases Arabs and Muslims, an influence discovered in various subplots: "The Jewish Berenson is married to an Indian Hindu 'brown' woman (perhaps cementing the Indian Hindu-Israel Jewish right-wing alliance against Arabs and Muslims in the minds of the scriptwriters.)"[27] Massad offers no evidence of such an alliance. However, virtually every reference to Berenson mentions his Jewish identity, despite the fact that his ethnicity is largely incidental and that he identifies as "American." Massad sees the hands of Ashkenazi Jews in scripting this plot, and claims that Arabic dialog has a distinct, Ashkenazi accent reminiscent of Benjamin Netanyahu.

He finds other subplots revealing. A Saudi diplomat with three wives and ten children "is declared by the Jewish Berenson to be gay 'on account of frequenting a gay bath house.'" The reviewer suspects that this subplot reveals that the show's creators and their Jewish Israeli advisors intend to convince the public that "Arab society is so horrific that it forces gay men not only to marry one woman, but three!"[28]

Finally, Massad believes the show's second season opened with "Goebbels-like propaganda": Israel bombs Iranian nuclear installations—an obvious attempt to prepare the public for an American-backed Israeli attack on Iran. Perhaps Massad hadn't viewed subsequent episodes that reveal the unexpected, harrowing consequences of Israeli actions. In the author's view, the show functions on several levels to promote a perverse ethic: a Jewish Israeli justification for demonizing Arabs and Muslims, both foreign and domestic.

Propaganda-lite

Writing for the Harvard Institute of Politics, Julianna Aucoin reiterates a common criticism: All the bad guys threatening the homeland are Muslims. Brody, the closet Muslim, is uniquely pernicious: elected to Congress, he's being groomed as a vice-presidential candidate. Given his family values and previous loyalties, he's conflicted. So is the reviewer: "I have struggled to balance my love of the show and its characters with my aversion to such a potentially marginalizing characterization of Islam."[29]

There is no difficulty finding instances of racism. Seeking out terrorists, the CIA prioritizes focusing on "dark-skinned" individuals. Stereotyping and profiling are excusable given exigent circumstances: Carrie and her cohorts struggle to stop Abu Nazir—a bin Laden clone—from visiting another 9/11 catastrophe (or worse) upon the United States. Initially, Nazir is portrayed as a cartoon-like, Middle Eastern caricature of evil. Painfully aware of this and other racist propaganda, Aucoin expresses a *very* guilty pleasure: "Enjoying *Homeland* seemed illicit and wrong."

Even so, she finds the propaganda leavened by portraying US government officials "as unlikeable and corrupt as possible." Another Obama favorite, *House of Cards,* portrays officials as shameless opportunists who would embarrass Machiavelli. *Homeland* depicts so-called good guys as child killers, murderers of children. Suddenly, a bad guy such as Abu Nazir is not an ineffable evil: He's avenging the murder of his son Issa and the other children. Even Islam gets favorable treatment: Brody, torn by conflict, always gets a moment of serenity on his prayer rug. In short, the show departs from the usual Manichean narrative and offers a more decent take that humanizes jihadists. Accordingly, the author conditionally approves of watching *Homeland*—an addictive mixture of prejudice and enlightenment.

Well-Crafted Entertainment

Are the previous takes on *Homeland* over-determined? Do reviewers read too much into what is simply a captivating drama? As co-creator Howard Gordon explains: "Alex and I, just as storytellers, wanted to find a character unlike Jack Bauer." They did—Nicholas Brody. Gordon and his colleague hoped we'd get hooked; we'd become voyeurs witnessing the tumult and unfolding of Brody's inner life. We'd witness an all-American Marine forfeiting all that he cherished. Likewise, Carrie, a brilliant piece of damaged goods, is far more intriguing than the usual femme fatale.

Writing in the *Huffington Post,* Maureen Ryan suggests the show effectively invokes ancient dramatic devices immersing us in the characters' moral predicaments. Ryan argues that *Homeland*'s best moments narrate decidedly unheroic moral journeys: harrowing journeys of conflicted individuals haunted by all-too-human questions: "Is what I see and think real, or is it all in my head? Who can I really trust?"

Terrorism is but a pretext for entering the high drama of the personal lives of intriguing, conflicted individuals: We're hooked; what happens next? What makes Carrie tick? She despises Brody as a traitor, a terrorist who would wreak havoc on her homeland. And yet, she passionately embraces him. Can individuals love what they hate? Freud thought so. Or could it be that Carrie just plays Brody to seduce a confession? As Ryan suggests, *Homeland* captivates because it improvises such daunting questions. Can individuals trust one another? Do only the naïve trust organizations that purport to look after their well-being? And what happens next in ambiguous situations when individuals with a will to believe are plagued by doubt?[30]

Homeland is admittedly ambiguous. Perhaps it's something more than engrossing entertainment. Considering his role in the production, Lewis ruminates about our fractured, collective consciousness. Perhaps Carrie is the avatar of the public who hates and fears terrorism but can't get enough of it on primetime TV? Lewis laments: "It's . . . bleak that the one person who represents hope [Carrie] is a broken-down, polarized person who represents a broken, polarized America."[31] Stay tuned.

NOTES

1. Quoted in "'Homeland' Raises the Anxiety Level," accessed August 23, 2014, http://nytimes.com/2012/09/16/arts/television/homeland-returns-for-second-season-on show.

2. Cited by Garry Wills, "What is a Just War?" in *New York Review of Books*, Vol. LI, No. 14, November 18, 2004, 34.

3. CNN.com, "Bush takes heat for WMD jokes," May 3, 2004, http://www.cnn.com/2004/ALLPOLITICS/03/26/bush.wmd.jokes/.

4. David Corn, "MIA WMDs—for Bush It's a Joke," *The Nation*, March 25, 2004, http://www.thenation.com/blog/156077/mia-wmds-bush-its-joke.

5. Andrew Bacevich, "He Told Us to Go Shopping. Now the Bill Is Due," *Washington Post*, October 5, 2008, accessed August 20, 2014, http://www.washingtonpost.com/wp-dyn/content/article/2008/10/03/AR2008100301977.html.

6. Susan Faludi, *The Terror Dream: Myth and Misogyny in an Insecure America* (New York: Henry Holt and Co, 2007), Kindle Edition, 2.

7. Ibid., 5.

8. Ibid., 60–61.

9. Ibid., 8.

10. Ibid., 59–71.

11. Stacy Takacs, *Terrorism TV: Popular Entertainment in Post-9/11 America* (Lawrence: University Press of Kansas, 2012), 13.

12. Ibid., 14.

13. Neil Postman, *Amusing Ourselves to Death: Public Discourse in the Age of Show Business* (New York: Penguin, 1984), Kindle edition, Locations 1638–39.

14. Al Gore, *The Assault on Reason* (New York: Penguin, 2007), 58.

15. Postman, Locations 269–71.

16. Cavan Sieczkowski, "'Honey Boo Boo' Ratings Match Bill Clinton DNC Speech On CNN," *The Huffington Post*, September 7, 2012, accessed August 25, 2014, http://www.huffingtonpost.com/2012/09/07/honey-boo-boo-ratings-bill-clinton-dnc-speech_n_1864145.html.

17. Matt Richenthal, "Here Comes Honey Boo Boo Review: Mud, Maxi Pads & Mullets," January 17, 2014, accessed August 7, 2014, http://www.tvfanatic.com/2014/01/here-comes-honey-boo-boo-review-mud-maxi-pads-and-mullets/#ixzz39kW2.

18. Richard Hofstadter, *Anti-Intellectualism in American Life* (New York: Vintage, 1962).

19. Eric Boehlert, "Team Bush declares war on the New York Times" (Suskind story), *Democratic Underground.com*, October 19, 2004, accessed August 6, 2014, http://www.democraticunderground.com/discuss/duboard.php?az=view_all&address=103x79790.

20. Ron Suskind, Faith, "Certainty and the Presidency of George W. Bush," *New York Times Magazine*, October 17, 2004, http://www.nytimes.com/2004/10/17/magazine/17BUSH.html?_r=0; also see "Team Bush Declares War on the New York Times," *Democratic Underground.com*, October 17, 2004, accessed July 5, 2014, http://www.democraticunderground.com/discuss/duboard.php?az=view_all&address=103x79790.

21. Daniel Bolger, "Why We Lost in Iraq and Afghanistan," *Harpers*, Vol. 329, No. 1974, September 2014.

22. Karl Marx, *The Communist Manifesto*, accessed July 31, 2014. https://www.marxists.org/archive/marx/works/1848/communist-manifesto/ch01.htm.

23. A version of "Picnicking in the Afterglow. . . ." first appeared in *Antique Children*, July 6, 2010.

24. "Families infuriated by 'crass commercialism' of 9/11 Museum gift shop," Washington Post.com, May 19, 2014. Accessed August 6, 2014, http://www.washingtonpost.com/news/post-http://www.washingtonpost.com/news/post-nation/wp/2014/05/19.

25. Sheila Marikar, "Inside 'Homeland,' the Terrorism Tale Turned TV Triumph," October 27, 2011, ABC News.com, accessed August 9, 2014, http.//abcnew.go.com/Entertainment/inside-homeland-terrorism-tale-turned-tv-trimph/story?id=.

26. Andrea Peterson, "Yes, Terrorists Could Have Hacked Cheney's Heart," *Washington Post*, October, 23, 2013, accessed August 23, 2014, http://www.washingtonpost.com/blogs/the-switch/wp/2013/10/21/yes-terrorists-could-have-hacked-dick-cheneys-heart/.

27. Joseph Massad, "'Homeland,' Obama's Show." *Al Jazeera English*, October 25, 2012, accessed August 15, 2014, http://www.aljazeera.com/indepth/opinion/2012/10/2012102591525809.

28. Ibid.

29. Julianna Aucoin, "Homeland: Islamophobic Propaganda or Progressive Masterpiece?"; *Harvard University Institute of Politics*, accessed August 24, 2014, http://www.iop.harvard.edu/homeland-islamophobic-propaganda-or-progressive-masterpiece.

30. Maureen Ryan, "What The Heck Is Going On With This Show?" *Huffington Post*, October 20, 2013, accessed August 25, 2014, http://www.huffingtonpost.com/maureen-ryan/homeland-review_b_4125281.html.

31. Ibid.

BIBLIOGRAPHY

Abizaid, John P., and Rosa Brooks. *Recommendation and Report of The Task Force on US Drone Policy.* Stimson Center, http://news.genius.com/Task-force-on-us-drone-policy-executive-summary-annotate.

Acheson, Dean. "Homage to Plain Dumb Luck." In *The Cuban Missile Crisis*, Robert Divine, ed. Chicago: Quadrangle Books, 1971.

Akbar, Ahmed. "Terror the Hidden Source." *New York Review of Books*, October 24, 2013: 23.

Allison, Graham. *Nuclear Terrorism: The Ultimate Preventable Catastrophe.* New York: Holt, 2005.

Allison, Graham and Morton Halperin. "Bureaucratic Politics: A Paradigm and Some Policy Implications." In *Classics of International Relations, 3rd ed.* John A. Vasquez, ed. Upper Saddle River, NJ: Prentice Hall, 1996.

Alperovitz, Gar. *The Decision to Use the Atomic Bomb.* New York: Vintage, 1996.

Ambrose, Stephen. *Nixon, vol.2.* New York: Simon & Schuster, 1989.

Aucoin, Julianna. *Homeland: Islamophobic Propaganda or Progressive Masterpiece?* Cambridge: Harvard University Institute of Politics, February 20, 2013. http://harvardpolitics.com/books-arts/homeland-islamophobic-propaganda-or-progressive-masterpiece.

Bacevich, Andrew. *The Limits of American Power: The End of American Exceptionalism.* New York: Metropolitan Books, 2008.

_____. *Washington Rules: America's Path to Permanent War.* New York: Metropolitan Books, 2010.

_____. *Breach of Trust: How Americans Failed Their Soldiers and Their Country.* New York: Henry Holt and Co., 2013.

Bernays, Edward. *Propaganda.* Brooklyn: Ig Publishing, 2005.

Betts, Richard K. *Nuclear Blackmail and Nuclear Balance.* Washington: The Brookings Institution, 1987.

Blight, James G., and David A. Welch. *On The Brink: Americans and Soviets Reexamine the Cuban Missile Crisis.* New York: Hill and Wang, 1989.

Blight, James G., and Janet M. Lang. *The Armageddon Letters: Kennedy/Khrushchev/Castro in the Cuban Missile Crisis.* Lanham, MD: Rowman and Littlefield, 2012.

Brulin, Remi. "Defining Terrorism: The 1972 General Assembly Debates on International Terrorism." *New York Times*, September 30, 2013.

Brzezinski, Zbigniew. "Terrorized by War on Terror." *Washington Post*, March 25, 2007, http://www.washingtonpost.com/wdyn/content/articles/2007/03/24/AR2007032301613.html.

Butler, General Lee. *National Press Club Remarks, December 4, 1996.* PBS American Experience References. http://www.pbs.org/wgbh/amex/bomb/filmmore/reference/primary/leebutler.html.

Canaday, John. *The Nuclear Muse.* Madison: University of Wisconsin Press, 2000.

Carroll, Eugene. "Nuclear Weapons and Deterrence." In *The Nuclear Crisis Reader,* by ed. Gwyn Prins. New York: Vintage, 1984.

Casey, Steven. *Cautious Crusade: Franklin D. Roosevelt, American Public Opinion, and The War Against Germany.* New York: Oxford University Press, 2001.

———. *Selling the Korean War: Propaganda, Politics, and Public Opinion in the United States 1950–1953.* New York: Oxford University Press, 2008.

Change, Laurence, and Peter Kornbluh. *The Cuban Missile Crisis, 1962.* New York: New Press, 1992.

Chomsky, Noam. "Distorted Morality: America's War on Terror." *Harvard.* Cambridge, 2002.

———. *The Culture of Terrorism.* Boston: South End Press, 1988.

———. "The evil scourge of terrorism: Reality, construction, remedy." *Erich Fromm Lecture.* Stuttgart, Germany, 2012.

Church, Frank. *Church Committee Report.* Washington. http://www.democracynow.org/2009/4/24/flashback_a_look_back_at_the. . . ., 1973.

Clarke, Jeffrey J. *War in the Persian Gulf: Operations Desert Shield and Desert Storm August 1990–March 1991.* 2010: http://www.history.army.mil/html/books/070/70-117-1/CMH_70-117-1.

Clarke, Richard A. *Against All Enemies: Inside America's War on Terror.* New York: Free Press, 2011.

Cody, C. A. J. "Bombing and the Morality of War." In *Bombing Civilians,* in Tanaka.

Cohn, Carol. "Nuclear Language and How We Learned to Pat the Bomb." *Bulletin of the Atomic Scientists,* 1987.

Coordinator for Counterterrorism. *Country Reports on Terrorism.* Washington: United States Department of State, 2007.

Corn, David. "MIA WMDs—for Bush It's a Joke." *The Nation,* March 25, 2004.

Cottrell, Robert. *Vietnam: The 17th Parallel.* New York: Chelsea House, 2004.

Creation of SIOP-62. The National Security Archive, Washington, July 13, 2004, http://www2.gwu.edu/=NSAEFF/NESEFF130/PRESS.HTM.

Critchley, Simon. "Abandon (Nearly) All Hope." *New York Times,* April 2014.

Crowther, Bosley. "Review of 'Mission to Moscow.'" *New York Times,* April 3 1943. http://www.tcm.com/tcmdb/title/76858/The-Great-Dictator/articles.html.

Cumings, Bruce. *The Korean War.* New York: Modern Library, 2010.

Dallek, Robert. "Three New Revelations About LBJ." *The Atlantic Monthly,* April 1998.

Department of the Air Force. *White Paper: Air Force Performance in Desert Storm.* http://www.pbs.org/wgbh/pages/frontline/gulf/appendix/whitepaper.html., 2003.

Dower, John. *Cultures of War.* New York: W.W. Norton, 2010.

———. *Embracing Defeat: Japan in the Wake of World War II.* New York: W.W. Norton, 1999.

———. *War Without Mercy.* New York: Pantheon Books, 1986.

Draper, Robert. *Dead Certain: The Presidency of George W. Bush.* New York: Free Press, 2007.

Ellsberg, Daniel. "A Call to Mutiny." In *Protest and Survive,* by eds. Dan Smith and E.P. Thompson. New York: Monthly Review Press, 1981.

Engelhardt, Tom. *The American Way of War.* Chicago: Haymarket Books, 2010.

Faludi, Susan. *The Terror Dream: Myth and Misogyny in an Insecure America.* New York: Henry Holt, 2007.

Ferrell, Robert H., ed. *The Autobiography of Harry S. Truman.* Boulder: University of Colorado Press, 1980.

Festinger, Leon. *A Theory of Cognitive Dissonance.* Stanford: Stanford University Press, 1957.

Filene, Peter G. *American View of Soviet Russia, 1917–1965.* Homewood, IL: Dorsey Press, 1968.

Fleischer, Ari. "Press Conference." *Washington Post,* September 26, 2001. http://www.washingtonpost.com/wpsrv/nation/specials/attacked/transcripts/fleischertext_0.

Freedman, Lawrence. *The Price of Peace.* New York: Henry Holt, 1986.

Freud, Sigmund and Albert Einstein. *Einstein-Freud Correspondence (1931–1932).* 1932. http://www.public.asu.edu/~jmlynch/273/documents/FreudEinstein.pdf.

Frum, David, and Richard Perle. *An End to Evil: How to Win the War on Terror.* New York: Random House, 2003.

Fukuyama, Francis. *The End of History and the Last Man.* New York: Free Press, 1992.

Fulwood, Sam, and Nick B. Williams Jr. "170,000 Iraqi Children Face Death, Health Study Finds." *Los Angeles Times,* May 21, 1991.

Fussell, Paul. *The Great War and Modern Memory.* New York: Oxford University Press, 1975.

_____. *Wartime.* New York: Oxford University Press, 1986.

Gaddis, John. *We Now Know.* New York: Oxford University Press, 1987.

Garthoff, Raymond. *Reflections on the Cuban Missile Crisis.* Washington: The Brookings Institution, 1987.

Glynn, Peter. *Closing Pandora's Box.* New York: Basic Books, 1992.

Goodwin, Richard N. "President Lyndon Johnson: The War Within." *New York Times Magazine,* August 21, 1988.

Gore, Al. *The Assault on Reason.* New York: Penguin, 2007.

Grayling, A. C. *Among The Dead Cities: The History and Moral Legacy of Bombing Civilians in Germany and Japan.* New York: Walker & Company, 2006.

Hedges, Chris, and Laila Al-Arian. *Collateral Damage: America's War against Iraqi Civilians.* New York: Nation Books, 2008.

Herken, Gregg. "The Earthly Origin of Star Wars." *The Bulletin of the Atomic Scientists,* 1987: 114.

_____. "The Nuclear Gnostics." In *The Security Question,* by ed. Douglas MacLearn, 15. Totowa: Rowman & Allanheld, 1984.

_____. *Counsels of War.* New York: Oxford University Press, 1987.

Herring, George C. "Cold Blood: LBJ's Conduct of Limited War in Vietnam." *United States Air Force Academy Harmon Lecture #33.*

Hirschbein, Ron. *Massing the Tropes: The Metaphorical Construction of American Nuclear Strategy.* New York: Praeger Security International, 2005.

_____. *Newest Weapons/Oldest Psychology: The Dialectics of American Nuclear Strategy.* New York: Peter Lang, 1989.

_____. *What If They Gave a Crisis and Nobody Came: Interpreting International Crises.* Westport: Praeger, 1997.

Hoffman, Bruce. *Inside Terrorism.* New York: Columbia University Press, 2006.

Kahn, Herman. *On Escalation: Metaphors and Scenarios.* New York: Praeger, 1965.

_____. *Thinking About the Unthinkable in the 1980s.* New York: Simon & Schuster, 1984.

Kaplan, Fred. *The Wizards of Armageddon.* New York: Simon & Schuster, 1983.

Kennan, George F. *American Diplomacy.* Chicago: University of Chicago Press, 1984.

Kennedy, Robert F. *Thirteen Days: A Memoir on the Cuban Missile Crisis.* New York: W.W. Norton, 1969.

Kesby, Rebecca. "North Vietnam, 1972: The Christmas Bombing of Hanoi." *BBC Newsmagazine,* December 24, 2012.

Kissinger, Henry. *The White House Years.* Boston: Little Brown, 1979.

Koppes, Clayton and Gregory D. Black. *Hollywood Goes to War.* New York: Free Press, 1987.

Kovic, Ron. *Born on the Fourth of July.* New York: McGraw-Hill, 1976.

Kramer, Cheri. "The Legality of Targeted Drone Attacks as U.S. Policy." *Santa Clara Journal of International Law,* February 4 , 2011: 375.

Lasch, Christopher. *Culture of Narcissism.* New York: W.W. Norton, 1991.

Lavine, Harold, and James Wechsler. *War Propaganda and the United States*. New Haven: Yale University Press, 1940.

LeBow, Richard Ned. "Thucydides and Deterrence." *Security Studies*, 2007: 163–88.

Lifton, Robert Jay. *The Broken Connection*. New York: Simon & Schuster, 1979.

Lilienthal, David. *Change, Hope and the Bomb*. Princeton: Princeton University Press, 1963.

Littauer, Raphael, and Norman Uphoff. *The Air War in Indochina*. Ithaca: Cornell University Press, 1971.

Luttwak, Edward. *Strategy: The Logic of War and Peace*. Cambridge: Harvard University Press, 1987.

MacArthur, John A. *Second Front: Censorship and Propaganda in the Gulf War*. New York: Hill and Wang, 1992.

Mahajan, Rahul. *We Think the Price is Worth It*. Fair, http://fair.org/extra-online-articles/we-think-the-price-is-worth-it/, 1996.

Massad, Joseph. "Homeland, Obama's Show." *Al Jazeera English*, October 25, 2012. http://www.aljazeera.com/indepth/opinion/2012/10/2012102591525809.

McManus, Sean. "How My Dad Covered the Munich Massacre." *The Hollywood Reporter*, July 27, 2012.

McNamara, Robert S. *In Retrospect*. New York: Times Books, 1995.

Miller, Arthur. "Introduction to Collected Plays." In *Willy Loman*, by ed. Harold Bloom. New York: Chelsea House, n.d.

Miller, David, and Tom Mills. "The terror experts and the mainstream media: the expert nexus and its domination in the news media." *Critical Studies on Terrorism, Vol. 2, No. 3*, 2009.

Miller, John. *Frontline Interview with bin Laden*. http://www.pbs.org/wgbh/pages/frontline/shows/binladen/who/interview.html., 1998.

Minimum Nuclear Deterrence. Washington: SAIC Strategic Group, 2003.

Moss, Peter. "Rhetoric of Defense in the United States: Language, Myth, and Ideology." In *Nukespeak Today*, by ed. Paul Chilton, 58–71. London: Frances Pinter, 1983.

Mueller, John, and Mark Stewart. "The Terrorism Delusion." *International Security*, n.d.

Nathan, James A. *The Cuban Missile Crisis Revisited*. New York: St. Martin's Press, 1992.

Natanson, Stephen. *Terrorism and the Ethics of War*. Cambridge: Cambridge University Press, 2011.

Niebuhr, Reinhold. *The Irony of American History*. Chicago: University of Chicago Press, 1952.

Orwell, George. *You and the Atomic Bomb*. http://orwell.ru/library/articles/ABomb/english/e abomb, n.d.

Postman, Neil. *Amusing Ourselves to Death: Public Discourse in the Age of Show Business*. New York: Penguin, 1984.

Pratkanis, Anthony, and Aronson, Elliot. *Age of Propaganda*. New York: Henry Holt, 2001.

Pringle, Peter, and James Speigelman. *The Nuclear Barons*. New York: Holt, Rinehart, & Winston, 1981.

Pyle, Ernie. *Last Chapter*. New York: Henry Holt & Co., 1945.

Record, Jeffrey. *The Wrong War: Why We Lost in Vietnam*. Annapolis: Naval Institute Press, 1998.

_____. "Why the Bush Administration Invaded Iraq." *Strategic Studies Quarterly, Vol. 2, No. 2*, 87., 2008.

Richard, Carl H. *When the United States Invaded Russia: Woodrow Wilson's Siberian Disaster*. Lanham, MD: Rowman and Littlefield, 2013.

Roosevelt, Franklin D. *The Public Papers and Addresses of Franklin D. Roosevelt, 1939: War and Neutrality*. New York: MacMillan, 1941.

Rorty, Richard. "Ironists and Metaphysicians." In *The Truth about The Truth*, by ed. Walter Truett Anderson, 101–102. New York: Putnam, 1995.

Rose, Gideon. *How Wars End*. New York: Simon & Schuster, 2010.

Rotblat, Joseph. "Leaving the Bomb Project." *Bulletin of Atomic Scientists*, August 1985: 16–19.

Rumsfeld, Donald, Paul Wolfowitz, et al. *Open Letter to the President.* http://www.iraqwatch.org/perspectives/rumsfeld-openletter.gtm, 1998.

Ryan, Maureen. "What The Heck is Going On With This Show?" *Huffington Post*, October 20, 2013: http://www.huffingtonpost.com/maureen-ryan/homeland-review_b_4125281.html.

Schell, Jonathan. "The Village of Ben Suc." *New Yorker*, July 7, 1967.

———. "Reflections." *New Yorker*, 1982: 45–52.

Schelling, Thomas C. *The Strategy of Conflict.* New York: Oxford University Press, 1963.

Sieczkowski, Cavan. "Honey Boo Boo Ratings Match Bill Clinton DNC Speech On CNN." *Huffington Post*, September 7, 2012: http://www.huffingtonpost.com/2012/09/07/honey-boo-boo-ratings-bill-clinton-dnc-speech_n_1864145.html.

Sontag, Susan. "Talk of the Town." *New Yorker*, September 24, 2001. http://www.newyorker.com/magazine/2001/09/24/1256341.

———. *Regarding the Pain of Others.* New York: Farrar, Straus, and Giroux, 2003.

Stampnitzky, Lisa. *Disciplining Terror.* Cambridge: Cambridge University Press, 2013.

Stanford Human Rights and Conflict Resolution Clinic and New York University School of Law. *Living Under Drones: Death, Injury and Trauma to Civilians from US Drone Practices in Pakistan.* http://www.livingunderdrones.org/download-report/, 2013.

Stiglitz, Joseph E., and Linda J. Barnes. *The Three Trillion Dollar War: The True Cost of the Iraq Conflict.* New York: W.W. Norton, 2008.

Suskind, Ron. "Certainty and the Presidency of George W. Bush." *New York Times Magazine*, October 17, 2004.

Takacs, Stacy. *Terrorism TV: Popular Entertainment in Post-9/11 America.* Lawrence: University Press of Kansas, 2012.

Tanaka, Yuki, and Marily, Young. *Bombing Civilians: A Twentieth-Century History.* New York: The New Press, 2010.

Tirman, John. *The Deaths of Others: The Fate of Civilians in America's War.* New York: Oxford University Press, 2011.

Toner, Christopher. "Just War and the Supreme Emergency Exemption." *The Philosophical Quarterly*, Vol. 55, #221, n.d.: 54–56.

Turner, Victor. *Dramas, Fields, and Metaphors.* Ithaca: Cornell University Press, 1971.

Turse, Nick. *Kill Anything That Moves: The Real American War in Vietnam.* New York: Henry Holt, 2013.

United States Committee on Foreign Relations. *Impact of the Vietnam War.* Washington, DC: U.S. Government Printing Office, 1971.

United States Department of Defense. *The Pentagon Papers—U.S.–Vietnam Relations, 1945–1967.* Kindle Edition, n.d.

United States Department of State Office of the Historian. *NSC68-1950.* Washington, DC: https.history.state.gov/milestones/1945-1952/NSC68., 1950.

United States Department of War. "United States Strategic Bombing Survey: Summary Report (Pacific War)." Washington, DC, 1946.

Walt, Stephen. "The Myth of American Exceptionalism." *Foreign Policy*, October 11, 2011.

Walzer, Michael. *Just And Unjust Wars.* New York: Basic Books, 1977.

Wicker, Tom. *One of Us: Richard Nixon and the American Dream.* New York: Random House, 1992.

Williams, William Appleman. *The Tragedy of American Diplomacy.* New York: W.W. Norton, 1959.

Wills, Gary. "What is a Just War?" *New York Review of Books*, November 18, 2004.

Wittgenstein, Ludwig. *Philosophic Investigations, 3rd ed., Trans. G.E.M. Anscombe.* Malden, MA: Wiley Blackwell, 2001.

Wohlstetter, Albert. "The Delicate Balance of Nuclear Terror." *Foreign Affairs*, Vol. 37, no. 2, 1959.

Zinn, Howard. *Terrorism and War.* New York: Seven Stories Press, 2002.

Zuckerman, Solly. "Nuclear Fantasies." *The New York Review of Books*, June 14, 1984: 28.

ACKNOWLEDGMENTS

My barbershop quip was telling: I spent a year writing about strategic fictions that often led to murder. Concluding by acknowledging my indebtedness is a sorely needed pleasure. Given the controversial nature of the book and errors yet to be discovered, the usual caveat must be taken very seriously: None of the people mentioned bear responsibility for my arguments or errors.

Lee, my wife of thirty-five years, read my ruminations several times. Her criticism and insight were invaluable, as always.

Speaking of good fortune, special thanks to Marie-Claire Antoine—there is no better editor. Her encouragement, suggestions, and congenial nature made the project possible. Speaking of good fortune, special thanks to Marie-Claire Antoin—there is no better editor. Her encouragement, suggestions, and congenial nature made the project possible. Special thanks to Elaine McGarraugh for her patience and skill. And special thanks to Jim Lopez for assistance.

I profited from the research and insight of a variety of scholars cited throughout the work. I am especially indebted to Reinhold Niebuhr, Andrew Bacevich, Lisa Stampnitzky, John Dower, John Tirman, Richard Rorty, Chris Hedges, Neil Postman, A. C. Grayling, Paul Fussell, and Daniel Ellsberg. Noam Chomsky, usually ignored in mainstream accounts of terrorism, deserves special mention for demythologizing American exceptionalism: America is not the best-behaved nation.

I owe a special debt to Steve Nathanson for his clear, incisive writing and friendship over the years. Brooke Moore invariably asked the right questions about my argument: whether they're properly answered is another matter.

INDEX

Abizaid, John, 157, 169
Abu Ghraib, 161
Abu Nazir, 190
Acheson, Dean, 46, 73, 97, 101, 111
Afghanistan, 116, 142, 144, 148, 168, 181, 183
Ahmadinejad, Mahmoud, 94
Ahmed, Akbar, 170
Al-Arian, Laila, 163
Albright, Madeleine, 155
Allen, Woody, 110
Allison, Graham, 73, 147
All Quiet on the Western Front (Remarque), 14
Alperovitz, Gar, 30, 31
America First, 18
American Caesar (Manchester), 102
American Century, 1, 59, 68, 100
American Eighth Army, 100
American exceptionalism, 1, 17, 137
"Americans Are from Mars, Europeans Are from Venus" (Kagan), 158
America West Airlines, 153
Aristotle, 84
Arnold, Henry (Hap), 29
Aronson, Elliot, 25
Article 9, Japanese constitution, 41
Atlantic Charter, 112
atomic bomb, 28, 30–32, 58; picnicking in shadow of, 184–186
atomic diplomacy, 69

Atomic Energy Commission, 58
Aucoin, Julianna, 189
al -Awalki, Anwar, 167
Axis of Evil, 144, 157
Axis Powers, 2, 9, 20, 24, 29, 41, 96; just terrorism theory to defeat, 133; three questions about pursuit of victory over, 9–10; *Why We Fight* series regarding, 36

Baader-Meinhof gang, 135
Bacevich, Andrew, 95, 155, 179
balance of power, 7, 75, 134
"Ballad of the Green Berets", 123
Bao Dai, 112
Bay of Pigs, 73, 115
Behind the Rising Sun, 27
Bell, George, 33
Berlin, extended deterrence failure in, 69–70
Berlin Wall, 70, 73, 115
Bernays, Edward, 12, 18, 19, 38
Betts, Richard, 61
Biden, Joe, 3
bin Laden, Osama (Usama), 94, 131, 144, 145, 146, 148; on Desert Storm, 154
Black, Gregory D., 27
Blackhawk Down, 180
Black Panthers, 135
Black Sea, 73
Black September, 132–133, 134–135

ABOUT THE AUTHOR

Ron Hirschbein has a PhD in social science from Syracuse University. His research includes numerous papers, articles, and books offering humanistic accounts of the causes of war and prospects for peace. He writes in a more lighthearted vein in various philosophy and popular culture series.

Teaching at California State University, Chico, he created a concentration in war and peace studies. He served as a visiting professor in peace and conflict studies at University of California campuses in San Diego and Berkeley, and at the United Nations University in Austria. He also served as president of Concerned Philosophers for Peace (the largest group of North American philosophers and other academics involved in peace studies).

He is married with two adult children. He and his wife live in California. He currently offers online graduate courses at Walden University.

CPSIA information can be obtained at www.ICGtesting.com
Printed in the USA
BVOW05*1657120415

395597BV00003B/3/P